EMERGING CONCEPTIONS OF WORK, MANAGEMENT AND THE LABOR MARKET

RESEARCH IN THE SOCIOLOGY OF WORK

Series Editor: Steven Vallas

Recent Volumes:

Volume 11: Labor Revitalization: Global Perspectives and New Initiatives

Volume 12: The Sociology of Job Training

Volume 13: Globalism/Localism at Work

Volume 14: Diversity in the Workforce

Volume 15: Entrepreneurship

Volume 16: Worker Participation: Current Research and Future Trends

Volume 17: Work Place Temporalities

Volume 18: Economic Sociology of Work

Volume 19: Work and Organizations in China after Thirty Years of Transition

Volume 20: Gender and Sexuality in the Workplace

Volume 21: Institutions and Entrepreneurship

Volume 22: Part 1: Comparing European Workers
Part A: Experiences and Inequalities
Part 2: Comparing European Workers
Part B: Policies and Institutions

Volume 23: Religion, Work, and Inequality

Volume 24: Networks, Work and Inequality

Volume 25: Adolescent Experiences and Adult Work Outcomes: Connections and Causes

Volume 26: Work and Family in the New Economy

Volume 27: Immigration and Work

Volume 28: A Gedenkschrift to Randy Hodson: Working with Dignity

Volume 29: Research in the Sociology of Work

RESEARCH IN THE SOCIOLOGY OF WORK   VOLUME 30

EMERGING CONCEPTIONS OF WORK, MANAGEMENT AND THE LABOR MARKET

EDITED BY

STEVEN VALLAS
Northeastern University, USA

emerald
PUBLISHING

United Kingdom – North America – Japan
India – Malaysia – China

Emerald Publishing Limited
Howard House, Wagon Lane, Bingley BD16 1WA, UK

First edition 2017

Reprints and permissions service
Contact: permissions@emeraldinsight.com

British Library Cataloguing in Publication Data
A catalogue record for this book is available from the British Library

ISBN: 978-1-78714-460-6 (Print)
ISBN: 978-1-78714-459-0 (Online)
ISBN: 978-1-78714-934-2 (Epub)
ISBN: 978-1-83867-924-8 (Paperback)

ISSN: 0277-2833 (Series)

INVESTOR IN PEOPLE

CONTENTS

EDITORIAL ADVISORY BOARD   *vii*

LIST OF CONTRIBUTORS   *ix*

INTRODUCTION: EMERGING CONCEPTIONS OF WORK,
MANAGEMENT AND THE LABOR MARKET   *xi*

LINKEDIN OR LINKEDOUT? HOW SOCIAL
NETWORKING SITES ARE RESHAPING THE LABOR
MARKET
    Ofer Sharone   *1*

DEALING WITH DOWNSIZING: NEW
ORGANIZATIONAL CAREERS IN FINANCIAL
SERVICES AFTER THE GREAT RECESSION
    Corey Pech   *33*

NEO-NORMATIVE CONTROL AND VALUE
DISCRETION IN INTERACTIVE SERVICE WORK: A
CASE STUDY
    Sarah Jenkins and Rick Delbridge   *59*

ENGINEERING MEDICINE: THE DEPLOYMENT OF
LEAN PRODUCTION IN HEALTHCARE
    William Attwood-Charles and Sarah Babb   *87*

DOING MORE WITH LESS: INTENSIVE CARE AND THE
LOGIC OF FLEXIBLE TEAMWORK
    Jason Rodriquez   *117*

RACE, RECESSION, AND SOCIAL CLOSURE IN THE
LOW-WAGE LABOR MARKET: EXPERIMENTAL AND
OBSERVATIONAL EVIDENCE
    Mike Vuolo, Christopher Uggen and Sarah Lageson   *141*

WORKFORCE DOWNSIZING AND SHAREHOLDER
VALUE ORIENTATION AMONG EXECUTIVE
MANAGERS AT LARGE U.S. FIRMS
Taekjin Shin   *185*

ABOUT THE EDITOR   *219*

INDEX   *221*

EDITORIAL ADVISORY BOARD

LIST OF CONTRIBUTORS

William Attwood-Charles	Sociology Department, Boston College, Chestnut Hill, MA, USA
Sarah Babb	Sociology Department, Boston College, Chestnut Hill, MA, USA
Rick Delbridge	Cardiff Business School, Cardiff University, Cardiff, UK
Sarah Jenkins	Cardiff Business School, Cardiff University, Cardiff, UK
Sarah Lageson	School of Criminal Justice, Rutgers University, Center for Law and Justice, Newark, NJ, USA
Corey Pech	Department of Sociology, The Ohio State University, Columbus, OH, USA
Jason Rodriquez	College of Liberal Arts, University of Massachusetts Boston, Boston, MA, USA
Ofer Sharone	Department of Sociology, University of Massachusetts Amherst, Amherst, MA, USA
Taekjin Shin	Fowler College of Business, San Diego State University, San Diego, CA, USA
Christopher Uggen	Department of Sociology, University of Minnesota, Minneapolis, MN, USA
Mike Vuolo	Department of Sociology, The Ohio State University, Columbus, OH, USA

INTRODUCTION: EMERGING CONCEPTIONS OF WORK, MANAGEMENT AND THE LABOR MARKET

In recent decades, there has been no shortage of speculation about the structural and cultural changes that have gripped work, management practices and the labor market in virtually all the advanced capitalist societies. Yet, little clarity has emerged concerning the nature of the new, post-Fordist regimes, the forces shaping them, and how distinct groups and classes are likely to fare in the new economy. The present volume is intended to fill these gaps. The chapters it contains draw on a diverse set of theoretical and methodological strategies. But what unites them is their shared concern with the changing economic landscape, its impact on the meaning of work, and way authority relations are shifting with the rise of neo-liberal capitalism. In this introduction to the volume, I will briefly sketch the intellectual context in which these chapters have emerged, and then address the distinctive ways in which each chapter advances our knowledge in this field.

From one perspective, of course, the transformation of market-based work represents nothing new; what was once called the "labor question" is, after all, as old as modern capitalism. Centuries of debate have unfolded regarding the brutalizing nature of wage labor and the destructive uses to which industrial technologies have been put. For decades following the introduction of the assembly line, a temporary solution had emerged in which workers relinquished their claim over job control, receiving in exchange varying measures of job security and rising wages. By the late 1970s, even this temporary solution – which came to be known as Fordism – had come undone, and the question arose as to the structure and meanings that work would assume in a post-Fordist period.

For a time, especially during the late 1980s and early 1990s, scholars envisioned a world in which an enhanced quality of employment seemed possible or even likely for many workers. Literature in this vein foresaw a weakening of centralized, hierarchical controls over work and the emergence of a horizontal logic empowering both skilled manual and mental workers alike (see Arthur & Rousseau, 2001; Piore & Sabel, 1984; Powell, 2001; Saxenian, 1994). Envisioned here was a logic of *flexibility*, a term that conjured work in a more creative and egalitarian form than Fordist regimes had allowed (Florida, 2003; Pink, 2001).

Since that time, a different and far more dystopian set of images has governed scholarly and public discussion of work, careers, and employment relations. This shift is partly due to the growing frequency and severity of economic crises, and partly to a growing awareness (and fear) of the risks to which workers have been exposed (Beck, 1992; Hacker, 2006; Harvey, 2005). Indeed, if "words are witnesses" (Hobsbawm, 1962, p. 17), then ours is a moment best described in terms of *precarity* — a term that has appeared with growing prominence appeared in many languages. As Bauman notes, "French theorists speak of '*precarite*', the Germans of *Unsicherheit* and *Risikogestellschaft*, the Italians of *incertezza* and the English of insecurity — but all of them have in mind the same aspect of the human predicament" (2000, pp. 160–161), in which workers stand more fully exposed to market volatility (see Kalleberg, 2011; Pfeffer & Baron, 1988; Pugh, 2015). This trend is perhaps most evident in the rising use of downsizing and outsourcing as managerial strategies by even highly profitable firms. It can be glimpsed in the disproportionate growth of jobs that are temporary, that offer highly uncertain or limited working hours (e.g., the British "zero hours" contract), or that apportion work on a project basis, offering contracts of limited duration. If precarious work is defined in this relatively stringent way, then the share of workers holding non-standard jobs had risen to one-sixth of the U.S. labor force in 2015 (Katz & Krueger, 2016), a 50% increase since 2005. Indeed, according to Katz and Krueger, the expansion of non-standard jobs accounted for virtually all of the job growth since 2005. The number of workers employed in such jobs is now more than twice as large as the number who belong to labor unions (Pugh, 2015).

The importance of these developments involves more than a matter of aggregate numbers, and cannot be attributed to purely subjective or irrational fears. Indeed, theorists have increasingly concluded that "precarity is not a passing or episodic condition, but a *new form of regulation* that distinguishes [our] historical time" (Butler, 2015, pp. vii–viii). In this view, "precarity has itself become a regime, a hegemonic mode of being governed, and of governing ourselves." Put differently, economic precarity has given rise to a "*mode of domination* of a new kind" (Bourdieu, 1998, pp. 83, 85, emphasis in the original). The notion here is that the "end of organized capitalism" (Lash & Urry, 1987) has now given way to a different, neo-liberal form of capitalism; and that in place of the Fordist regimes there has emerged newer and more protean regimes governed by a logic of "flexible accumulation" (see Bauman, 2000; Clegg & Baumeler, 2010; Davis, 2016; Harvey, 1989). Here, the performance of labor ceases to provide the central organizing principle of the firm; indeed, as Davis shows (2016), the most prosperous firms hardly need employ large aggregates of labor at all. The result can at times impose managerial domination in a largely *negative* form, based largely on economic coercion or fear. But at other times, managerial domination assumes a more positive or *affirmative* guise, as with discourses that advice workers to embrace a "career management" ideology that construes workers as "entrepreneurs of themselves" (Brockling, 2016; Freeman, 2014; Ho, 2009; Lane, 2011; Vallas & Cummins, 2015).

European theorists have paid particular attention to the latter forms of managerial regime. Thus, du Gay (1996) viewed work organizations as increasingly informed by what he termed "enterprise culture," a set of practices and beliefs in which workers adopt the outlook of the "sovereign consumer" toward their own work. Alvesson and Willmott (2002) developed a theory of identity regulation, in which the ability to shape worker identity becomes a critical component of the neo-liberal firm. And Clegg and Baumeler (2010) envision contemporary firms through the lens of what Bauman called "liquid modernity" (2000). All these conceptions essentially extend the general proposition, reiterated in recent decades, that managerial power and authority have come to rest in its control over the discourses, norms, and identities that arise within the workplace itself (Boltanski & Chiapello, 2005; Kunda, 1992).

These claims have provoked much discussion, debate, and empirical research. Yet the literature that has emerged is as yet marked by a number of absences and ambiguities. First, owing to the abstract level at which much of the discussion has been pitched, we have little clear understanding of precisely how neo-liberal employment regimes operate. How are the new forms of subjectivity and identity established or policed? How do the new regimes "work" to elicit consent on the part of employees? And what is the role of technology in shaping the identity norms to which employees are expected to comply?

Second, the question arises as to how disparate groups and categories of employees are affected by the new precarity. Here, it is important to acknowledge the ways in which racial, gender, and class privilege have all differentially positioned workers in the labor market. Rather than assume that precarity represents a "collective mentality" that is "common to the whole epoch" (Bourdieu, 1998, pp. 83, 85), research on job and labor market insecurity cannot afford to accept a single, overarching narrative, least of all at a time when primordial affiliations based on race and gender seem so powerful, often prompting workers to assume a defensive and even reactionary stance (Atkinson, 2007; Wacquant, 2009).

Third, and related to the above, is the matter of agency, or the ways in which workers themselves can act to modify, negotiate, or resist managerial authority (Courpasson & Vallas, 2016; Hodson, 1995, 2001). The question of resistance has been well developed in the field of organization studies, where a rich tradition of theory and research has developed (see Vallas, 2016). Yet the connection between precarity and worker agency has not been well explored. Occasional eruptions of worker mobilization, as in the Euro May Day movements during the early years of this century, prompted a number of claims regarding the self-styled "precariat" (Standing, 2011), whose validity remains open to doubt. Our may not be a time in which a "new dangerous class" has emerged, but rather on in which an old class struggles desperately to restore its previous economic position.

In varying ways and using diverse approaches, each of the contributions to the current volume has sought to address such absences and ambiguities as these. Sharone's analysis, for example, scrutinizes a previously unexamined feature of the labor market: its growing reliance of digital platforms such as LinkedIn, which harbor structural constraints and normative presuppositions that impose on job seekers an array of subtle yet powerful pressures and dilemmas (Marwick & boyd, 2010; van Dijck, 2013). Having a "complete" profile on this site virtually requires the posting of a photograph, with obvious implications for labor market stratification. The very structure of LinkedIn rules out the impression management tactics (such as the tailoring of resumes to fit particular audiences) on which job seekers have long relied. Social networking sites expand the visibility of job seekers' skills, but they do so by subjecting workers to the watchful gaze of potential employers. Implied here are subtle institutional forces that shape workers' orientations toward work, the labor market, and the self, thus contributing to the workings of the new managerial regimes.

The chapters by Pech and by Jenkins and Delbridge also inquire into the exercise of managerial authority. Using the case of mid-level workers in the financial industry, Pech asks what happens when workers face the clear and present danger of downsizing (Ho, 2009). Do workers exhibit pattern of continuing loyalty to their employers, even in the absence of firm reciprocity? Or do they withdraw their affiliation and adopt a more self-interested orientation? Pech's findings support the former point of view. The effect of job and labor market uncertainty seems to incline workers to narrow their job horizons, redoubling their willingness to identify with their current employer. Here is a good example of the tenacity of what Pugh (2015) has called the "one-way honor code."

The chapter by Jenkins and Delbridge runs parallel to that by Pech. Here workers exhibit a similar form of loyalty or allegiance to the firm, in spite of the unrewarding nature of the job as measured by wages. In this case, involving workers in an upscale call center, the reason is not rooted in the pursuit of career opportunities (as in the chapter by Pech). Instead, the efficacy of management's regime lies in its willingness to allow workers the capacity to exercise "value discretion" − that is, the ability to rule on the firm's behalf. Here we encounter a regime that bears more than a passing resemblance to what popular writers have termed "liberation management," and what Fleming and Sturdy (2009) have called "neo-normative control." Here, firms achieve control over employees by enabling them to "just be themselves" − thus lending managerial authority an informal and even "natural" quality to which no one could reasonably object. A subtle form of colonization occurs here, Jenkins and Delbridge conclude, in which workers embody the interests of the firm, now on their own account.

The chapters by Attwood-Charles and Babb and by Rodriquez both address a terrain that stands in particular need of attention − the provision of medical care − given the health care industry's growing embrace of privatization, profit imperatives, cost controls, and new managerial constructs (e.g., "lean production" and "team" systems). Indeed, the adoption of the latter practices by the health care industry attests to the pervasive presence that neo-liberal logic has achieved across broad swaths of the economy. Notably, both these chapters speak to the capacity of medical practitioners to subvert normative practices they find to be alien to their own professional orientations. In the case of the Attwood-Charles and Babb chapter, doctors easily marginalized the lean regimes their employers had proposed, but in highly variable ways. In one site, doctors invoked their professional autonomy, refusing lean medicine by defining it as too profit-oriented, and thus as foreign to their professional norms. In a second site, however, lean medicine failed to gain traction for very different reasons: largely because it seemed at odds with the efficiency- and profit-generating needs that administrators sought to address. These findings provide a healthy reminder of the limits of managerial regimes, and of the nuanced patterns of contention that arise within work organizations, even in the face of economic restructuring and organizational consolidation (Kellogg, 2011). Parallel processes unfold in Rodriquez's account. Here, management introduced a new, team-based regime with great promise, only to see this effort crash and burn. The reason did not stem from the resistance of either professionals or administrators; indeed, "team" discourse seemed wholly acceptable to both groups. Instead, the failure of the new regime stemmed from the contradictions implied within the new regime itself – its promise of enhanced quality, cooperation, and autonomy on the one hand, versus its imposition of a regime of austerity and rationalized cost-cutting on the other hand.

As noted, we have as yet only a meager understanding of the ways in which ascribed statuses shape the unfolding of labor market uncertainty in the current period. For this reason, the chapter by Voulo, Uggen, and Lageson, which explores the relation between recession and racial hierarchies, is especially welcome. The question Vuolo and his colleagues have posed whether the labor market privileges that whites enjoy tend to expand during periods of substantial downturn (as social closure theory might suggest); or alternatively, whether racial hierarchies within the labor market exhibit the qualities that Tilly (1998) once called "durable inequality." Both scenarios seem plausible. It is conceivable that hiring managers would respond to a recessionary economy by exhibiting a preference for white labor, even within low-wage jobs, especially if doing so would advance the firm's prestige. The alternative possibility is that racial hierarchies are so deeply institutionalized as to persist as part of the "natural" order of things, with racial disparities in the labor market remaining as a constant over time. As Vuolo et al. report, the "durable" outcome seems to obtain, suggesting that racial disparities and status hierarchies are powerfully institutionalized within the low-wage labor market. Perhaps most strikingly, the job rewards that black workers receive even during flush times remain less generous than those which their white counterparts receive during recessionary times (see Pager, 2003). The Vuolo, Uggen, and Lageson chapter stands as a strong example of the need to sort out the workings of the categorical inequalities that are brought forward into the neo-liberal economy.

The final chapter in this volume, that by Shin, investigates the link between what has become the *lingua franca* of contemporary corporate life – the view of the firm as a platform for the enrichment of shareholders – and the rolling out of downsizing campaigns as a result layoffs. Carefully studying CEO reports, Shin finds evidence of a close connection between their content – that is, their embrace of the "shareholder value" discourse – and correlative shifts in employment levels (the use of downsizing as a weapon against alleged inefficiencies within the firm). These findings provide a cautionary note against neo-institutionalist accounts that encourage us to view corporate announcements as discursive performances that uncoupled from the internal operations of the firm. Discourse, Shin finds, has real consequences; it seems closely bound up with managerial practices that operate to the disadvantages of millions of employees.

Much remains unknown about the nature of the economic era into which we have been so blindly propelled. Some scholars, such as Beck (2000) speak of a looming crisis of the "work society," suggesting that the modernization process has begun to erode its own sources of stability. Certainly, the onset of precarity has disrupted longstanding assumptions and orientations regarding the meaning of work and the employment relation itself. Needed are studies such as those collected here, the better to map out the ways in which work organizations and labor market institutions have evolved – and to explore the space in which alternative arrangements might conceivably emerge.

Steven Vallas
Editor

REFERENCES

Alvesson, M., & Willmott, H. (2002). Identity regulation as organizational control: Producing the appropriate individual. *Journal of Management Studies, 39,* 619–644.

Arthur, M. B., & Rousseau, D. (2001). *The Boundaryless career: A new employment principle for a new organizational era.* Oxford: Oxford University Press.

Atkinson, W. (2007). Beck, individualization, and the death of class: A critique. *The British Journal of Sociology, 58,* (3), 349–366.

Bauman, Z. (2000). *Liquid modernity.* Cambridge: Blackwell.

Beck, U. (1992). *Risk society: Towards a new modernity.* London: Sage.

Beck, U. (2000). *The brave new world of work.* Cambridge: Polity.

Boltanski, L., & Chiapello, E. (2005). *The new spirit of capitalism.* London: Verso.

Bourdieu, P. (1998). *Acts of resistance: Against the tyranny of the market.* New York, NY: New Press.

Brockling, U. (2016). *The entrepreneurial self: Fabricating a new type of subject.* Thousand Oaks, CA: Sage.

Butler, J. (2015). Foreword. In *Isabell Lorey, state of insecurity: Government of the precarious* (pp. vii–xi). London: Verso.

Clegg, S., & Baumeler, C. (2010). From iron cages to liquid modernity in organizational analysis. *Organization Studies, 31*(12), 1713–1733.

Courpasson, D., & Vallas, S. P. (2016). Resistance studies: A critical introduction. In D. Courpasson & S. P. Vallas (Eds.), *The SAGE handbook of resistance studies*. London: Sage.

Davis, G. F. (2016). *The vanishing corporation: Navigating the hazards of a new economy*. Oakland, CA: Berrett-Koehler.

Du Gay, P. (1996). *Consumption and identity at work*. Thousand Oaks, CA: Sage.

Fleming, P., & Sturdy, A. (2009). "Just be yourself!": Towards neo-normative control in organisations? *Employee Relations, 31*(6), 569–583.

Florida, R. L. (2003). *The rise of the creative class: And how it's transforming work, leisure, community and everyday life*. New York, NY: Basic Books.

Freeman, C. (2014). *Entrepreneurial selves: Neoliberal respectability and the making of a Caribbean middle class*. Durham, NC: Duke.

Hacker, J. (2006). *The great risk shift*. New York, NY: Oxford.

Harvey, D. (1989). *The condition of postmodernity: An enquiry into the origins of cultural change*. Oxford: Blackwell.

Harvey, D. (2005). *A brief history of neo-liberalism*. Oxford: Oxford University Press.

Ho, K. Z. (2009). *Liquidated: An ethnography of wall street*. Durham, NC: Duke University Press.

Hobsbawm, E. (1962). *The age of revolution: Europe 1789–1848*. New York, NY: Vintage.

Hodson, R. (1995). Worker resistance: An underdeveloped concept in the sociology of work. *Economic and Industrial Democracy, 16*, 32.

Hodson, R. (2001). *Dignity at work*. New York, NY: Cambridge University Press.

Kalleberg, A. (2011). *Good jobs, bad jobs: The rise of polarized and precarious employment systems in the United States, 1970s–2000s*. New York, NY: Russell Sage Foundation.

Katz, L. F., & Krueger, A. B. (2016). *The rise and nature of alternative work arrangements in the United States, 1995–2015*. Retrieved from http://krueger.princeton.edu/sites/default/files/akrueger/files/katz_krueger_cws_-_march_29_20165.pdf

Kellogg, K. (2011). *Challenging operations: Institutional reform and resistance in medical work*. Chicago, IL: University of Chicago Press.

Kunda, G. (1992). *Engineering culture*. Cambridge, MA: MIT Press.

Lane, C. (2011). *A company of one: Insecurity, independence, and the new world of white collar unemployment*. Ithaca, NY: ILR/Cornell.

Lash, S., & Urry, J. (1987). *The end of organized capitalism*. Madison, WI: University of Wisconsin Press.

Marwick, A. E., & boyd, D. (2010). I tweet honestly, I tweet passionately: Twitter users, context collapse, and the imagined audience. *New Media and Society, 12*(1), 114–133.

Pager, D. (2003). The mark of a criminal record. *American Journal of Sociology, 108*, 39.

Pfeffer, J., & Baron, J. (1988). Taking the workers back out: Recent trends in the structuring of employment. *Research in Organizational Behavior, 10*, 46.

Pink, D. (2001). *Free agent nation: How America's new independent workers are transforming the way we live*. New York, NY: Warner Books.

Piore, M. J., & Sabel, C. F. (1984). *The second industrial divide: Possibilities for prosperity*. New York, NY: Basic Books.

Powell, W. W. (2001). The capitalist firm in the twenty-first century: Emerging patterns in western enterprise. In P. DiMaggio (Ed.), *The twenty-first century firm* (pp. 33–68). Princeton, NJ: Princeton University Press.

Pugh, A. (2015). *The tumbleweed society*. New York, NY: Oxford.

Saxenian, A. L. (1994). *Regional advantage: Culture and competition in Silicon Valley and route 128*. Cambridge, MA: Harvard University Press.

Standing, G. (2011). *The precariat: The new dangerous class*. New York, NY: Bloomsbury.

Tilly, C. (1998). *Durable inequality*. Berkeley, CA: University of California Press.

Vallas, S. P. (2016). Working class heroes or working stiffs? Domination and resistance within business organizations. *Research in the Sociology of Work, 28*, 101–126.

Vallas, S. P., & Cummins, E. R. (2015). Personal branding and identity norms in the popular business press: Enterprise culture in an age of precarity. *Organization Studies, 36*(3), 293–319.

Van dijck, J. (2013). 'You have one identity': Performing the self on Facebook and LinkedIn. *Media, Culture & Society, 35*(2), 199–215.

Wacquant, L. (2009). *Punishing the poor*. Durham, NC: Duke.

LINKEDIN OR LINKEDOUT? HOW SOCIAL NETWORKING SITES ARE RESHAPING THE LABOR MARKET

Ofer Sharone

ABSTRACT

The rapid growth of online social networking sites ("SNS") such as LinkedIn and Facebook has created new forms of online labor market intermediation that are reconfiguring the hiring process in profound ways; yet, little is understood about the implications of these new technologies for job seekers navigating the labor market, or more broadly, for the careers and lives of workers. The existing literature has focused on digital inequality — workers' unequal access to or skilled use of digital technologies — but has left unanswered critical questions about the emerging and broad effects of SNS as a labor market intermediary. Drawing on in-depth interviews with unemployed workers this paper describes job seekers' experiences using SNS to look for work. The findings suggest that SNS intermediation of the labor market has two kinds of effects. First, as an intermediary for hiring, SNS produces labor market winners and losers involving filtering processes that often have little to do with evaluations of merit. Second, SNS filtering processes exert new pressures on all workers, whether winners or losers as perceived though this new filter, to manage their careers, and to some extent their private lives, in particular ways that fit the logic of the SNS-mediated labor market.

Keywords: Labor market; social networking; human resources; Internet; digital technologies

Emerging Conceptions of Work, Management and the Labor Market
Research in the Sociology of Work, Volume 30, 1–31
Copyright © 2017 by Emerald Publishing Limited
All rights of reproduction in any form reserved
ISSN: 0277-2833/doi:10.1108/S0277-283320170000030001

Over a decade ago leading scholars of the American labor market began
observing that the "Internet is bringing radical change to corporate recruiting"
(Cappelli, 2001, p. 139), and predicted that a "spectacular rise" in online labor
market intermediation "will change the way employer-employee matches are
made" (Autor, 2001, p. 25). While academic research in this area remains
sparse, the existing data suggest, as these scholars foresaw, that the use of the
Internet for recruiting has rapidly risen. Since 2006 a majority of new hires
have been "sourced" from the Internet (Cober & Brown, 2006), but little is
known about the implications of this transformation for workers.

The use of the Internet for hiring has come in two great waves. The first
wave was marked by the rise of online job boards, such as Monster.com, where
employers post ads and job seekers post resumes. This first wave replaced local
newspaper ads with a globally accessible database of jobs listings and resumes
that is continuously updated. A second wave of technological change – the
explosive growth of online social networking sites ("SNS") – has created new
forms of online labor market intermediation that are currently reconfiguring
the hiring process in even more profound ways that have no pre-digital equiva-
lents. SNS are online platforms on which users create profiles, connect (or
"friend") other users, and make themselves visible and searchable to network
contacts and potential employers. A report by the Society for Human Resource
Management (SHRM), the largest association for human resource professionals
in the United States, revealed that among a random sample of its 250,000 member companies the use of SNS for recruiting increased from 34% in 2008 to
56% in 2011 to 77% in 2013 (SHRM, 2013). By 2015 another industry survey
found that 92% of recruiters used social media as part of their candidate search
(Jobvite, 2015). SNS provide recruiters who pay a fee the ability to search their
entire database of profiles, review potential candidates' work histories, pictures,
and contacts, and send a personal message to any potential candidate of interest.
SNS are being used to recruit for a wide range of jobs, from executives to hourly
employees, with the highest rates of usage for hiring of "non-managerial salaried
employees" (SHRM, 2013). One study suggests that even in cases where job
applicants initiate contact using traditional resumes, and in which no links to
social media are provided, up to a third of U.S. firms nonetheless search SNS
for information about the applicant (Acquisti & Fong, 2013). Despite these
trends, little is understood about the implications of SNS for job seekers navigating the labor market, or more broadly, for the careers and lives of working
professionals. This paper is the first to my knowledge to use interview data with
job seekers to explore the implications of the rise of SNS for workers.

The literature on digital technologies and labor markets has to date largely
focused on the issue of digital inequality: job seekers' unequal access to digital
technologies and various barriers to the effective use of these digital technologies (DiMaggio, Hargittai, Celeste, & Shaer, 2004). The literature's focus on
digital inequality implicitly takes for granted the career benefits of using SNS
and is concerned about workers who do not have access to these benefits.

While barriers to the use of SNS technology are undoubtedly important, this focus has left unanswered critical questions about the broader effects of SNS as an emerging labor market intermediary for all workers.

A dominant narrative has emerged among policy-makers and career professionals that SNS *empower* job seekers, and correspondingly the central issue of policy concern has been the ability of job seekers to access and effectively use SNS. This perspective is a subset of the more general concern over a growing *digital divide* or digital inequality in which technological change is largely perceived as beneficial to all who are able to use it; a perspective which may overlook how new technologies may have unanticipated consequences for generating new forms of inequalities or for reproducing existing inequalities.

This paper breaks new ground by pointing to a range of previously overlooked tensions and dilemmas that exist for the growing numbers of job seekers who have full access and capacity to use SNS. Drawing on in-depth interviews with unemployed job seekers using SNS to look for work, and participant observations at workshops to train job seekers to use SNS, this study finds that while job seekers perceive certain benefits to using SNS, the use of SNS also raises a range of difficulties and potential obstacles. At core, SNS increase the exposure of job seekers, and this exposure is double-edged. The same visibility that makes it easier for job seekers to expand their networks and for employers to find and recruit them, also makes it possible for employers to classify, compare, and screen out entire categories of job seekers on the basis of job seekers' pictures or political activities. Moreover, for reasons that will be described in this paper, SNS mediation of the labor market may disadvantage workers who wish to simultaneously pursue different kinds of jobs, or whose work histories are not optimally presented in a reverse chronological order. Reflecting this double-edge, the job seekers I interviewed share deep ambivalences and anxieties about the effects of using SNS. In various ways these anxieties all point to a perceived loss of control over one's narrative and image, and to concerns about the implications of such lost control for one's ability to find work. Job seekers' experiences suggest that SNS intermediation of the labor market has two kinds of effects. First, as a filtering mechanism for hiring, SNS may generate labor market winners and losers on the basis of information that has little to do with merit. Second, these filtering mechanisms may exert new disciplinary pressures on all workers (Foucault, 1977), whether winners or losers, to manage their careers and private lives in ways that fit the logic of the SNS-mediated labor market.

JOB SEARCH AND DIGITAL INTERMEDIARIES

Since scholars first observed that digital technologies are changing the nature of hiring (Autor, 2001; Cappelli, 2001) most studies of this change have focused on digital inequality in access and use. In the early 2000s research revealed a substantial "digital divide" along the traditional stratification lines of education, income, race, and initially gender. For example, a national survey in 2002 showed that Internet access and adoption rates were higher for those with higher incomes and education levels (Hargittai, 2008). Over the past decade access and use of digital technologies has become much more widespread, and although some studies continue to examine inequalities in access − particularly as measured by bandwidth (Hilbert, 2016; Pick, Sarkar, & Johnson, 2015) − the literature has largely shifted its focus from access and use to inequalities in skills, capacities and know-how to make *effective use* of digital technologies (see DiMaggio et al., 2004; Duerson & Dijk, 2014; Halford & Savage, 2010; Hargittai, 2008; Lee, Park, & Hwang, 2015; Robinson, 2009). For example, Duerson and Dijk (2014) recently found that lower levels of education are associated with *more* hours of Internet usage − a finding that turns traditional digital divide concerns on their head − but also that higher socioeconomic status individuals are better skilled at gaining valuable information from digital technologies. Lee et al. (2015, p. 46) similarly discuss the importance of focusing on the skilled use of digital technology, nothing that "the rise of social network sites (SNS) is intensifying the use of participatory online activities," which require a host of digital skills, and the lack thereof risks "social, cultural, and economic exclusion" (p. 54).

While inequalities in skills and capacities to utilize digital technologies are important, I hypothesize that there are other important emergent mechanisms of stratification that are both underexplored and under-theorized. The focus on digital inequality has potentially obscured the ways in which new technologies are not simply empowering all skilled users but may make some workers − including skilled users of SNS − more vulnerable to systematic exclusion from the labor market. Additionally, the focus on digital inequality also leaves unexamined the ways in which digital technologies may exert new disciplinary pressures on all workers (Foucault, 1977) to manage their careers and private lives in ways that fit the logic of the SNS-mediated labor market.

The focus on digital inequality misses the significant effects of the rise of SNS in reconfiguring the architecture of the labor market and redesigning the space in which job seekers and employers see and are seen. Drawing on Goffman (1959, p. 12) this paper shows how SNS construct new virtual "settings" in which workers present themselves to potential employers; and its features constitute the "furniture, décor, physical layout and other background items which supply the scenery and stage props" for job seeker performances. This architecture's distinct features shape and delimit the possible presentations of self by, for example, limiting the capacity for job seekers to erect barriers for the purpose of "segregating" their audiences for different performances (Goffman, 1959, p. 137). This paper also builds on an important line of more recent literature which expands Goffman's insights and analysis of presentations of self beyond physically bounded and face-to-face interactions and recognizes that interactions are increasingly "disembedded from local settings" but nonetheless bound together by emerging virtual "microstructures" (Cetina & Brugger, 2002, p. 908). As Cetina (2009, p. 63) argues there is nothing "analytically prior" about face-to-face contexts, and the need to update concepts and theories rooted in presumptions of geographically bounded face-to-face interactions is evident given the increasing number of interactions that now routinely occur in virtual settings whether we are chatting, shopping, working, learning, or hiring. For example, Marwick and boyd (2014b, p. 1188) observe that "in most American high schools social media have replaced the street or coffee shop as the 'place' where much discussion, interaction, and 'hanging out' between teens goes on."

By shaping and constraining workers' presentations of self, SNS architectures redesign the ways in which workers are categorized, compared, filtered, and excluded. Foucault (1977, p. 172) discusses how architectures can facilitate forms of disciplinary power using "calculations of openings, of filled and empty spaces, passages and transparencies." Disciplinary power operates on two levels simultaneously. On the one hand, it individuates subjects by constructing hierarchies of "qualities, skills and aptitudes" (Foucault, 1977, p. 181), entailing a continuum of winners and losers. On the other hand, it creates "constant pressure to conform to the same model," entailing that all individuals are "subjected to 'subordination [and] docility" (Foucault, 1977, p. 183). As Foucault summarizes it, disciplinary power "compares, differentiates, hierarchizes, homogenizes, excludes. In short, it *normalizes*" (1977, p. 183, italics in the original).[1]

While Foucault developed the theory of disciplinary power in the context of prisons and criminal justice he explicitly treats these as particular manifestations of a broader pattern of disciplinary power embedded in the design of modern institutions. In *The Birth of Biopolitics* (2008) Foucault analyses the design of markets. Although neoliberal discourses depict markets as neutral spaces in which buyers and sellers spontaneously interact, Foucault shows that exchange within markets is not a "natural process," but takes place "insofar as an institutional framework and positive rules have provided them with their conditions of possibility" (2008, p. 163). In analyzing the SNS-mediated labor market, we are thus guided by Foucault to be particularly mindful of the effects of the market's specific design. This paper argues that the rise of SNS mediation has meaningfully changed the design of the labor market by reshaping what, when, and to whom particular slices of job seeker information are visible, in what sequence such slices are visible, and with what salience. This changed design is perceived by workers as exposing them in new ways to the employers' gaze, and as opening the door to new employer filtering processes – both conscious and subconscious – through which applicants are selected or rejected.

In short, as the architecture that increasingly houses our professional selves, SNS makes visible and salient certain dimensions of the self, and thus brings into play both levels of disciplinary power. First, SNS generates new technologies of classification, producing new filters that sort winners and losers. Second, it exerts new forms of discipline on all job seekers, winners and losers alike, through practices and discourses that create pressures on subjects to become particular kinds of selves. Far from a straightforward tool of empowerment for digitally savvy workers, the effects of SNS are more complex and double-edged than is often assumed, and have significant but overlooked implications for modern subjects as workers as well as citizens.

DATA AND METHODOLOGY

To explore the social networking practices and experiences of American job seekers I primarily draw on 76 in-depth semi-structured interviews with unemployed white-collar American workers. The paper focuses on unemployed workers because as a group these workers are particularly motivated to use all available means to find work, including SNS, and therefore the focus on this group is likely to yield uniquely rich data about the uses of SNS to find work. All interviewees were living in the greater Boston area and were between the ages of 25 and 65. Each interview lasted approximately 90 minutes. The sample included a broad range of white-collars occupations, including managers, technical workers, administrative assistants, and teachers. In terms of its racial and ethnic composition the sample was 84% white, which reflects the demographics of site where job seekers were recruited (discussed later) but which means that the data are of limited applicability with respect to the experiences of racial and ethnic minorities. Table 1 summarizes the basic demographic characteristics of the interviewees.

During the interviews open-ended questions were used to probe, among other things, whether job seekers used SNS to look for work, details about the variety of ways they used SNS in their search, the perceived benefits and costs of using this technology, and how the use of SNS affects the day-to-day

Table 1.   Sample Demographics.

	Interviewed Job Seekers
Number of Interviewees	76
Percentage Female	54%
Age (median)	53
Race/ethnicity	
White	84%
African-American	7%
Asian-American and other	9%

experiences of job searching. The interviews were transcribed and coded, initially using broad concepts that inductively emerged from the interviews. Codes that corresponded to large amounts of data were subsequently broken down into several sub-codes.

Approximately half of the interviewees were recruited at general introductory workshops for unemployed workers at a One Stop center in the greater Boston area. I chose to recruit at this workshop because unemployed workers were required to attend this workshop as a condition to receiving unemployment benefits. This requirement means that there was minimal self-selection in attending these workshops but only in agreeing to participate in this study, for which participants were paid US $20.

Since this study focuses on the use of SNS to job search, and less than half of the job seekers recruited at these mandatory workshops actively used SNS to job search (pointing to the persistence of digital inequality), I also recruited job seekers at a workshop offered at the same One Stop center which specifically focused on how to use SNS to job search. This group of job seekers, by definition, had some interest in using SNS. Recruiting at this workshop purposively aimed at self-select job seekers who chose to develop their SNS job search skills so as to gather rich data on the experiences of using SNS. When recruiting in this group I attempted to obtain a sample that varied along potentially significant independent variables (Lamont & White, 2009; Small, 2009; Trost, 1986), including occupation, gender, and age. The ultimate number of interviews was determined by saturation; the point at which further interviews provided little new and surprising information (Small, 2009). This purposive recruiting approach has been recognized as appropriate when seeking to understand particular processes, with the aim of developing or extending theories (Becker, 1998; Burawoy, 1998; Trost, 1986).

I also gathered data through participant observations at SNS workshops. As a participant-observer I was able to supplement my primary interview data with observations of job seekers discussing with classmates and with the instructor their concerns and responses to using SNS for job searching. Each class had between 10 and 20 students. Finally, to further supplement my data and provide context, I also interviewed five HR professionals who recruit for a broad range of industries about their use of SNS in the hiring process. I was introduced to these HR professionals by the staff at the One Stop center.

THE LURE AND BENEFITS OF SOCIAL NETWORKING TECHNOLOGIES

When seeking advice on how to find work in the current labor market, unemployed job seekers who visit state-funded "one stop" centers in the Boston area are told that finding work begins with social networking. In Massachusetts, the

Secretary of Labor and Workforce Development declared: "It is becoming clear that understanding *online networking tools* is critical in order to get ahead and successfully find your next job."[2] Accordingly, one stops career centers in Massachusetts, as elsewhere around the United States, have begun to provide trainings for unemployed job seekers focused on how to use SNS in their job search, particularly "LinkedIn," the most popular SNS for career purposes. When attending such workshops I repeatedly heard two assertions: First, that SNS and particularly "LinkedIn has revolutionized job searching." And second, that "if you are not on LinkedIn you are invisible." At one workshop the facilitator emphasized to the 20 job seekers in the room: "For the purposes of networking, *if you're not on LinkedIn you don't exist*." She then elaborated:

> You wouldn't use an old tennis racket to play in a professional competition. Same thing for networking: The rules have changed and the tools have changed. LinkedIn is one of the new tools that changes how the game is being played, and it isn't going away.

Striking a more positive tone, at another workshop the facilitator excited the job seekers by explaining:

> We often talk about the black hole of the applications. Well, LinkedIn is one way to get around that. With my first degree contacts I can get introduced to up to eighty two thousand people. That's a lot of people. With my second degree contacts I can be introduced to over five million people.

The five million number drew several audible "wows" from workshop participants. [3]

Along the same lines, a growing number of career-advice books claim that the social media "revolution" provides a great boost to those job seekers who know how to make use of it. The purported benefits of SNS include increased visibility of job seekers to potential employers and an easy and efficient tool to expand their network.

SNS allow users, free of charge, to create a profile page that includes their career history, educational background and picture, connect to other members or join various "groups" of members, and post updates of recent activities or ideas (Brown & Vaughn, 2011). Once connected members can browse each other's contacts. Members can also conduct keyword searches of their entire "network," which on SNS like LinkedIn includes their direct contacts, their contacts' contacts (called "second degree" contacts) and the contacts of their second degree contacts ("third degree" contacts). Typically, a person who has 100 direct contacts will have around 10,000 second degree contacts, and 1,000,000 third degree contacts. The million members of the extended network are searchable by occupation, university, workplace, location, or other keywords.

The SNS most widely used for career purposes is LinkedIn, which in 2016 was the 16th most visited website in the world.[4] The most widely used SNS in the world is Facebook, which has a more social focus and which in 2016 was the 3rd most visited website in the world behind Google and YouTube.[5] As Fig. 1 shows, membership in the SNS platform LinkedIn grew at breakneck speed between 2009 and 2016.

Why is LinkedIn growing so rapidly? My interviews suggest that workers perceive concrete benefits to joining. Most American job seekers put great emphasis on networking (Lane, 2011; Sharone, 2013), and job seekers perceive that SNS provide a useful tool to identify and connect with networking targets who may be helpful in their job search. Moreover, networking in person is often a dreaded activity and the promise of SNS is of an easier and more efficient way to connect with others. Job seekers primarily use LinkedIn to reconnect with old contacts. As Helen explains:

> People that you've worked with have gone in different ways. There's a tremendous amount of people that I know of that had gone in different ways. Or if you've lost touch you can look them up. You can always say, "Hi, so-and-so, I noticed your name, I would like to connect up with you if possible in pursuit of a position." So that's another opportunity.

Job seekers use SNS is to perform what I call "reverse networking," a new form of networking made possible by SNS. While in traditional networking job seekers first approach members of their network and ask for information and referrals to possible job openings, in reverse networking the job seeker starts by identifying a particular company that has posted an opening and *then* searches for any connections, including second or third degree contacts, who are presently working in that company and thus in a position to provide a referral. SNS makes this kind of reverse networking possible because it renders ones' extended network instantly visible. In the past such networking would have been implausible

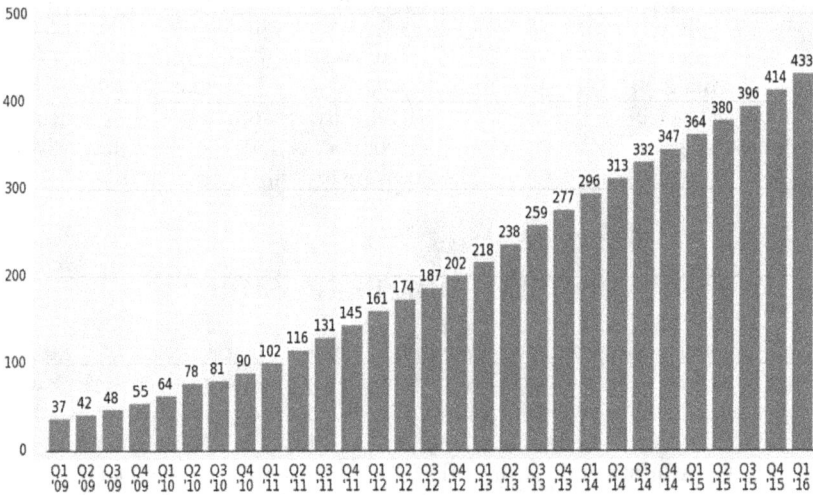

Fig. 1. The Rise of LinkedIn Membership. *Source*: LinkedIn.

as it would have required one to ask all their contacts whether they or *anyone* they are connected to, know anyone at a particular company. In short, SNS not only makes networking easier, it transforms the way networking is practiced.

SNS can also be used to balance the informational asymmetries between the interviewee and interviewer. While job seekers have always submitted their resumes in advance of interviews, with LinkedIn, they can now look up their interviewers and, as Sarah put it: "see what *their* credentials are." More broadly, one can learn about the hiring company by viewing the credentials and work histories of other workers presently in the company who are in the position that one is seeking. Learning about the hiring manager's background and experiences is particularly useful for knowing how to optimally present oneself at an interview to increase the likelihood of a positive interaction. It may also help job seekers feel at ease. As Carolyn explained:

> I have a job interview next week and I've looked up all the people that are going to be inter-
> viewing me and I tried to find them all on LinkedIn, and it's very helpful that way. If you
> find the people you can get an idea of their background, sometimes you get a picture, which
> is very helpful. So then when you get to the interview you know who's who before you get
> introduced. So I think it helps provide more of a comfort level for me.

Some job seekers also perceive value from joining groups of SNS members that share particular occupations or professional interests. Groups range in size from less than 100 to over 100,000 members, and some job seekers report that these groups are a valuable source of professionally relevant information. Jack finds in such groups a source of "sharing solutions," or as Bruce put it, "techni-cal, professional-related advice" that is specific to his field. Beyond the intrinsic value of the information, joining a group can also be a signal to employers that one is an active member in a given profession. Debbie explains: "There's a tre-mendous amount of groups that you can become affiliated with. People that are in the same caliber professionally that you are, [and] you can sort of get yourself affiliated." Dave explained that comments he makes in groups help "me brand myself as an expert in the field." By creating a profile, connecting with others, joining groups, and making comments SNS provide a new way for job seekers to gain exposure; yet, the exposure is double-edged.

DOUBLE-EDGED EXPOSURE

Although the above-discussed potential benefits lure job seekers to explore using SNS, job seekers also discuss deep anxieties and ambivalences. As Karen expressed it: "I have my profile out on LinkedIn, although I have to say I hate the whole idea of LinkedIn. I feel *exposed* on LinkedIn. You can't select who you share you information with, really." Or as John put it: "I feel like it's a sort of an invasion of privacy. I want to share my information with who I want to share it with."

The anxiety and ambivalence from the disclosure of information about one-self are pervasive. While the previously described digital inequality literature focuses on the negative consequences for individuals who do not have the capacity to effectively use SNS, it overlooks the tensions and dilemmas that exist for job seekers who have full capacity to use SNS but fear it may under-mine them.

A minority of job seekers expressed a sense of generalized fear related to making public personal information. For example, Heather explained her hesi-tation in putting information on LinkedIn:

> I don't like to put a lot of personal information out there... With anything that deals with social media you should be careful because you don't know who your audience may be... I've known people that have gotten spammed, and been targets of phishing. There were times that I would get spammed... You have to be astute and just be conscientious when you give out information.

Yet, such generalized fears being spammed or scammed were the least com-mon type of concerns shared by job seekers. The most common concerns were more distinct and specific to the job-searching context, and to the management of information about oneself as a job candidate.

The remainder of this paper will unpack the multiple dimensions of this anxiety. I will in turn discuss varied types of exposures that arise via SNS, which generate a sense of lost control over key dimensions of self-presentation, image, and narrative.

EXPOSURE OF ONE'S IMAGE

A salient form of exposure occurs with the posting of one's picture on the SNS profile. The picture entails a highly significant change in the *sequence* of the fil-ters which job seekers must pass through before being hired; specifically, mak-ing considerably *earlier* the timing of when the employer scrutinizes a job seeker's looks. In the pre-SNS world this scrutiny would typically happen only after successfully passing through other filters and reaching the interview stage. However, SNS labor market intermediation makes one's picture a slice of the information that is provided upfront, and likely among the most salient pieces of information. As one recruiter explained: "I definitely prefer to see a picture [on LinkedIn profile]. It's priceless... I also check them out on Facebook, get a sense of the person." Prior research shows the significant effects of candidate pictures in hiring decisions (Marlowe, Schneider, & Nelson, 1996; Ruffle & Shtudiner, 2013). An industry study, which uses eye-tracking technology, found that recruiters looking at the LinkedIn profiles of potential candidates spend 19% of their time examining the candidate's picture (Ladders, 2012), and a study in Belgium found that over 40% of recruiters agreed with the statement that SNS profile pictures signal applicant's level of "extraversion" and "maturity" (Caers & Castelyn, 2011).

To contextualize the salience of job seeker pictures it is important to consider prior research revealing the extent to which employers form impressions and make decisions about candidates on the bases of intangible qualities or gut feelings (Rivera, 2015; Moss & Tilly, 2001; Watkins & Johnston, 2000), and the link between such employer impression and candidate appearance. For example, examining the work of headhunters Finlay and Coverdill (2002, p. 130) report the central importance employer's attach to intangible qualities of fit or "chemistry," and add that in assessing these intangible qualities the candidates' physical appearance matters, with particular attention paid to beauty and weight. In the context of temp agencies Smith and Neuwirth (2008) likewise find that intangible characteristics are critically important and assessed through interviews. Like the headhunters, the temp agency recruiters report that candidates' appearance is important, and their assessment of possible recruits includes a section on "grooming," and requires ranking candidate's appearance as "management and professional material," "fit for light industrial and manual labor," or "unacceptable" (Smith & Neuwirth, 2008, p. 83). These pre-SNS studies suggest the importance that employers attach to intangible characteristics, but also that the institutions which mediated hiring in the pre-SNS labor market structured a typical sequence in which employers would first review documents, such as resumes and cover letters, and then invite the few candidates who made the first cut to a personal interview in which intangible qualities, including appearance, would be evaluated. The dramatic change brought on by the SNS-mediated labor market is the disruption of this sequence by frontloading the candidate's image, and thus making more likely an evaluation based on appearance at the very start of the filtering process.

Job seekers are fully aware that images make a difference, and report substantial ambivalence about the exposure of their image. They see both advantages and risks. Some job seekers discuss practical advantages of posting a picture for networking such as making it easier for others to recognize you "when you meet for coffee." It can also help when people seek to connect online. Sally explains: "When people want to connect with me I don't necessarily know who they are, but if I look at their picture I go, 'Oh, I know that person!' So I thought maybe that might happen to somebody else." Chris adds another practical consideration: "I have a very common name, so I include a picture just so that when people try to find me, it makes it easier."

More often the kinds of advantages job seekers discussed were not strictly practical but related to how their image can enhance their likelihood of getting beyond employers' initial filters. Some job seekers perceived that posting pictures provide a way to establish their professionalism, or as one put it, their "normalcy." These job seekers believe they have a professional look that will appeal to employers. Lisa explained:

> I think a lot of people still subconsciously may be judging people based on how they look or what they're wearing... They don't want you to show up with tattoos on your face and whatever if it's like a specific type of job... I would never judge them by their appearance, because you could get a totally benign-looking person who couldn't get the job done.

Maryann likewise believed that her professional image would help her:

> I don't know. I mean it probably helps. Maybe if they see you with a suit and a nice blouse on or something they'll say "Oh, they look professional." They might think, "Oh, yeah, she would fit into our office." She doesn't have a bone sticking out of her nose or something.

Another perceived advantage of posting a picture was the possibility of fostering a sense of connection. As Alex explained: "It makes you more personal, it puts a face behind it. You know, when you would just send out a resume, all they have is a piece of paper. They don't have a human connection to it. So if you have a photo I think it sort of personalizes it a little bit." Fiona believed that her happiness could be seen in her picture and would help: "I'm a pretty happy person, and it's a pretty happy photo. And I think people want to work with happy people ... It gives somebody a sense of who I am."

But the exposure is double-edged. Job seekers also discuss the risks that come with a picture. They share a range of concerns and anxieties rooted in the same insights underlying the perceived benefits. In both cases it is understood that images have powerful effects. The assessment of risks and benefits depends on the extent to which this powerful form of communication is expected to attract or repel potential employers. Anxieties were expressed through insecurity about how one looks in pictures. As Lena put it: "I'm not photogenic so I don't put a photo on there." One job seeker described a chicken and egg situation, feeling that having a picture is important for finding work, but also expressing that she will only feel *confident* enough to post a picture once she had a job: "Once I get a full-time job I think I will have more confidence to put a profile that will include a picture." Job seekers' insecurity is rooted in the sense that any number of assumptions could be made about them based on their pictures. In the same way that a picture may help establish one's "normalcy," or help the viewer connect, it could also drive them away. As Karen put it:

> I think it would make a huge difference. If you can see somebody, connect with them, you might think they look like a friendly person. And they can just get a better feel for you. But on *the flip side* again, people make assumptions based on pictures, and those assumptions could be wrong.

The most common specific concern that job seekers articulated focused on the fact that, as Marie put it, the picture "definitely opens the door for possible discrimination." Jerry explains: "I think it does make a difference to an employer, but if you were to ask them they would probably say no. I don't know, it could be kind of racist, or it could be ageist or sexist or whatever." Jerry is 48-year-old white male and he is clearly aware of the possibility of age discrimination:

> I'd say my age and my photograph on LinkedIn could definitely be a factor ... In this industry, I mean, why would you hire somebody in their 40s when you could hire somebody in their 20s? You can get a lot more mileage out of the younger person, maybe not the experience, but it's a pretty physically demanding job.

Just like age, discrimination based on ethnicity was also a concern. As Veronica put it: "I actually was really hesitant to put up a photo. My name is just very Caucasian, so if you don't see a photo of me, you don't know that I'm an Asian-Pacific Islander." Given that my sample is largely white, with a median age of 53, the data likely understate the extent of job seeker concern about possible racial and ethnic discrimination (Ruggs, Speights, & Walker, 2013), and perhaps over-represents age-related concerns.[6]

Despite these concerns there are several reasons job seekers feel pressured or compelled to include a picture on their LinkedIn profile (76% of interviewees). First, on LinkedIn, profiles are categorized as "incomplete" if they are missing pictures. In LinkedIn workshops job seekers are made aware of the fact that to optimize their profile's visibility to recruiters — that is, to make it more likely that their profile will come up near the top on searches by recruiters — their profiles need to be deemed 100% complete. Completion, among other things, requires a picture.

The SNS's algorithm for determining which job seekers will appear at the top of a keyword search is a critical dimension of the design of the SNS-mediated market, and since only a limited number of job candidates appear at the top of a recruiter search, this design creates a new terrain of competition. In this context, notwithstanding job seekers' ambivalence and awareness of the ways that visibility and exposure may disadvantage them, the design of the SNS-mediated market works to generate competition for scarce visibility. Specifically, it produces a strong pressure on job seekers to complete their SNS profile for the sake of search engine optimization (SEO), which foremost requires adhering to the requirements for profile completeness, including posting a profile picture.

Why would LinkedIn condition the completeness of a profile, and thus search engine optimization, on the inclusion of a picture? Gillespie (2010) argues that when analyzing technological platforms owned by for-profit firms it is important to explore the relationship between the architecture and the business model; for example, Gillespie shows how the YouTube platform is shaped by catering to the desires of advertisers. Following Gillespie (2010) in analyzing the SNS-mediated labor market we hypothesize that the design, and specifically the conditioning of profile's search engine optimization on the inclusion of a picture, is driven by the needs of the playing clients, which in the case of LinkedIn are recruiters. As previously discussed, a long line of research establishes employers' keen interest in candidates' intangible characteristics, and the explicit or implicit link between such intangible characteristics and job applicants' appearance.

Beyond the pressure to include a picture in order to optimize the likelihood of appearing in recruiter searches, LinkedIn workshops and career-advice books emphasize that job seekers "raise question marks" if they do not show up on SNS with their image. The following was a typical exchange between a job seeker and workshop facilitator:

> Facilitator: People with no pictures show up as a silhouette. You'll be more attracted to networking with people with photos. People respond to other human beings. I suggest a close up headshot, that's well-lit. It's nice to have a smile.
>
> Job seeker: If I am over 50, should I post a picture?
>
> Facilitator: Posting a picture is up to you. If you don't want to use a picture you can use an avatar. It's all subjective and depends on you. This can be a delicate issue, but its up to the individual.

This facilitator's refrain of "its up to the individual" avoids discussing the thorny dilemma that older job seeker's face by making it a matter of "subjective" preference. At another workshop the same question surfaced and the facilitator did her best to allay concerns: "In terms of discrimination, if someone found your profile they are looking for a skill set and trying to solve a problem. Something obviously led them to your profile in the first place." Although optimistic facilitator responses such as this allowed the workshop to avoid difficult discussions of discrimination, the persistence of workers' concerns about discrimination was clear during in-depth interviews.

While at interviews and during workshops job seekers consistently expressed anxiety about posting their pictures, over three quarters of the interviewees ultimately opted to post pictures. Jack explains: "The silhouette [that appears if there is no picture] is just kind of lame. It's kind of like you're participating but you're not. Or you're kind of just lurking in the background... You need your photograph to be 100% participating."

A widely shared notion among job seekers was that if one does not post their picture they are presumably trying to hide something about themselves. Alex explained the pressure to post: "It's one of these things, I think you have to do it just because it's expected now. If you don't have a picture out there it may hurt you, because someone may say 'Well, what is this person trying to hide?'" This pressure creates dilemmas. As Patricia puts it: "If you put [a picture] it could go against you, but if you do not have it on, what are you trying to hide? I feel between a rock and hard place. I don't look like I am in my 20s... You are damned if you do and damned if you don't."

Given the possibility of age discrimination, job seekers also face dilemmas about what kind of picture to post. Kenny considered dying his hair but resisted, explaining: "If I post my picture people will find out that I have white hair. If I colored it, it would be a surprise to anyone who knows me." Facing a similar predicament Sandy decided to dye her hair:

> My hair was sort of grey and white and I really liked it and I've had it that way for a long time. And I had an interview several weeks ago. I can't stand dealing with the prejudice involved around age so I had it colored. My photo sort of makes my hair look blonde. (Laughs) These are the things I obsess about. I felt the photo was really important.

In sum, most SNS users I interviewed post pictures but with great ambivalence. Recruiters' ability to see applicant pictures at the *initial* screening stage represents an important change in the labor market architecture, which substantially alters the sequence and extent of job seeker exposure. Job seekers perceive that based on physical characteristics some will be screened out while others may gain an edge. In addition, beyond the early stage filtering based on appearance in pictures, with its winners and losers, all job seekers are presumably affected by becoming more widely exposed to the employers' "gaze" (Foucault, 1977) and thus face pressure to look young and "normal" by, for example, coloring one's hair. Cathy's articulation of the feeling of "damned if you do and damned if you don't" is a sentiment that encapsulates many job seekers' overall feeling about the use of SNS. It is at once necessary in order to network and be visible to potential employers as a candidate, and at the same time, it makes visible factors that may be used to screen them out.

EXPOSURE AND THE ONE-PROFILE DILEMMA

Another important dimension of exposure and of job seekers' loss of control is what I call the one-profile dilemma. Traditionally job seekers adjust their presentation-of-self to the targeted audience. The pre-SNS labor market architecture contained multiple separate "settings" for job seeker "performances" (Goffman, 1959) such that workers could tailor their cover letters, resume, networking appeals, and personal pitches to the perceived needs and preferences of the targeted employer. Most workers have varied experiences and skills that can be framed and highlighted in varied ways. Equally important, most job seekers are able to fine-tune their personal style and image to fit the targeted job. This targeted self-presentation is a specific case of the broader phenomenon famously discussed by Goffman (1959, p. 136) wherein people find it advantageous to give the "impression that the role they are playing at the time is *their most important role* and that the attributes claimed by or imputed to them are *their most essential* and characteristic attributes" (emphasis added). For example, in the context of job search, a person with work experience in both engineering and management, and who is open to both kinds of jobs, will typically want to create different cover letters, and to claim in one cover letter that *at core* they are really engineers, and in the other that *at core* they are really managers. Maintaining these distinct self-presentations for distinct audiences requires that the audiences be segregated. As Goffman explains: "when individuals witness a show that was not meant for them they may, then, become disillusioned about this show, as well as about the show that was meant for them" (1959, p. 136).

The architecture of SNS prevent audience segregation by requiring users to have a single profile for their professional identity, which declares to one and all, *who*, as a professional, one is. The strict requirement of a single identity is common to all dominant SNS platforms, including Facebook and LinkedIn, and is defended on moralistic grounds by the companies controlling SNS. For example, Facebook founder Marc Zuckerberg is quoted as saying: "You have one identity ... Having two identities is an example of lack of integrity" (quoted in van Dijck, 2013, p. 199). But beyond moral concerns, scholars have suggested that "platform owners have vested interest in pushing the need for a uniform online identity" because advertisers, and more relevant in this context recruiters may find it useful to have users' "truthful' data" (van Dijck, 2013, pp. 200, 211).

While it may be advantageous for recruiters to know that a job seeker is not claiming to be a passionate manager in one application and a passionate engineer in another, for workers the new SNS architecture mandating a singular professional identity is experienced as limiting. As one job seeker explained: "One disadvantage is that if you're going after very different targets, you can only really have one profile. It makes sense because you're an individual, but individuals have multiple things." Brian explains the problem this way: "You write a different resume depending on the job you apply for, [but] in LinkedIn it's the same resume to every person." Brian most recently worked as a chef in a restaurant. Seeking more autonomy over his schedule he decided to focus on trying to become a self-employed "home chef." He created an SNS profile with the top line saying "home chef" and in his description of his past jobs he highlights relevant experiences. While being a home chef is Brian's preference, given the difficulty of starting a successful new business, he is also open to considering restaurant chef positions. But using SNS, Brian explains, "I am foreclosing going back to the restaurant business by declaring that I am a personal chef. There are jobs that I might apply for, and am qualified for. So the LinkedIn profile does close off some doors." Brian cannot simultaneously have a profile in which his title is "home chef" and make a compelling case that he is committed to working in a restaurant environment.

Kenny found himself in a similar predicament because he wants to apply to jobs in biomechanics and in engineering. He explains:

> [having one LinkedIn profile] will be a problem for me because I want to do biomechanics but have not done it since 1977. So any resume I send out [for biomechanics] would emphasize the 1977 experience and deemphasize stuff not relevant. But when I apply to engineering jobs I would leave out the biomechanics work. So LinkedIn having it all visible to everybody, it's a problem.

At LinkedIn workshops anxious questions from job seekers about this one-profile dilemma were almost as common as questions about posting pictures. Typically, job seekers ask whether it's possible to create two profiles, and the facilitators, somewhat apologetically explain that in fact this is not possible. As one facilitator put it: "Actually, LinkedIn is very strict about people having only one profile, so this is against their terms of use." Or, as another put it: "It's against company policy. It creates all kinds of problems. But you can represent both interests on the same page." Facilitators' seemed somewhat uncomfortable in providing these answers because of the implicit reminder that the ultimate customers, which SNS company policies serve, are employers not job seekers. From the job seekers' perspective, the one-profile rule is a game-changer that favors employers in the information exchange game, depriving job seekers' of their traditional strategy of customizing information for different audiences.

The one-profile dilemma goes beyond which skills or experiences to highlight and reaches back to the less tangible matter of image. In an earlier section, I discussed the *timing* of the exposure of a picture of the physical self and concerns about discrimination. But the posting of a picture also presents tensions regarding what kind of image of the self to simultaneously expose to multiple audiences. In a pre-SNS world where one's appearance is only revealed in an in-person interview, one's appearance and style can be customized, to some extent, using mode of dress and other "props" (Goffman, 1959), to fit the expectations of the employer. But the posting of a picture upfront requires making a choice about the singular personal style and person one wishes to highlight to *all* potential employers and network contacts.

A similar concern arises with respect to posting updates or comments on SNS. Dan never posts "status updates" on social media like LinkedIn or Facebook. He explains:

> I hesitate to post because it is like saying something to one person, and then another person says I hear you. Facebook give me that feeling. I have 250 friends. To talk to everyone its just weird to me… *It's the "you've got your pants down" feeling all the time.*

The sense of being exposed from having your "pants down" arises because one cannot easily compartmentalize different presentations of self across different audiences. Whatever dimension of the self is presented to one audience is now visible to all. As Goffman notes "when audience segregation fails… difficult problems in impression management arise" (1959, p.139).

Studies of how SNS mediate the social lives of teenagers reveal striking parallels. The challenges of managing a single identity to multiple audiences arises due to what boyd (2014, p. 31) calls "context collapse," wherein "people are forced to grapple simultaneously with otherwise unrelated social contexts that are rooted in different norms and seemingly demand different social responses." For teenagers such tensions typically arise when teachers or parents observe a teen's presentations of self to other teens, or when teens present themselves simultaneously to different groups of peers. For example, Marwick and boyd (2014b, p. 1194) describe the everyday struggle of teens whose SNS posts aim at one group of friends but create negative social repercussions when seen by another group of friends. In short, teens report experiencing a "lost privacy" (Marwick & boyd, 2014a, p. 1056) that is strikingly similar to the experiences described by unemployed job seekers in this paper, and this similarity suggests that the challenges posed by SNS cannot be understood as limited to the context of unemployment but are broader and deeper. Moreover, the fact that teenagers − presumably the most native users of SNS technology in society − are experiencing these challenges undercuts arguments that the challenges described by the unemployed workers in this paper are merely a product of their older age and possible discomfort with digital technologies.

Both teenagers and unemployed workers report that there is no easy and effective individual way of dealing with context collapse. Marwick and boyd (2014a, p. 1056) show that privacy settings offered on SNS are not a reliable solution but are "complicated, confusing, and rarely provide meaningful protection." Job seekers take a few different strategic approaches to dealing with the single profile dilemma.[7] One approach is to present oneself as a generalist who can be potentially valuable to different kinds of employers. To remain viable for different kinds of jobs, David explains, "you make [the profile] very general." The tradeoff, as David explains, is that with a "pared down version of yourself" you are not "the best version of yourself for any particular audience," but at least "you are not alienating the various people you want to connect to." Or as Sheila put it: "I try to convey my work ethics, what I'm strong at, like say at communication and bringing people together, that kind of stuff that I was good at my job, which can be transferrable. So I'm trying to make it so all the skills that I think are transferrable." Kenny likewise explains: "I deal with this by leaving in whatever I want *everybody* to see."

Most interviewees, however, avoided the generalist approach because they believed that such self-presentation would not be effective. Their belief comports with the typical advice of career coaches who claim that in the SNS-mediated labor market, where recruiters can find countless potential workers with a keyword search, a general profile means the job seeker has no chance of standing out as the unique right fit for any specific job opening. Instead, job seekers are increasingly urged to create a clear and unique personal "brand," as can be seen in the dramatic rise in career-advice books focusing on personal branding (Vallas & Cummins, 2015). Sarah, a job seeker explains: "You need a clear picture of what you can do. The description of the profile needs to back up what you say. You can't be jack of all trades. You need a focus." While a clear focus, and the claiming of a particular niche, can indeed help some job seekers, it is also perceived as a high-risk strategy. Job seekers are pushed to become more like entrepreneurs, selling a differentiated product, and putting their financial future in the one basket of this product. Most job seekers are hesitant and anxious about this strategy, wishing to keep more options open, but nonetheless feeling pressure to identify a single niche.

Again we see the dual effects of SNS. First, the redesign of the labor market architecture may advantage some and hurts others. Specifically, the single profile identity may be helpful to job seekers who are specialists and who seek to make visible their distinct niche, but disadvantageous to many workers who have varied experiences and who wish to target varied potential jobs. Second, beyond winners and losers, SNS may generate pressure on all workers to choose and define their "personal brand," and clearly differentiate from others. In this way SNS contribute to broader forces shaping what Foucault (2008) calls the "enterprise of oneself," as will be discussed in the conclusion.

Aside from the pressure to choose a single career niche, a further source of subjective anxiety and potential disadvantage stems from job seekers' loss of control over how their career narrative is revealed and how it is packaged. In crafting traditional resumes job seekers maintain considerable degree of control over the construction of their career narratives. A critical dimension of any career narrative is the sequence in which information is presented, and particularly which information comes first. Whatever information is provided first (i.e., at the top) has disproportionate importance because in many cases resumes or profiles are only given a few seconds by screeners and the first few lines are therefore the only ones that are ever read (Ladders, 2012). Moreover, even if the screener reads beyond the first few lines, the work experience that is first highlighted provides the frame for their reading of further experiences. Given the importance of order, job seekers constructing resumes use a variety of formats. If their most recent job happens to be the most useful for making their case to the prospective employer then a traditional reverse chronological format may be used, but if the most relevant experience was three jobs ago then a "functional" resume may be preferred, which is organized around descriptions of various professional experiences and highlights the most relevant experience at the top.

SNS severely limit job seekers' flexibility in constructing their career narratives by imposing a strict reverse chronological presentation of career history. Carolyn provides an illustrative case. She explains:

> I was only at my last two jobs for a short time because I was laid off twice. People frown on that, they think, "Oh, gee, she doesn't stay at a job." So that's one reason I'm hesitant to use it.... They can look at your information and just make an assumption and rule you out based on whatever assumption that might be.

Carolyn is worried that a negative impression will be created by her short tenure at her two recent jobs, and the structure of SNS profiles requires job seekers to put their positions in reverse chronological order, and to specify the dates. The standardization of formats may benefit employers trying to quickly sift through profiles, but from the perspective of job seekers whose career narratives are not optimally communicated in reverse chronological format, standardization means that their ability to avoid being routinely screened out is diminished. Cathy, who is searching for work as a tutor, focuses on a similar predicament. She explains: "the relevant stuff, the teaching [experience], is at the beginning of my career. There are lots of middle years when I did lots of things. If I do a functional paper resume it can be more vague, but on LinkedIn they want to see dates."

As with other dimensions of the redesigned labor market architecture the standardized package of information is perceived by job seekers to be favorable to recruiters because it limits their own flexibility in how they present their narratives and thus allows for easier — but perhaps more superficial — categorizing and screening out. Specifically, because it makes salient what a worker has done most recently, the loss of control over one's narrative is likely to be particularly disadvantageous to anyone with an non-standard career trajectory, wishing to make a career change, or to return to work they have done in the not recent past. Beyond winners and losers, it can be expected that this architecture exerts pressure on all workers to normalize their careers; to manage their careers in a way that will fit the standardizing conventions and logics of the SNS-mediated labor market.

EXPOSURE OF THE SOCIAL-POLITICAL SELF

A final category of anxiety discussed by job seekers concerns exposure of their social or political selves to potential employers. With the dramatic rise in recent years of SNS and other social media tools such as YouTube and Twitter, which are widely used to communicate about personal, social, and political matters, job seekers worry that such communications may negatively affect their image as appropriate and appealing professionals to employers. As Karla put it: "I really don't want employers looking at my personal life. Making assessments of me."

This concern leads job seekers to monitor the content of their online interactions. Alan explained: "You have to maintain a professional demeanor on LinkedIn. Because even if you make one off-color comment or something you could screw yourself over *forever*... It can come back to haunt you, so you really have to be careful with what you put on electronic media."

Most job seekers have heard stories of inappropriate pictures of drinking or partying leading to employers to disqualify candidates. To deal with this type of challenge some job seekers take the approach of being much more selective of what images to post online, even on more social SNS platforms such as Facebook. Jeff explains that as he began his job search he cleaned up his online image: "Before I was living in Italy, cooking for students, and I had put pictures of me drinking. I took that down. I took down things that look like partying, or do not look serious. I now monitor photos." Sarah likewise explained: "I don't put my family's photos on there. I have one of my pictures and the only other pictures I have my friends have put on there, you know like tagged you. Which, whatever, I can't stop them." With private lives increasingly being lived through SNS such as Facebook, the cleaning up of one's image for employers is not trivial.

The attempt to maintain a sharp line between one's visible professional identity and other forms of identify (e.g., social, political) can be seen in the norms of behavior in LinkedIn groups. Strikingly, LinkedIn group discussions never go beyond technical and professional matters. These groups of workers, facing similar labor market conditions, never discuss their job search experiences, salaries, or difficult bosses. The discussions are also free of any negative emotions or hardships. For unemployed job seekers the sharing of negative emotions or hardships may lead to their exclusion from consideration as job applicants (Sharone, 2013). But even for those who are currently employed there is a perceived risk of open communication. For example, Sherry explained:

> Yeah, that's why I don't put anything on there. I don't write any weird things on there. I still think that's not cool for HR to go in and look at your Facebook, but if you're trashing the company you work for it's not cool either. And some people do that. And we had some managers that were pretty vindictive.

In recent decades, institutions that bring together workers to discuss shared interests and concerns, like labor unions, have declined. While LinkedIn groups provide a new space where such sharing could potentially take place, it is a space that is sharply constrained by visibility and fear of employer scrutiny. When I asked job seekers to explain why the group conversations never go beyond the narrowly technical, there was a consensus explanation. Discussions in the groups, or for that matter in any other non-anonymous online context, are viewable by potential employers and therefore one must strategically present oneself in a manner that will appeal to employers.

For example, in the fall of 2011 the "Occupy Wall Street" (OWS) protests received considerable media attention. Yet, not a single word was mentioned about OWS in the many SNS group discussions that I followed. As one job seeker explained: "I'm sure if I were a prospective employer, and if I learned of candidate's involvement with OWS, or if somebody pointed it out to me, you definitely take it into consideration." The awareness that employers may take such involvement into account goes well beyond individual activity on LinkedIn and spills over to all online activities that may appear on Internet searches.

Social media are heralded as new venues for politics. As former Secretary of State Hilary Clinton put it: "Social media have become the public space of the 21st century," akin to the physical public squares of the 20th century (Coll, 2011). Yet, as social media has facilitated political participation, job seekers have grown concerned about their political and private selves being scrutinized by potential employers. As Helen explains: "Let's say someone was commenting on something, a topic of discussion, maybe they were having a conversation with someone else on Facebook. That comment can be viewed. *Anything can be viewed.*" The sense of exposure leads to many job seekers to abstain from online political activity even during periods of historically high levels of unemployment. As Susan put it:

> I think, yeah, if somebody has very strong political opinions and if they're out there and easy to find on the Internet that could definitely work against them. In the job search the best thing is to appear to be as neutral as possible until you get the job. You don't want to advertise you're for this or for that, because people may have strong adverse reactions. But, you know, there are some people who just don't care. I don't have the luxury to take that attitude.

Maryann explained a similar concern:

> You have to understand that you could actually put your job on the line if you participated in sit-ins or protests. A lot of people kind of walk on eggshells. Even if they watch the news at home they might agree with [the protestors]. They might keep it to themselves, because they don't want [employers] to think that they're too radical or too independent or too left-wing. I mean if they had a mortgage to pay, and two kids to feed, they're not gonna put their job on the line and post: "Hey, I'm gonna go down there at lunchtime and sit in with the Occupy guys."

Andrew echoed the same type of concern: "It could have a negative effect. [Employers] may have a negative view of the Occupy Wall Street crowd, so if they see postings, that could hurt you... So I keep it more at the dinner table with my wife or my social groups versus posting the stuff online. But I think it could have an awful effect, regardless of your opinion."[8]

The belief that there would be repercussions for political activity online was almost universally held. Only one person expressed a view that employers' hiring decisions would not be affected. Everyone else believed there would be an effect and only two interviewees expressed a defiant attitude of maintaining their political involvement online despite this effect. Bruce was one such defiant job seeker: "If they do not hire me because of my political views. I don't want to work for them. So I am pretty open." But Bruce was in a distinct minority.

In the pre-SNS era job seekers would surely refrain from discussing politics in job interviews for the same reasons as articulated above. The difference is that with SNS, and social media more broadly, even if a job seeker does not proactively discuss their politics, job seekers are keenly aware that the employer may nonetheless easily stumble upon online traces of their political activities while browsing the mix of information that may appear about the job seeker on various SNS, social media, and the Internet more broadly. The concern about exposure from posting "inappropriate" social or political information is also intensified by the sense that, as Paul put it, once information is posted "it's there forever." As with pictures, singular profiles, and career narratives, exposure likely produces winners and losers, and exerts a disciplinary (Foucault, 1977) and depoliticizing pressure on all workers.

Looking at research outside the unemployment context we can see similar effects. For example, when examining the practices of users of the micro blogging platform Twitter Marwick and boyd (2010) find that context collapse leads to self-censorship. Specifically, Marwick and boyd (2010, p. 124) find that "people refrain from discussing certain topics on Twitter," including "complaining about an employer" or "one's job," and that most consider discussions of politics as risky and "dangerous" (p. 127). Given their market vulnerability unemployed workers may indeed be more sensitive than others to the risks of exposure, but studies like Marwick and boyd (2010) suggest that what may be clearly seen in interviews with unemployed workers may likely play out more broadly, albeit in less visible ways, across our SNS-mediated society.

IMPLICATIONS AND CONCLUSION

The existing literature on SNS and the labor market has focused on the problem of digital inequality and unequal access and skilled use of SNS. The data presented in this paper suggest the need for greater attention to questions that go beyond such issues and focus on the complex effects of intermediation of labor markets by SNS. Specifically, this paper points to important but previously overlooked effects of SNS in significantly reshaping the space in which job seekers and employers see and are seen.

SNS increase workers' exposure, and this exposure is double-edged. On the one hand, it is beneficial for increasing visibility to employers, growing one's network, and for engaging in practices like reverse networking as described in the first part of this paper. However, on the other hand, it is also the source of new vulnerabilities. Unlike the sharing of information during in-person conversations, in the SNS-mediated labor market one cannot customize the extent or nature of the disclosed information depending on the audience, the context, or the level of established trust. Unlike in-person conversations, sharing information on SNS is not done gradually and reciprocally with each side sharing more in turn. SNS sharing has neither contextual customization nor reciprocity. Most striking, audience segregation (Goffman, 1959) – a timeless strategy for navigating multiple presentations-of-self – is simply not allowed in the SNS house. Information sharing is *upfront* and standardized and visible to all.

Dominant career-advice discourses focus on the benefits of utilizing SNS to workers, and declare that workers not on SNS are rendering themselves practically "non-existent." But even if opting out of SNS is not a viable option for those seeking employment, stepping back, particularly in light of the considerable ambivalences and anxieties expressed by job seekers in this paper, important questions arise that merit further consideration. The first set of questions that should be further explored are whether and how workers are unequally advantaged and disadvantaged by being more visible. Put another way, who are the winners and who are the losers of this new form of labor market intermediation? Does this new sorting of winners and losers correspond to our notions of meritocracy and fairness? Based on the experiences and perceptions of job seekers described in this paper the rise of SNS may indeed produce new forms of stratification. Job seekers' perceive that winning in this new game hinges on factors that are of little relevance to their merit as workers, including their abilities to digitally convey images and narratives that fit the screening logics of the SNS-mediated market. Examples discussed in this paper include how the SNS labor market brings one's physical image to an earlier stage of filtering, which may disadvantage those whose image may not fit employers' expectations or preferences. The SNS labor market may also disadvantage workers who are pursuing two or more kinds of jobs and wish to customize their presentations-of-self for each kind of employers, and workers whose career trajectory and work history are not optimally presented in a reverse chronological format. While there is an emerging literature on the effects of SNS on the evaluation of candidates (Acquisti & Fong, 2013; Bohnert & Ross, 2010), much more research along these lines is needed.

While this paper primarily draws job seekers' experiences and perceptions, on the issue of winners and losers there is reason to believe that SNS may have additional implications that are not easily observable to job seekers themselves. Specifically, future research may examine whether among the effects of increased recruiting through SNS is the increased systematic exclusion of specifically *unemployed* job seekers. A survey of HR professionals by the Society of Human Resources Management reports that the *most* important reason employers offer for using SNS for recruitment is "to recruit *passive* job candidates" (SHRM, 2013). Passive job candidates are typically individuals who are currently employed but are open to considering new opportunities. The stigma of unemployment may lead employers to prefer currently employed candidates as revealed in recent audit studies (Eriksson & Rooth, 2014; Ghayad, 2013), and SNS make it significantly easier and cheaper for recruiters to find, contact, and recruit employed candidates instead of relying on their pool of active – and more likely unemployed – applicants. The extent to which SNS represents a dramatic shift in the ease of recruiting passive job seekers is indubitable when considering Finlay and Coverdill's (2002) fascinating account of the laborious and creative ruses headhunters used in the pre-SNS era just to obtain the contact information for potential passive candidates. One example is tricking receptionists to reveal the names of employees who do certain jobs in their organization by pretending to be a student writing a term paper. The fact that with SNS this information has become very easy and cheap to obtain, often with one just a few clicks, likely benefits those workers that employers most wish to contact and recruit: the currently employed. As a result, the erstwhile advantage unemployed job seekers' enjoyed from having the time and the lower opportunity costs to actively reach out with applications and resumes to potential employers may have greatly diminished. To the extent that use of social networking websites decreases the cost of recruiting currently employed workers for new positions, it would constitute another distinct mechanism by which SNS mediation of the market may provide advantage to the already privileged and further leave behind marginalized unemployed job seekers.

Increased SNS mediation of labor markets raises two kinds of concerns. One concern discussed above focuses on new forms of inequality or mechanisms of reproducing traditional inequalities and exclusions. The other concern may be more difficult to measure but is of no less importance and focuses on the intensification of disciplinary pressures to shape the self in accordance with the demands of the market. The starting point for this analysis is Foucault (1977) insight: Exposure disciplines. This paper argues that the exposure built-in to the design of SNS-mediated labor market disciplines individuals as workers, social beings, and political citizens.

To understand this broad intensification of discipline it is important to note how exposure in the SNS-mediated labor market is of particular slices of information about job seekers, which are thereby made more salient. Two examples from this paper are one's appearance as conveyed in a picture, and one's career narrative as conveyed in strict reverse chronology. It is by calling forth and compiling these specific slices of information that the SNS-mediated labor market facilitates the proliferation of a set of homogenizing standards, against which all workers are measured, ranked, and compared (Foucault, 1977). This process is described by Gutting (2005, p. 84) across a growing variety of modern social contexts in which individuals or institutions are rated and ranked, and as such disciplined to conform. For example, Sauder and Espeland (2009) find that law schools responding to the discipline of regularly published rankings experience intense pressure to conform to the standardized demands and logics of the new metrics. These conforming pressures affect the shape of law schools even when law school deans are aware that given the norms underlying the rankings "student bodies may become homogenized, as admissions officers select for high GPAs instead of students with unique career goals" or "diverse backgrounds" (Sauder & Espeland, 2009, p. 73). As suggested throughout this paper, the rise of SNS as a labor market intermediary may similarly create pressures to normalize professional careers to fit the logic of the SNS labor market. Moreover, beyond careers, for individuals in their private lives as social beings and political citizens, the use of SNS for labor market filtering may also exert pressures to normalize their social selves and refrain from political or otherwise potentially controversial activities that may find a trace online.

The SNS mediation of the labor market thus appears to be one of the forces in the forging of the disciplined and homogenized subject that Foucault variously refers to as the "entrepreneur of himself" (2008, p. 226) or the "enterprise of oneself" (2008, p. 230). The pressure to present a marketable self can be seen as part of what Foucault describes as the "generalization of the 'enterprise' form" which gives rise to a particular "model of social relations and of existence itself" (p. 242) where society is "subdivided, and reduced, not according to the grain of individuals, but according to the grain of enterprises" (p. 241). While Foucault could not have anticipated the SNS-mediated labor market, this paper has shown the variety of ways in which SNS generates disciplinary pressures on subjects to shape themselves as marketable enterprises. For example, because SNS undermines individuals' ability to engage in Goffmanesque audience segregation and construct different presentations of self for different target audiences, individuals are not only constrained with reduced flexibility in seeking different kinds of jobs, but also, and perhaps more profoundly, inhibited in expressing or developing non-marketable dimensions of the self. boyd (2014, pp. 37–38) notes the irony that Internet-based technologies, which a mere 20 years earlier where perceived as holding the promise of enabling radical self-experimentation in which subjects would be free of "the burdens of their 'material' – or physically embodied – identities," have now become entwined with very forces constraining and disciplining subjects through dominant forms of SNS. boyd's particular concern is the ability of teens to develop a self under ever-present surveillance of parents who "hover, lurk, and track." (2014, p. 74). In light of the findings in paper, we may extend boyd's concern and wonder about the free development of all selves under the ever-present gaze of the SNS-mediated market.

This paper reveals the curtailment of online political activities among unemployed workers, but less clear is the breadth of such curtailment. Might the same logic that leads to the curtailment of online political activity also make it less likely that individuals will participate in support groups for health-related issues fearing that the exposure of illness will lead employers screen them out? What other practices and behaviors might be disciplined into extinction because once exposed these might be deemed less than marketable? While it awaits further research to explore the full implications of SNS reshaping of the labor market, as an increasing proportion of modern life is mediated by SNS we may expect that correspondingly workers' concerns about employability will have increasingly profound effects on all realms of modern social life.

Can the disciplinary pressures described in this paper be successfully resisted and countered? It is worthwhile reflecting on Crossley's (1993, p. 407) simple but provocative question of whether being exposed must always be "experienced anxiously or as controlling." In considering the conditions that make exposure controlling it is striking that precarity is the common link between the unemployed adults discussed in this paper, and the other group of individuals where prior research reveals similarities in experiences with SNS – teenagers living with their parents. While different in obvious ways these two groups nonetheless do share the vulnerability of having their SNS-mediated selves scrutinized by parents and employers, respectively, on whom they are materially dependent. Future research might explore the hypothesis that disciplinary effects of visibility vary in relation to the degree of one's precarity. For example, we expect that in the university context visibility would exert more discipline on precarious adjunct faculty than on tenured faculty. If this hypothesis is correct then it follows that institutions that counteract precarity would also diminish the force of disciplinary pressures.[9]

Addressing precarity offers an indirect way of countering disciplinary power. A more direct approach would be to contest aspects of the design of the SNS-mediated labor market. The precondition for any such contestation is recognition that this market, and the technology that undergirds it, do more than provide a neutral space for the spontaneous interactions of buyers and sellers. As Foucault (2008) recognizes, all markets are sites of regulation and discipline. Foucault's insight can be extended in critically examining, problematizing, and politicizing technologically mediated labor markets. Building on Gillespie (2010), it is important to develop an understanding of the interests and logics underlying the specific designs of technologically enabled "platforms" like SNS, and how such designs shape uses and outcomes. At least since passage of civil rights legislation in the 1960s the United States has recognized that hiring practices — even in the private sector — are public matters, and this is reflected in regulations prohibiting various forms of discrimination in the hiring process. Given the growing role of SNS in mediating the labor market, and the varied effects of such mediation as described in this paper, it is vital to recognize and grapple with questions of SNS architecture as *public* issues, and to facilitate democratic participation in assuring that SNS are designed in ways that serve the broad public interest.

With the bulk of our interactions migrating to online spaces, we are living in a new social architecture with levels of visibility unimaginable only two decades ago. This architecture disciplines workers, teens, and tweeters alike; yet, unlike Foucault's (1977) panopticon, it is important to note that visibility in SNS is not only vertical — of the watchtower — but also horizontal — of the other inmates — and therefore holds the potential of being an emerging space where those with shared hardships and grievances can find each other and develop horizontal solidarity. The findings in this paper suggest that any such horizontal solidarity will be constrained so long as the architecture structuring our SNS interactions does not facilitate horizontal visibility which is free of vertical surveillance.

NOTES

1. While the theories of Goffman and Foucault are very different this paper draws on both given their shared concern about the ways in which institutional contexts shape the performative nature of the self.
2. Press release from Labor and Workforce Development on February 3, 2011.

3. The workshop trainers are employees of the One Stop center and establish their legitimacy to teach these materials on the basis of their past experience supporting job seekers learn how to effectively use SNS.

4. While at the time of writing LinkedIn is the dominant SNS for job seekers, and therefore most examples in this paper draw on experiences with LinkedIn, this paper is not only about LinkedIn or any specific SNS or feature thereof. Given the rapid changes in this sector it is possible that any particular feature of LinkedIn or other SNS discussed in this paper may change; yet, I contend that the overall direction of changes in the architecture of SNS-mediated labor market are likely to continue pointing toward the double-edged forms of exposure discussed in this paper.

5. Data base on Ranking.com accessed on June 3 2016 at http://scripts.ranking.com/data/report_domain.aspx

6. It is also worthy of noting that while interviewees did not often discuss a possible employer bias in favor of physically attractive candidates, the previously described research suggests that physically attractive job candidates are advantaged in the hiring process and we can accordingly expect that this form of bias is also exacerbated by the availability of photos at the early screening stage.

7. Some teens attempt to navigate context collapse by engaging in "social stenography," the "encoding [of] a meaningful message to a narrow, desired audience" (Marwick & boyd, 2014a, p. 1058). The practice of phrasing a communication in a way that is decodable by the targeted audience but not by others appears similar to politicians' use of dog-whistle messages to targeted audiences, but is not a strategy discussed by any of the unemployed workers I interviewed.

8. Consistent with the findings of Marwick and boyd (2010) most interviewees did not trust "privacy settings" on SNS to limit the exposure of information. Some cited the example of Facebook updating its platform in a way which made generally visible information previously set to only be visible to a limited audience. To avoid exposure individuals can and do use Internet platforms that allow for anonymity but such platforms lack the potential impact of open discussions among workers who share personal networks.

9. It is notable that in Foucault's (1986) own writing the clearest case of visibility that is not associated with discipline are the practices of self-examination which enhance the autonomy of ancient Greek men with sufficient economic resources to afford the time for such practices.

REFERENCES

Acquisti, A., & Fong, C. M. (2013). *An experiment in hiring discrimination via online social networks.* SSRN Working Paper No. 2031979.

Autor, D. H. (2001). Wiring the labor market. *Journal of Economic Perspectives, 5*(1), 25–40.

Becker, H. S. (1998). *Tricks of the trade: How to think about your research while you're doing it.* Chicago, IL: University of Chicago Press.

Bohnert, D., & Ross, W. (2010). The influence of social networking web sites on the evaluation of job candidates. *Cyberpsychology, Behavior and Social Networking, 13*(3), 341–347.

boyd, D. (2014). *It's complicated: The social lives of networked teens.* New Haven, CT: Yale University Press.

Brown, V., & Vaughn, D. (2011). The writing on the (Facebook) wall: The use of social networking sites in hiring decisions. *Journal of Business and Psychology, 26*(2), 219–225.

Burawoy, M. (1998). The extended case method. *Sociological Theory, 16*(1), 4–33.

Caers, R., & Castelyn, V. (2011). LinkedIn and Facebook in Belgium: The influences and biases of social network sites in recruitment and selection produces. *Science and Computer Review*, *29*(4), 437–448.

Cappelli, P. (2001). *Making the most of online recruiting*. Boston, MA: Harvard Business.

Cetina, K. K. (2009). The synthetic situation: Interactionism for a global world. *Symbolic Interaction*, *32*(1), 61–87.

Cetina, K. K., & Bruegger, U. (2002). Global microstructures: The virtual societies of financial markets. *American Journal of Sociology*, *107*(4), 905–950.

Cober, R., & Brown, D. (2006). *Direct employers association recruiting trends survey*. Washington, DC: Booz Allen Hamilton.

Coll, S. (2011). The Internet: For Better or for Worse. *New York Times Magazine*.

Crossley, N. (1993). The politics of the gaze: Between Foucault and Merleau Ponty. *Human Studies*, *16*(4), 399–419.

DiMaggio, P., Hargittai, E., Celeste, C., & Shaer, S. (2004). Digital inequality: From unequal access to differentiated use. In K. Neckerman (Ed.), *Social inequality* (pp. 355–400). New York, NY: Russell Sage Foundation.

Duerson, A., & van Dijk, J. (2014). The digital divide shifts to differences in usage. *New Media and Society*, *16*(3), 507–526.

Eriksson, S., & Rooth, D.-O. (2014). Do employers use unemployment as a sorting criterion when hiring? Evidence from a field experiment. *The American Economic Review*, *104*(3), 1014–1039.

Finlay, W., & Coverdill, J. (2002). *Headhunters: Matchmaking in the labor market*. Ithaca, NY: ILR Press.

Foucault, M. (1977). *Discipline and punish: The birth of the prison*. London: Allen Lane.

Foucault, M. (1986). *Volume 3 of the history of sexuality the care of the self*. New York, NY: Vintage Books.

Foucault, M. (2008). *The birth of biopolitics*. New York, NY: Palgrave Macmillan.

Ghayad, R. (2013). *The jobless trap*. Working Paper. Retrieved from http://media.wix.com/ugd/576e9a_684e84d83d694fef8c58c4d176cd4c4b.pdf

Gillespie, T. (2010). The politics of 'platforms'. *New Media & Society*, *12*(3), 347–364.

Goffman, I. (1959). *The Presentation of Self in Everyday Life*. New York, NY: Doubleday Anchor Books.

Gutting, G. (2005). *Foucault: A very short introduction*. Oxford: Oxford University Press.

Halford, S., & Savage, M. (2010). Reconceptualizing digital social inequality. *Information Communication and Society*, *13*(7), 937–955.

Hargittai, E. (2008). The digital reproduction of inequality. In D. Grusky (Ed.), *Social stratification* (pp. 936–944). Boulder, CO: Westview Press.

Hilbert, M. (2016). The bad news is that the digital access divide is here to stay. *Telecommunications Policy*, *40*(6), 567–581.

Jobvite. (2015). *Recruiter nation survey*. Retrieved from https://www.jobvite.com/wp-content/uploads/2015/09/jobvite_recruiter_nation_2015.pdf

Ladders. (2012). *Keeping an eye on recruiter behavior*. Retrieved from http://cdn.theladders.net/static/images/basicSite/pdfs/TheLadders-EyeTracking-StudyC2.pdf

Lamont, M., & White, P. (2009). *Interdisciplinary standards for systematic qualitative research*. National Science Foundation Workshop for Cultural Anthropology, Law and Social Sciences, Political Science, and Sociology Programs; 2005 May 19–20; Arlington, VA.

Lane, C. M. (2011). *A company of one: insecurity, independence, and the new world of white-collar unemployment*. Ithaca, NY: Cornell University Press.

Lee, H., Park, N., & Hwang, Y. (2015). A new dimension of the digital divide: Exploring the relationship between broadband connection, smartphone use, and communication competence. *Telematics and Informatics*, *32*(2015), 45–56.

Marlowe, M., Schneider, S. L., & Nelson, C. E. (1996). Gender and attractiveness biases in hiring decisions: Are more experienced managers less biased? Journal of *Applied Psychology*, *81*(1), 11–21.

Marwick, A., & boyd, D. (2010). I tweet honestly, I tweet passionately: Twitter users, context collapse, and the imagined audience. *New Media & Society, 13*(1), 114−133.

Marwick, A., & boyd, D. (2014a). Networked privacy: How teenagers negotiate context in social media. *New Media & Society, 16*(7), 1051−1067.

Marwick, A., & boyd, D. (2014b). 'It's just drama': Teen perspectives on conflict and aggression in a networked era. *Journal of Youth Studies, 17*(9), 1187−1204.

Moss, P., & Tilly, C. (2001). *Stories employers tell: Race, skill, and hiring in America.* New York, NY: Russell Sage Foundation.

Pick, J., Sarkar, A., & Johnson, J. (2015). United States digital divide: State level analysis of spatial clustering and multivariate determinants of ICT utilization. *Socio-Economic Planning Sciences, 49*(2015), 16−32.

Rivera, L. (2015). *Pedigree: How elite students get elite jobs.* Princeton, NJ: Princeton University Press.

Robinson, L. (2009). A taste for the necessary: A Bourdieuian approach to digital inequality. *Information, Communications and Society, 12*(4), 488−507.

Ruffle, B. J., & Shtudiner, Z. (2013). Are good-looking people more employable? SSRN. Retrieved from http://ssrn.com/abstract=1705244

Ruggs, E., Speights, S., & Walker, S. (2013). Are you in or out? Employment discrimination in online and offline networks. *Industrial and Organizational Psychology, 6*(4), 457−462.

Sauder, M., & Espeland, W. (2009). The discipline of rankings: Tight coupling and organizational change. *American Sociological Review, 74*, 63−82.

Sharone, O. (2013). *Flawed system/flawed self: Job searching and unemployment experiences.* Chicago, IL: University of Chicago Press.

Small, M. L. (2009). 'How many cases do I need?': On science and the logic of case selection in field-based research. *Ethnography, 10*(1), 5−38.

Smith, V., & Neuwirth, E. (2008). *The good temp.* Ithaca, NY: Cornell University Press.

Society for Human Resources Management. (2013). *Social networking websites and recruiting selection.* Retrieved from http://www.shrm.org/Research/SurveyFindings/Articles/Pages/SHRM-Social-Networking-Websites-Recruiting-Job-Candidates.aspx

Trost, J. E. (1986). Statistically nonrepresentative stratified sampling: A sampling technique for qualitative studies. *Qualitative Sociology, 9*(1), 54−57.

Vallas, S., & Commins, E. (2015). Personal branding and identity norms in the popular business press: Enterprise culture in an age of precarity. *Organization Studies, 36*(3), 293−319.

Van Dijck, J. (2013). 'You have one identity': Performing the self on Facebook and LinkedIn. *Media, Culture and Society, 35*(2), 199−215.

Watkins, L. M., & Johnston, L. (2000). Screening job applicants: The impact of physical attractiveness and application quality. *International Journal of Selection and Assessment, 8*(2), 76−84.

DEALING WITH DOWNSIZING: NEW ORGANIZATIONAL CAREERS IN FINANCIAL SERVICES AFTER THE GREAT RECESSION

Corey Pech

ABSTRACT

The literature on precarious and insecure work rarely examines how workers with jobs in large bureaucratic firms experience insecurity. Current theories suggest two approaches. First, workers might focus on their individual occupation and detach their commitment from firms that no longer reciprocate long-term commitments. Second, employees might respond with increased organizational commitment because leaving an employer creates risks of uncertainty. Based on in-depth interviews with 22 financial services professionals, this paper refines our understanding of when workers focus on intra-organizational career development. This happens when large firms offer opportunities for advancement and foster loyalty. I develop the terms spiral staircase and serial monogamy career. A spiral staircase career results when workers take entrepreneurial approaches to advancement that include lateral job changes and vertical promotions within a firm. When the local labor market has multiple firms in their sector, career advancement may take an intermediate form, in which workers spend medium-to-long-term stints with multiple organizations. I call this the serial monogamy career. My research

Emerging Conceptions of Work, Management and the Labor Market
Research in the Sociology of Work, Volume 30, 33–57
Copyright © 2017 by Emerald Publishing Limited
ISSN: 0277-2833/doi:10.1108/S0277-283320170000030003

*shows how sector characteristics and geography can impact worker commit-
ment and mobility in insecure environments.*

Keywords: Boundaryless careers; new organizational careers; precarious
work; insecurity

INTRODUCTION

U.S. firms laid off workers in large numbers during the Great Recession
(Ydstie, 2010). The post-recession reality allows for an exploration of how
workers in large bureaucratic organizations view insecurity and mobility during
and after economic downturns. It remains unclear how workers in large firms
would react to their job seeming precarious. The decline in job security and the
rise of precarious work has been well-studied for almost 30 years (Lane, 2011;
Newman, 1988). There is also a smaller literature on surviving downsizing that
focuses on decreases in well-being either among survivors or comparatively
with laid off workers (Knudsen, Johnson, Martin, & Roman, 2003; Parks-
Yancy, 2004; Snorradottir, Tomasson, Vilhjalmsson, & Rafnsdottir, 2015).
There is even less literature on workers experiencing firm restructuring (Lam
et al., 2015). There are two competing ideas for how workers will respond to
turbulence. First, literature on precarious work suggests workers will feel
detachment from their firm (Lane, 2011). Similarly, theories of boundaryless
careers, in which workers develop careers over multiple organizations, suggest
workers will respond with increased firm mobility (Arthur & Rousseau, 1996).
Second, some career literature suggests workers might still feel commitment to
their firm and take an intra-organizational approach to career development
(Clarke, 2013).

This study addresses the question, what happens when workers in large
bureaucratic firms experience employment insecurity? What are the effects on
their organizational commitment and attitudes toward career development?
This paper is based on in-depth interviews with 22 employees at financial services firms in New York City and Columbus, Ohio. They all have either been
laid off or witnessed downsizing during or since the recession. Many of the
financial professionals under study do not expect job security anymore, but still
framed attachment to their firm through the new organizational career framework. This relatively new and highly suggestive concept has been introduced by
Clarke (2013). Clarke suggests new organizational careers are co-managed by
employers and employees in a way that fosters commitment. In this model,
advancement is entrepreneurial, hence the need for co-management. This
approach stands in contrast to traditional organizational careers in which firms
provided structured job ladders (Clarke, 2013).

I show how respondents frame their preference for the new organizational career and I extend Clarke's (2013) term. My data speaks to two distinct variants of the new organizational career which I refer to as the serial monogamy and spiral staircase careers. The serial monogamy career involves medium- or long-term tenures at multiple firms. These attachments are expected to be stable and enduring. The spiral staircase model involves a career in one firm that develops through a mixture of lateral job changes and vertical advancement. Geography is one factor that can shape which variant workers experience. In New York, the serial monogamy career was more prevalent, while more workers in Columbus had spiral staircase careers. I show that depending on sector characteristics, increased insecurity does not necessarily lead to lessened commitment and increased mobility. I also provide insights into workers' commitment to new firms after layoffs.

PRECARIOUS WORK AND INSECURITY

Discussions of precarious work tend to focus on job insecurity. There has been particular interest in the rise of white-collar insecurity, beginning with Newman's (1988) classic study of laid off professionals. More contemporary studies tend to focus on either contingent workers (Hatton, 2011; Smith, 2002) or unemployed workers (Lane, 2011). While it may be difficult to define precarity, it is usually linked to increased insecurity. Therefore, an increase in layoffs, either experienced or observed, can be said to make a job, or all jobs within a firm, seem more precarious. Likewise, a pattern of downsizing across organizations in a sector can be said to make work in that sector seem precarious.

There is attitudinal evidence to support the claim that workers in general feel more insecure. Many individuals are concerned with both job loss and their ability to find new jobs if they are laid off (Fullerton & Wallace, 2007; Schmidt, 1999). Kalleberg and Marsden (2013) find that job security is now the benefit workers most desire in a job. They argue the increase in the preference for security is directly related to its widespread decline. Vallas and Prener (2012), in an overview of popular business publications, find an explosion in an individualist and entrepreneurial rhetoric of career advancement. However, some authors argue that the new rhetoric of insecurity is more of an academic construction than a reflection of empirical reality (Fevre, 2007; Rodrigues & Guest, 2010).

Regardless of whether jobs have become more insecure or if workers just feel more insecure, there are still implications for how workers view their relationship with their firm. Cohen and Mallon (1999) find portfolio workers (workers who package individual skills and sell them) feel detached from firms that hire them. This detachment is perceived as reflecting the zeitgeist, not as a quirky or alternative career path. Lane's (2011, chapter 2) concept "the company of one," and Pugh's (2014, pp. 18-19) concept "the one-way honor system," both suggest workers accept that firms provide little reciprocation to employee attachment. Pugh makes an exception, however, for workers who have stable jobs. The winners in the new economy, according to Pugh (2014), Lane (2011), and Sennett (1998) discuss flexibility and not longevity. At their core, these approaches document a shift toward an occupational career outlook, where individuals are tied more to a job than a firm. This contrasts with a career focused on organizational commitment. However, the white-collar workers in all three studies are itinerant. Lam and colleagues (2015) find workers in restructuring firms feel increased insecurity, though this can be mitigated somewhat by their managers. None of the above authors studied workers with white-collar careers in large bureaucratic firms, except for Lam and colleagues who study the IT sector, one notorious for a lack of attachment to firms (Saxenian, 1996). There is older literature that suggests size of firm is positively correlated to levels of employee satisfaction and commitment (Pfeffer & Baron, 1988).

Recent literature on downsizing shows that female managers are harmed more than men (Haverman, Broschak, & Cohen, 2009); and both women and minorities are expected to see declines in social capital (Parks-Yancy, 2004). However, all survivors do report feeling more job stress and less perceived organizational support (Knudsen et al., 2003). In the long run increased insecurity works as a chronic stressor and can have negative health effects (Glavin, 2015). Yet, survivors still score comparatively better than those who were laid off on measures of health and well-being (Snorradottir et al., 2015). Lastly, when organizations take a "caring" approach to recessions and downsizing, workers may not lose commitment or perceived reciprocity (Grdinovac & Yancey, 2012). Caring approaches are defined as treating people humanely and the scale used by Grdinovac and Yancey include questions like whether executives took larger pay cuts than lower level employees (see Grdinovac & Yancey, 2012, pp. 11−13). While we know about the effects of demographic characteristics and organizational approaches on downsizing, we know little about how firm structure or sector characteristics affect workers.

What the sociological literature on insecurity and precarious work lacks is a way to talk about comparative experiences based on organizational context. Even if there is a general rise in feelings of insecurity, workers will respond differently depending on their geography and/or sector characteristics. It makes sense that Lane's (2011) laid off tech workers would experience detachment from firms and no longer expect much professional development. Earlier publications on the tech industry also find that workers were not bound to traditional organizational careers (Saxenian, 1996). It also makes sense that workers who have not had stable careers would not expect firms to reciprocate their commitment (Pugh, 2014, chapter 2). Literature on precarious work suggests workers will respond to turbulence with detachment from their firm, reflecting the "zeitgeist" of increased insecurity (Cohen & Mallon, 1999; Vallas & Prener, 2012). Some contingent workers do identify with the firm by internalizing management ideologies (Padavic, 2005), but these workers do not express commitment in the style of the traditional career, rather they are more excusing the regime of detachment. Workers entrenched in corporate bureaucracies should have different outlooks. The new organizational career (Clarke, 2013), arising out of a debate over boundaryless and traditional organizational careers, provides another possible theory for workers' responses to insecurity.

BOUNDARYLESS AND TRADITIONAL/NEW ORGANIZATIONAL CAREERS

The traditional organizational career is spent with just one firm, internal labor markets provide advancement, and workers feel a strong sense of belonging to the organization, establishing a collectivist ethic (Whyte, 1956). However, this model was short-lived, limited to the post-war era, and largely only attainable by white men. As the 20th century neared a close, several publications emerged studying the decline of traditional organizational careers (Jacoby, 1999; Newman, 1988). The traditional organizational career model relied on a bifurcation between core and periphery workers (or good and bad jobs). Smith (2002) problematized that distinction to suggest insecurity and risk is manifest in many jobs and organizations in the contemporary economy. In her view risk and mobility can be either positive or negative for workers. To replace the traditional organizational career, the term boundaryless career was developed (Arthur & Rousseau, 1996). The concept was meant to demonstrate that new careers were marked by "independence from, rather than dependence on, traditional organizational career arrangements" (Arthur & Rousseau, 1996, p. 6). Boundaryless career studies often look at worker movement across organizations. In other words, inter-firm mobility is the most common way to empirically study boundaryless careers (see Inkson, Gunz, Ganesh, & Roper, 2012).

Studying inter-firm mobility provided mixed support for the prevalence of boundaryless careers. Some authors find that mobility is not higher in recent decades, as the boundaryless career theories would suggest (Jacoby, 1999). Other research finds that managers and professionals were still least likely to switch firms, the very people it was suggested would benefit most from boundaryless careers (Rodrigues & Guest, 2010). Even in industries where boundaryless careers might be expected, such as the technology sector, the phenomenon is far from universal (Ituma & Simpson, 2009; Lane, 2011; Saxenian, 1996). On the other hand, a recent study by Kim (2013) found that professional employees switched jobs at a higher pace in the 2000s than in the 1990s. Additionally, there is still evidence that job instability is on the rise; this trend has just been masked by women's increased labor market activity (Hollister, 2012).

Besides job mobility, scholars have also studied ideology, or the boundaryless career orientation. Scholars show that people generally prefer security and promotions, regardless of their age (Dries, Pepermans, & De Kerpel, 2008). Workers can also prefer staying with their current firm even when they consider themselves to be marketable (Wajcman & Martin, 2001). However, there is relatively low correlation between boundaryless career orientation and behavior (Briscoe, Hall, & DeMuth, 2006; Gubler, Arnold, & Coombs, 2014).

There are many critiques of the term boundaryless career, including calls for more nuanced discussion of institutional context and individual agency (Dany, Louvel, & Valette, 2011; Inkson et al., 2012; Pringle & Mallon, 2003). Recently, there have been calls for synthesis between organizational and boundaryless careers (Arthur, 2014; Gubler et al., 2014). Gubler and colleagues (2014) suggest that individuals often change occupations and move across geographic regions without switching firms. They argue this is a type of boundaryless career. Other scholars suggest occupations or geographic regions can serve as boundaries, limiting career movement (Rodrigues, Guest, & Budjanovcanin, 2015). Clarke (2013) instead argues for the term "new organizational careers" when individuals experience movement within a firm. In this framework, workers do not have traditional job ladders and must take on an entrepreneurial spirit toward training and promotion, but the firm helps co-manage this experience by encouraging networking and internal movement. This new organizational career provides a good middle ground for encompassing aspects of boundarylessness into a career that can be developed in one firm.

The distinction between boundaryless careers and new organizational careers provides a framework, counter to the precarious work literature, for thinking about how individuals respond to increased insecurity or precarity. Concepts from Lane (2011) and Pugh (2014) suggest more of a boundaryless outlook, in which employees in insecure jobs do not expect much employer reciprocity to their commitment. On the other hand, workers in big organizations that have been laid off or observe layoffs may still see the employment relationship as reciprocal and their careers as co-managed with their firm (whether it be a new firm or existing attachment). This latter attitude would be more in line with Clarke's new organizational career (2013). However, neither model allows room for workers that neither move firms frequently nor stay with one firm for their whole career. Workers who spend an intermediate amount of time with one firm or multiple firms, but experience these stints as relatively permanent employment, would fall outside the pre-existing boundaryless and new organizational frameworks that privilege occupation or organization, but not both simultaneously.

CAREERS IN FINANCIAL SERVICES

Finance is well-studied by scholars for several reasons. The financial services sector is one of the biggest and most powerful in the economy (Tomaskovic-Devey & Lin, 2011). Many non-finance firms look to the big finance companies as a model for new employment relationships (Ho, 2009; Sennett, 2007). Finance executives frequently move to non-finance firms to occupy managerial positions (Ho, 2009). And lastly, financial services firms were at the heart of the Great Recession.

Most studies of financial services careers focus on job insecurity (Ho, 2009; Tempest, McKinlay, & Starkey, 2004; Zaloom, 2010). The results seem unequivocal that finance professionals are becoming insecure workers. How this insecurity affects organizational commitment is less clear. Constant insecurity is reason to suggest finance workers may react with detachment; this is similar to how Ho's (2009) respondents discuss insecurity. Yet Ho (2009) only studies Wall Street investment bankers. It is unclear how other finance workers would react to insecurity. The large and bureaucratic nature of financial services firms makes them the ideal location for new organizational careers (Clarke, 2013).

DATA AND METHODS

The author conducted 22 interviews with professionals working in financial services. In-depth interviews were chosen because they allow individual accounts to be pieced together into a broader narrative (Weiss, 1994). It was the aim to see how individuals understand their career and attachment to their firm in their own words, a task that is not possible with a fixed-response survey. Ten respondents work in New York City and the other 12 respondents work in Columbus, Ohio (except for one who relocated from Columbus to Scottsdale, Arizona). New York is the epicenter of finance and opportunities for career advancement abound. Columbus is both a fairly representative U.S. city and home to large regional and national headquarters for financial services firms. Columbus also hosts multiple universities, corporate headquarters, and white-collar professional services firms. Since New York has a dense financial sector and Columbus is more representative, yet still has a large white-collar workforce, this helps ensure variation based on geography. Additionally, this study is strengthened by including workers from the same firm in multiple cities, including employees who formerly worked for a different firm in the set. All these steps were taken to maximize the salience of firm and sector characteristics in analysis. The effects of the recession were also slightly different for the two cities. New York City's unemployment declined at a lower rate than the national average from 2009 to 2012 (Kohli, 2014). In Columbus, by September 2014 there were more jobs than when the recession started (Williams & Gearino, 2015). However, given the small and heterogeneous sample, multiple factors can contribute to responses. For instance, the Columbus sample makes on average less money and is younger. But following others with small sample comparisons (see Blair-Loy, 2001, pp. 77–78), I can still make suggestive comparisons based on how respondents frame their experiences. Additionally, the respondents who overlap on many characteristics, such as the older Columbus workers, serve to confirm rather than contradict the trends found in the research.

Sampling was purposive to include well-compensated professionals with a variety of ages, backgrounds, and work functions. An initial informant was found through a colleague's referral. Next, respondent-driven sampling was used, but each respondent-driven line included a limit of three individuals to avoid selection bias. In total 16 of the 22 respondents were found via respondent-driven sampling, the rest were procured through colleague referrals. Because the study relied on snowball sampling and just two geographic locations, it is possible a set of more itinerant workers were excluded from the study. Those with good networks are likely to be longer tenured employees or those who approach their job with a more long-term mindset. However, the workers under study do represent one case contra to those previously studied, so we can learn particular frames used by this set of workers. Respondents occupy different areas of the sector: 12 work at banks and 10 work at insurance companies that offer financial services products. All the firms employing respondents are large, well-known, national, or global firms. Respondents hold a variety of jobs. A fuller description of respondents' demographics can be seen from Table 1. Approximately half of the respondents make six-figure salaries when including bonuses, including all 10 New York respondents. Most Columbus respondents made over $75,000 annually, with three exceptions — two employees who are early in their careers and one who lacks a college degree.

Interviews ranged from 45 to 75 minutes, with most approximating 55 minutes. Interviews were semi-structured to allow respondents stories to drive the interview. This process is consistent with Cohen's (2006) career narrative approach and has been used by others doing career research, such as Clarke (2013). Topics discussed included employment history, considerations employees had when deciding to change jobs or when they thought about changing jobs, what they like or do not like about their firm and employment, and how they would evaluate their benefits. Women make up 55% of the set and 55.7% of all finance and insurance workers.[1] Previous studies have shown that women face discrimination in finance (Blair-Loy, 2001; Turco, 2010). Yet those studies are looking at specific areas of financial services, Turco (2010) particularly looks at small firms. This is not to say respondents in this study did not face discrimination, but that was not a research question and did not come up during interviews.

Table 1. Respondents.

Name	Firm	Job Function	Tenure (Yrs.)	Age	Gender	Ethnicity	Income BaseK (bonus%)	City	Laid Off (Y/N)
Christine	East End Bank	Learning and Development	12	53	Female	Caucasian	160(25)	New York	Y
Beverly	East End Bank	Learning and Development	13	40	Female	African-American	125(15)	New York	Y
Penny	East End Bank	Community Development	17	50s	Female	African-American	Six figures	New York	N
Leslie	Southern Insurance	Human Resources	6	52	Female	Caucasian	135(15–20)	New York	Y
Betty	Park Bank	Auto and Student Loans	25	49	Female	Hispanic	120(30)	New York	N
Theodore	East End Bank	Banking	10	68	Male	Caucasian	Unreported	New York	N
James	East End Bank	Banking	3	52	Male	Caucasian	Six figures	New York	Y
Julia	East End Bank	Community Development	15	65	Female	Caucasian	140–160(20)	New York	N
Juan	Rockefeller Bank	Community Relations	6	48	Male	Hispanic	99.4(15)	New York	Y
David	Madison Bank	Financial Advising	6	43	Male	Caucasian	250–500	New York	N
Amelia	Park Bank	Compliance	3	35	Female	Caucasian	99(5–10)	Columbus	N
Peter	Central Insurance	Marketing	22	52	Male	Caucasian	100(15)	Columbus	N
Esther	Central Insurance	Learning and Development	28	50	Female	Caucasian	88(3–5)	Columbus	N
Donald	Central Insurance	IT	27	49	Male	Caucasian	50s	Columbus	N
Niles	Central Insurance	Compliance	1	24	Male	Caucasian	46(2)	Columbus	N
Belinda	Park Bank	IT	5	28	Female	Caucasian	75(2)	Columbus	N
Jennifer	Central Insurance	IT	6	31	Female	Caucasian	84(5)	Columbus	N

Table 1. (Continued)

Name	Firm	Job Function	Tenure (Yrs.)	Age	Gender	Ethnicity	Income BaseK (bonus%)	City	Laid Off (Y/N)
Carl	Central Insurance	Learning and Development	20	54	Male	Caucasian	80–110	Columbus	N
Priya	Central Insurance	Learning and Development	6	49	Female	Indian	74(3)	Columbus	Y
Mark	Central Insurance	Mortgage Foreclosure	3	32	Male	Caucasian	40(2)	Columbus	Y
Jane	Park Bank	Compliance	3	31	Female	Caucasian	80(3–5)	Columbus	N
Morris	Central Insurance	Analytics	4	34	Male	Caucasian	85–100(3–5)	Columbus	N

All 22 interviews were transcribed and coded by the author. Transcripts were analyzed thematically, a common approach for interview studies (Lamont, Morning, & Mooney, 2002). Themes such as insecurity, importance of employer-provided benefits, and career path were used for top-level coding. After that, the sections were grouped together and read closely for the induction of more detailed patterns. Interviewing concluded after the completion of 22 because all respondents' answers were easily categorized into the frames that had emerged. All names of respondents and companies are pseudonyms.

LARGE FINANCIAL FIRMS BECOME PRECARIOUS

The large and bureaucratic firms that employ the individuals under study are the type of firms that gave rise to the traditional organizational career. Yet, in the wake of the global financial crisis, all of the employees interviewed experienced downsizings either as a laid off worker or an observer of firm restructuring. Seven of the 22 respondents were laid off during, or since, the financial crisis. Restructuring as a process generally increases workers' perceptions of insecurity (Lam et al., 2015). This suggests that financial services jobs should seem more precarious. Wall Street workers do expect layoffs throughout their career (Ho, 2009), but many of those in the positions under study mentioned they first expected instability after the recession.

Leslie, an employee of Southern Insurance in New York, worked at Park Bank for 16 years. According to Leslie, "I thought I'd retire there. But they moved the credit card division I supported down to Delaware. I had the opportunity to stay or leave and they gave me a really nice severance package." After she moved to Southern Insurance, she continued to see massive downsizing, "talk about insecure and unstable. We've been having reductions in force every 2 weeks; we have one coming in April. They are eliminating jobs." She went on to say "we're always wondering which parts [of the firm] will go away." After creating a stable career at Park Bank, Leslie was laid off during the financial crisis and no longer expects sector stability.

Younger workers who have been hired since the financial crisis also experience the constant hiring and firing nature of their firms. Mark has only been at Park Bank for three years and yet he's seen the firm has "been laying a lot of people off ... we're talking 4/5 hundred people." The effects of reorganization have reached him directly when he was moved from a salaried to an hourly position. He says they were told they were "lucky" to have a job. Several respondents mentioned going through a firm reorganization where it was uncertain if their jobs would be eliminated, and if it was eliminated, it was unknown whether they would be moved to another position or if they would be laid off. This commonly took the form of a 60- or 90-day window to find a new assignment or be let go. Others suggested they could lose their job tomorrow or without warning. Belinda said "that [job security] is never a guarantee at a big company; I could lose my job tomorrow." Younger workers saw this insecurity as normal, as evidenced by Belinda saying it is never guaranteed at a big company. Older employees mentioned these layoffs were becoming more common, suggesting that job security no longer existed.

NEW ORGANIZATIONAL CAREERS IN FINANCIAL SERVICES

Workers' reactions to insecurity could fall under two broad frames. First, they could follow in the footsteps of laid off workers and adopt a company of one or boundaryless mentality, in which their career becomes occupationally focused (Arthur & Rousseau 1996, Lane, 2011). Alternatively, there could be a commitment to Clarke's (2013) concept of the new organizational career. Specifically, employees could focus on opportunities for development within an organization. Very few employees took the former approach; rather overwhelmingly there was a commitment to the new organizational career. It was expected there may be variation by geographic region, but this turned out not to be the case. Evidence for the new organizational career is presented in two ways. First, by demonstrating that workers under study applied to many internal jobs yet never considered external opportunities. Second, employees expressed loyalty to the firm. Both of these results are surprising given the recent layoffs experienced and literature studying different sets of workers.

Internal Movement as Evidence for the New Organizational Career

Mark, mentioned above, is 32 and works in mortgages/foreclosures at Park Bank in Columbus. Mark has a master's degree, is neither a husband nor a father, and ambitiously tries to get ahead within Park. In three years Mark has applied to 125 different internal jobs. When asked if he has applied to jobs outside the company, Mark responded, "I haven't actually looked." Mark has applied to *125 internal job postings, but zero external job postings.* Perhaps less surprisingly, long-tenured employees also had little interest in leaving the firm. Penny has been at East End Bank for 17 years and suggests if she became unhappy in her current position she would only look to move internally. This emphasis on internal mobility was a common frame.

Even individuals who identify with a particular profession attempted to move internally without external applications. Amelia works in compliance at Park Bank in Columbus. Her first assignment was in monitoring. She said her job "was boring, but it paid well," so she switched to the investigation team.

Though she switched teams to advance her career in compliance, she says "I wasn't wanting to leave the firm; I was just going to move internally, switch to another team." Christine, the only respondent who mentioned the possibility of leaving in the near future suggested she was only "passively" looking. Almost all respondents, regardless of demographic characteristics, spent little time looking for external opportunities. Though Gubler et al. (2014) found no significant difference in boundaryless career orientation by gender, women and minorities are more likely to be harmed from layoffs and downsizing than men (Haverman et al., 2009; Parks-Yancy, 2004). Additionally, people prefer security and promotions regardless of generation (Dries et al., 2008). This need for stability can endure in the face of firm uncertainty.

Searching for other opportunities within the firm can be a strategy for dealing with restructuring. It does not appear this outlooks need to be mutually exclusive with searching for external opportunity. However, many respondents in this study portrayed uneasiness when asked about moving externally. Juan has been at Rockefeller Bank in New York for six years. He has been contacted numerous times by recruiters. When asked what it would take for him to leave he responded, "that's a great question because it's been posed to me over and over again. And I've been recruited by other institutions ... *I'm not about to jump out of the frying pan and into the fire*" (emphasis added). Juan has two Ivy League degrees. He is a bilingual, Latino, unattached, and ambitious finance worker in New York. These attributes make him attractive to recruiters. He has had offers that would significantly increase his salary. Yet, he referred to the idea of leaving as jumping out of the frying pan and into the fire, associating tumult and uncertainty with switching institutions. This suggests that sector instability might actually decrease rather than increase employee mobility. When asked why he turned down jobs that paid more, he noted his comfort in current relationships and resources at his firm. The reverse could potentially be true as well, in booming economic times there might be less reticence toward switching firms.

Loyalty as Evidence for the New Organizational Career

Loyalty is hard to operationalize, however many respondents self-identified as loyal. They felt invested in the firm's success and reputation, and had an emotional attachment to their corporation. In return respondents thought their firm cared about employees, even after layoffs, which are justified as industry norms. Morris said his firm is invested in "employee engagement" and Juan said employees do "have a voice" in the organization, mentioning surveys and other mechanisms for feedback that he feels Rockefeller Bank takes seriously. Jennifer went so far as to say of Central Insurance, "they really value their people ... they really care about the people." While respondents acknowledged the firm's primary goal was profit, they did not feel that precluded commitment to employees' well-being. Some workers felt a survivor's camaraderie in the wake of the financial crisis. Leslie explains further:

> We had a lot of trouble with the government and people were spitting at us on the street. It was stupid. I think then I felt a lot of pride and loyalty funny enough because the issues that happened were just five or six guys at the top. It had nothing to do with us who were regular workers. For taxpayers to be complaining that the government bailed us out, well we're taxpayers too ... they said don't wear your Southern gear outside the building because some guy got beat up outside the subway. Then my sense of loyalty was high.

Leslie is demonstrating that for some workers the push back from the outside world garnered a sense of closeness to their fellow workers and loyalty to their firm.

Betty has a "tremendous" amount of loyalty adding she was a "true-blue Park employee." When asked about her loyalty to Park Bank, Betty said "I feel like I align personally with the values of this organization." She added "I grew up in this company and like I said I align with the values of the organization. I just feel like this is a place where I belong." Carl, who has been at Central Insurance for 20 years, has only worked for two large corporations in his career. He describes himself as a "pretty loyal" person. When asked if he saw himself at Central in 10 years he responded, "in 10 years I see myself still working here, but working here by choice not because I have to." Both Carl and Betty show a loyalty linked to their personal values. Long-tenured employees tend to show a commitment to the firm, sometimes framed as an alignment of values or growing up together. This is even true of workers who have been at multiple firms, such as Carl and Leslie. Leslie had an acrimonious departure from Park Bank and yet when Southern Insurance was going through a crisis she felt loyalty. Young workers also find reasons for loyalty, such as company culture and opportunity structure. Jane has been at Central Insurance in Columbus for three years, stating:

> I love Central, it's a great culture ... when I came to Central I was expected to set up a coffee date with leaders and meet with senior leaders ... I feel like people at that level will take the time out of their day to talk to you about your career and your plan and we're very good on volunteering and giving back to the community, which is important to me ... it's not just about coming in and doing your job, it's about more than that.

Jane claims working at Central is about more than just doing your job, she mentions community involvement and professional development as important to the company's culture. All of these add up to Jane saying she loves Central. Demographic variations can effect where the loyalty comes from, but very few respondents said they had no loyalty to their firm.

THE CO-MANAGEMENT OF CAREER PATHS

Respondents across firms discussed how the new organizational career differs from the traditional organizational career. Clarke (2013) describes new organizational careers as jointly managed by employers and employees. Organizational responses to the boundaryless career era are significant yet often overlooked (Currie, Tempest, & Starkey, 2006). The workers studied here said their organizations embraced aspects of boundarylessness that are essential to a new organizational career, such as fostering trainings and development, as well as promoting internal opportunities. Though workers had to seek these out, the firm did provide such opportunities and doing so helps firms retain talent. Respondents felt they had plenty of opportunity within their firm.

Many respondents suggested firms no longer offered a clear career path. Christine, who works at East End Bank in New York, sees plenty of opportunities at the bank, but she said "it's absolutely not delivered to you in a package by the firm." She went on to say that a "career track or a career path is also anachronistic today." Betty, an employee of Park Bank in New York said "if you want a bigger job, make your own job bigger." Both of these respondents make clear a belief that promotion and opportunity are entrepreneurial. It is in this way careers are co-managed, or at least seem co-managed to the employees under study. These results are not limited to New Yorkers. Peter and Esther, who both work for Central Insurance in Columbus, expressed the same sentiment that traditional career ladders no longer exist.

Despite the lack of a traditional path, respondents did think organizations provided substantial opportunities. Jennifer, who works at Central Insurance in Columbus, decided she needed to get a promotion to a project manager to advance her career. She looked around the company for that title in a different department. She said staying in her position "was going to hurt my career in the long run, I needed to be called Project Manager." She found a position in Scottsdale, Arizona. Despite possible career damage she said "I was thinking about moving on, but more sort of to a different department rather than outside of Central." She did not think Central would lack the necessary opportunities for her advancement. It appears this relocation strategy might be becoming more common for career advancement. Prior research has shown people willing to move for opportunity during increasingly insecure economic times (Pugh, 2014; Sennett, 1998).

Belinda made the point that an employee could find an opportunity regardless of their interest since large firms have many areas for development. Firms also help facilitate movement through self-paced trainings and networking opportunities. Christine feels East End does a good job helping people get ahead, "I do think they offer a lot, there's a lot of learning opportunities. We have a learning management system, we have tens of thousands of self-paced trainings that are free to the employee to take and their manager should be encouraging them to take." Christine went on to say, "I do think there is plenty of opportunity. It's part of the culture, it's part of the message."

Besides internal training, employees mentioned getting outside training or education sponsored by their firm. Peter said the "educational assistance is very good [at Central]. I have earned two professional designations at no expense to me and in fact I've even been given a reward trip for one of them, to the conferment ceremony in Seattle." These designations and trainings are not forced on the employee, but the company actively supports and pays for training. These characteristics align with Clarke's (2013) new organizational career concept.

Perhaps the most innovative way firms co-manage careers in the new organizational career model is with an emphasis on networking tools. Jane mentioned that Central Insurance created their own internal LinkedIn-type program to encourage networking and movement. She sees this as a dual responsibility between herself and the organization:

> I am constantly wanting to learn and be challenged and grow ... it's important for an organization to recognize that people are going to want to move across and see new things and maintain that talent ... and let people move across so that you're learning different parts of the organization ... getting different flavors.

Employees gave the impression that networking leads to opportunities to constantly grow without having to leave. Penny, mentioned above, said if she was unhappy at East End Bank she would just network and find a new position in the firm. Belinda said these networking opportunities happen often. Recently another employee reached out to her about an opportunity in a different department. Belinda had no experience in that area but applied "on a whim" and got the job. In sum, while employees must seek out opportunity, many of those in this study emphasized the firm's encouragement of internal training and movement. In this way, workers frame their careers as co-managed with the organization.

VARIATION IN NEW ORGANIZATIONAL CAREERS

The respondents in New York and Columbus shared key similarities – preference for the new organizational career when faced with increased uncertainty and the transition of internal labor markets from pre-defined ladders to entrepreneurial. However, the new organizational career was experienced in different ways as well. The New York set tended to experience new organizational careers in line with the analogy of serial monogamy. A serial monogamy career is defined by medium-to-long-term stints at multiple companies. Each company is expected to be a stable and enduring employer for the foreseeable future. Seven of the 10 members of the New York set experienced the serial monogamy career. In Columbus 11 of the 12 members of the set experienced the spiral staircase career. Spiral staircase careers are marked by internal movement within a firm that does not adhere to strict upward advancement, but also involves lateral changes and/or job function/department changes. These types are not necessarily mutually exclusive, but reflect differences in the cities' labor markets and other possible variations between the two groups of respondents.

The Serial Monogamy Model of New Organizational Careers

Many of the New York respondents expressed new organizational careers in a way that can be compared to the serial monogamy form of dating. This was the case for 7 of the 10 New York respondents. Five of the 7 had spent over 10 years with a previous firm before moving to their current position. This concept addresses an important gap in the career literature. Boundaryless careers imply workers are always moving firms and traditional or new organizational careers imply that workers never change firms. In reality, workers can spend many years with multiple organizations. This is not a form of boundarylessness because each firm is expected to be a stable and enduring employer; much like each new romantic partner is expected to last forever. Christine made this metaphor and explained it as such:

> a mutually satisfying relationship between the employer and the employee, and I think that it's like a serial monogamy type of thing. You know your career isn't going to be 30 years at one place now, but you might have, you know, 3 or 4 or 5 different things that you will do over the course of your professional life with different companies, they may be the same thing or they might be variations or different things. And there's no hard feelings on that.

Though Christine was the only respondent who used this metaphor, the concept was abundant in the New York sample.

Serial monogamy occupies a middle ground in current theories and respondents offered an outlook unique to this form of new organizational career. There was both a disdain for the traditional organizational career or company man model and a respect for longevity. Beverly, an employee at East End Bank, represents this viewpoint. "I think there are some folks that have been here 30, 40 years, who will complain to high heaven and are not leaving East End." Yet, Beverly had been at East End for 13 years. When pushed on this contradiction she expressed, "I think it is good to stay somewhere for a certain period of time, even 10 years is ok if it's not in the same role, and I think it's good to move around in the company, but I don't know about 30 years." Julia, also an employee at East End Bank, expressed a similar sentiment. For her, moving around every few years is a bad thing, but expressed it was also negative to stay with a company for 30 years. Yet Julia has been with East End for 15 years.

The serial monogamy model can be either forced or purposive, but often-times employees suggest they would like to stay at their current firm for their entire career. This is despite saying working for one firm for too long can be a mistake in the abstract. Julia, mentioned above, said in order for her to leave after 15 years a new opportunity would "have to be something really unique or different," suggesting it is unlikely she would move on. James worked at Park Bank for 25 years before coming to East End Bank three years ago. He moved laterally to East End after being laid off. Though James has experienced a lay-off, he plans to stay at East End Bank for the foreseeable future. He says he "is forgetting the past," and looking to "grow with the company." James shows a remarkable ability to re-establish commitment at a new firm. David left his pre-vious bank for Madison Bank when they changed their compensation formula. He now hopes to stay at Madison Bank until he retires saying "I have signifi-cant financial goals ... but I have the ability to obtain those, with no ceiling, here at this firm." Respondents were asked where they see themselves in 5 and 10 years. Not a single respondent said they expect leave the firm in five years. Answers became more ambivalent in 10 years, but no respondent said they actively envisioned switching firms. Respondents' commitment to the new firm is evidence that the serial monogamy model is a new organizational, rather than boundaryless, career.

The Spiral Staircase Model of New Organizational Careers

Eleven of the 12 respondents in Columbus experienced the spiral staircase model of the new organizational career. Though not necessarily mutually exclu-sive to the serial monogamy model, there was less firm-switching among the Columbus set. When a worker stays with a firm they are experiencing a spiral staircase career. A spiral staircase career can also become a serial monogamy career at any time. The serial monogamy career is analytically distinct because it relies on firm-switching rather than just department or job function changes. Peter, an employee at Central Insurance, provided the spiral staircase simile, "my career progression at Central has been more like a spiral staircase, I've moved up but I've also moved around as well." Elaborating on his career tra-jectory Peter stated, "I started off in property casualty market research, after a year I moved over to the life and health marketing team and after that I chan-ged either jobs or bosses or both on average once every 18 months." The spiral staircase analogy allows for short-term career transitions within a firm. Of course this is different from boundarylessness because Peter remained with Central Insurance for the long haul, 22 years at the time of the interview. This length would have seemed imprudent to many New York respondents.

I am not the first to compare careers to a spiral staircase. Turner, Keegan, and Crawford (2000) refer to project work as a spiral staircase career, suggesting people move from project to project. The conception in this paper is slightly different, since workers are not changing projects, but teams or departments. Like the serial monogamy model, the spiral staircase model can either be forced or purposive. Peter has charted his own course building a career in marketing. He has worked in many appendages of the organization. Carl is another example, he expressed that when he sees change coming he tries to get out to a different team before reorganization can reach his current department. Carl said "everything has a life cycle ... you kind of sense it's winding down and you start looking, you dust off your resume, you start putting your feelers out."

Mark and Priya both experienced the spiral staircase career as a result of organizational restructuring. As mentioned above, during reorganization Mark was re-assigned. He was moved from a salaried position to an hourly position. In fact, we can think of Mark as moving down the spiral staircase. This sort of demotion is also unaccounted for by current career literature. Mark has applied to 125 different jobs throughout the company. This is an example of the spiral staircase model because he is looking for variegated opportunities all over the company. Priya was given 60 days to find a new job during a firm reorganization. Fortunately, she was able to find an opportunity within Central Insurance. This was a move up the spiral staircase because Priya is much happier in her new job, saying of the transition "I had no control obviously when we merged ... I ended up being the person who was given 60 days ... I was lucky enough to find this one [job] and it was probably one of the best things that's ever happened to me." Overall, every member in the Columbus sample has had more than one job in their current firm, even younger workers. Niles, the least tenured respondent, received a new job assignment after just one year at Park Bank. Peter's analogy of the spiral staircase was prevalent among Columbus respondents.

DISCUSSION

Results are based on a small non-probability sample. However, there was an overwhelming trend found among the interviews. Almost all of the respondents expressed a desire for the new organizational career. This was evidenced by a reliance on seeking opportunity inside the firm rather than outside the firm and expressions of loyalty to the current employer. Even workers who had been laid off express loyalty to their current employer. These careers are not traditional organizational careers because promotion and advancement was largely entrepreneurial. We might expect New York workers to be unique, but the inclusion of Columbus as a research site helps suggest that geography is less important than sector characteristics. There are other possible variations between the two sets of workers, but including some overlap in firms (both as current and previous employer) and some overlap in functions help mitigate somewhat against this problem. In addition there is no reason to think one set of workers is more privileged than the other vis-à-vis local labor markets.

The desire to stay is not counter-intuitive, but what this study offers is an insight into how certain workers frame/justify that desire when their jobs are insecure, and perceived as increasingly insecure by older employees. Growing insecurity does not always lead to more mobility. Some workers did mention higher transaction costs to leaving the firm, such as a decline in accrued benefits, but staying was mostly presented as an active choice. There are many possible reasons workers chose to stay, but regardless of the specific mechanism the preference for the new organizational career emerged. When workers feel content with the opportunities their firm provides, self-identify as loyal, and find economic conditions unfavorable, they may stay with their organization and establish a spiral staircase career. When there are many firms in their sector this can take a more intermediate form, in the serial monogamy career. Tighter post-recession labor markets in New York could have contributed, but it is hard to determine the impact of specific labor markets. The role of the recession and short- versus long-term factors cannot be unpacked by this research, but the recession did spur downsizings. Downsizing made insecurity seem immediate to workers in a way that 30 years of gradual trends may have concealed.

The preference for the new organizational career is not surprising based on the literature. Pugh's (2014) term the "one-way honor system," and Lane's (2011) "company of one," do not preclude an individual wanting to spend their career with one firm. Pugh, however, does suggest only employees with stable secure jobs experience mutual commitment with their firm. Even contingent workers can develop commitment to their workplace (Kojima, 2015) or adopt management ideologies to justify insecurity (Padavic, 2005). However, the loyalty felt and reciprocity expected by the workers under study stands in contrast to the existing literature on precarious work, as do their limited attempts to seek employment/promotion outside their current firm. Despite this lack of security, the workers in this study remained committed to their firm.

These results make more sense when the debate between traditional/new organizational careers and boundaryless careers is integrated into the sociology of work. In their early critique of boundaryless careers, Pringle and Mallon (2003) noted the importance of structural and cultural factors. Respondents in this study did not expect job security because they assumed other firms did not provide it either. Respondents, did however, appreciate the entrepreneurial paths to advancement firms offered. These opportunities were not forced on the workers. However, since firms encouraged networking and self-paced trainings and education, the workers did feel their careers were co-managed. And workers were generally satisfied with the resources firms provided for advancement. These methods of advancement are outside the traditional organizational career/job ladder framework. These methods also do not coincide with a free-agent or boundaryless outlook. Employees might be embracing an entrepreneurial outlook that is popular in contemporary management literature (Vallas & Prener, 2012), but in a way that is focused toward their firm rather than their occupation. As a result, respondent frames are more indicative of the new organizational career developed by Clarke (2013).

Variation among the two cities was mostly found in the way the new organizational career was expressed. The best metaphors for these were provided by respondents as serial monogamy, experienced mostly in New York, and the spiral staircase, the dominant experience in Columbus. The spiral staircase model of the career is in line with Clarke's (2013) original conception of the new organizational career. The serial monogamy career fills an intermediate space that had previously been left out of the careers literature. A spiral staircase career can also turn into a serial monogamy career. Whether local labor markets or other variations explain the difference between the two research sites is less important than the analytical distinction that arose from the interviews. These two frames emerged to give empirical insight into how workers can experience new organizational careers when they have insecure jobs in large bureaucratic organizations.

CONCLUSION

This paper has examined the experience of white-collar professionals facing precarity in large bureaucratic firms. Their experience aligns with work on the new organizational career. The new organizational career concept allows for comparing worker responses to changing careers based on their particular context, such as geography or sector characteristics. As insecurity continues to rise, workers' responses continue to be of great importance. Common sociological approaches show some professional workers experience general detachment or lack of reciprocity (Lane, 2011; Pugh, 2014). However, these approaches do also suggest wide class variation in approaches to insecurity (Cooper, 2014; Pugh, 2014). Discussions of new organizational careers show that many workers, in a variety of sectors/occupations, still crave and experience attachment to, and reciprocity from, their employer (Clarke, 2013; Dries et al., 2008). What this study shows is how workers in a particular sector react to job insecurity.

There are limitations of this study. First, a respondent-driven sample could exclude individuals who have positive or frequent experiences changing firms. It is possible only those with good internal networks referred the author to others. There are likely more itinerant financial professionals who would feel differently from those under study here. Second, the financial sector is unique. It is dominated by few large firms that are venerated within the industry. A few respondents in both cities mentioned the prestige of their institution as a positive attribute. In other sectors where firms are not as prestigious, large, or bureaucratic, there might be less incentive to stay or other models of new organizational careers might emerge. Third, the set of workers under study, particularly within each city, is small. Results need to be interpreted as suggestive rather than conclusive.

This study has contributed to our knowledge of careers and worker attachment, showing that sector characteristics and geography can be of great importance. Additionally, this paper has shown ways workers can frame new firm attachments in the wake of layoffs, a particularly salient topic as scholars continue to study the aftermath of the Great Recession. Future research needs to examine other sectors and to make international comparisons. Future research could also benefit from a longitudinal approach, since we know insecurity can have different effects in the short and long term (Glavin, 2015). This paper can only speak to what happened after the Great Recession, not before. Future research can also use quantitative data to test whether geography, occupation, or other institutional arrangements matters most for experiencing the spiral staircase or serial monogamy career. Future research can also study employee experiences during economic expansion. Variation in organization type is influential in shaping employees' responses to increased insecurity (Lam et al., 2015). This study acts as a comparative case study to other industry/firm case studies. I provide a frame for comparing experiences based on geography or institutional arrangements rather than using a specific case study as a generalizable rule for other organizations/sectors. Hopefully future research will take the framework developed here and apply it to other industries, firms, and nationalities experiencing organizational turbulence (or growth). Because this study does suggest that there are workers who still take an organizational rather than occupational approach to their career.

NOTE

1. Number derived from Current Population Survey Labor Force Statistics as reported by the Bureau of Labor Statistics: http://www.bls.gov/cps/cpsaat18.htm

REFERENCES

Arthur, M. B. (2014). The boundaryless career at 20: Where do we stand, and where can we go? *Career Development International, 19*(6), 627−640.

Arthur, M. B., & Rousseau, D. M. (1996). Introduction: The boundaryless career as a new employment principle. In M. B. Arthur & D. M. Rousseau (Eds.), *The boundaryless career: A new employment principle for a new organizational era* (pp. 3−20). Oxford: Oxford University Press.

Blair-Loy, M. (2001). It's not just what you know, it's who you know: Technical knowledge, rainmaking, and gender among finance executives. *Research in the Sociology of Work, 10*, 51−84.

Briscoe, J. P., Hall, D. T., & Frautschy DeMuth, R. L. (2006). Protean and boundaryless careers: An empirical exploration. *Journal of Vocational Behavior, 69*(1), 30–47.

Clarke, M. (2013). The organizational career: Not dead but in need of redefinition. The *International Journal of Human Resource Management, 24*(4), 684–703.

Cohen, L. (2006). Remembrance of things past: Cultural process and practice in analysis of career stories. *Journal of Vocational Behavior, 69*(2), 189–201.

Cohen, L., & Mallon, M. (1999). The transition from organisational employment to portfolio working: Perceptions of 'boundarylessness'. *Work, Employment & Society, 13*(2), 329–352.

Cooper, M. (2014). *Cut adrift: Families in insecure times.* Oakland, CA: University of California Press.

Currie, G., Tempest, S., & Starkey, K. (2006). New careers for old? Organizational and individual responses to changing boundaries. *International Journal of Human Resource Management, 17*(4), 755–774.

Dany, F., Louvel, S., & Valette, A. (2011). Academic careers: The limits of the 'boundaryless approach' and the power of promotion scripts. *Human Relations, 64*(7), 971–996.

Dries, N., Pepermans, R., & De Kerpel, E. (2008). Exploring four generations' beliefs about career: Is 'satisfied' the new 'successful'? *Journal of Managerial Psychology, 23*(8), 907–928.

Fevre, R. (2007). Employment insecurity and social theory: The power of nightmares. *Work, Employment, & Society, 21*(3), 517–535.

Fullerton, A. S., & Wallace, M. (2007). Traversing the flexible turn: US workers' perceptions of job security, 1977-2002. *Social Science Research, 36*(1), 201–221.

Glavin, P. (2015). Perceived job insecurity and health: Do duration and timing matter? *The Sociological Quarterly, 56*(2), 300–328.

Grdinovac, J. A., & Yancey, G. B. (2012). How organizational adaptations to recession relate to organizational commitment. *The Psychologist-Manager Journal, 15*(1), 6–24.

Gubler, M., Arnold, J., & Coombs, C. (2014). Organizational boundaries and beyond: A new look at the components of a boundaryless career orientation. *Career Development International, 19*(6), 641–667.

Hatton, E. (2011). *The temp economy: From Kelly girls to permatemps in postwar America.* Philadelphia, PA: Temple University Press.

Haverman, H. A., Broschak, J. P., & Cohen, L. E. (2009). Good times, bad times: The effects of organizational dynamics on the careers of male and female managers. *Research in the Sociology of Work, 18*, 119–148.

Ho, K. (2009). *Liquidated: An ethnography of wall street.* Durham, NC: Duke University Press.

Hollister, M. N. (2012). Employer and occupational instability in two cohorts of the National Longitudinal Surveys. *The Sociological Quarterly, 53*(2), 238–263.

Inkson, K., Gunz, H., Ganesh, S., & Roper, J. (2012). Boundaryless careers: Bringing back boundaries. *Organization Studies, 33*(3), 323–340.

Ituma, A., & Simpson, R. (2009). The 'boundaryless' career and career boundaries: Applying an institutionalist perspective to ICT workers in the context of Nigeria. *Human Relations, 62*(5), 727–761.

Jacoby, S. M. (1999). Are career jobs headed for extinction? *California Management Review, 42*(1), 123–145.

Kalleberg, A. L., & Marsden, P. V. (2013). Changing work values in the United States, 1973–2006. *Social Science Research, 42*(2), 255–270.

Kim, Y. (2013). Diverging top and converging bottom: Labour flexibilization and changes in career mobility in the USA. *Work, Employment, & Society, 27*(5), 860–879.

Knudsen, H. K., Johnson, J. A., Martin, J. M., & Roman, P. M. (2003). Downsizing survival: The experience of work and organizational commitment. *Sociological Inquiry, 73*(2), 265–283.

Kohli, M. (2014). Persistence of a high unemployment rate in New York City during the recent recovery. *Beyond the Numbers, 3*(2), 1–8. Retrieved from http://www.bls.gov/opub/btn/volume-3/persistence-of-a-high-unemployment-rate-in-new-york-city.htm

Kojima, S. (2015). Why do temp workers work as hard as they do?: The commitment and suffering of factory temp workers in Japan. *The Sociological Quarterly, 56*(2), 355–385.

Lam, J., Fox, K., Fan, W., Moen, P., Kelly, E., Hammer, L., & Kossek, E. E. (2015). Manager characteristics and employee job insecurity around a merger announcement: The role of status and crossover. *The Sociological Quarterly, 56*(3), 558–580.

Lamont, M., Morning, A., & Mooney, M. (2002). Particular universalisms: North African immigrants respond to French racism. *Ethnic and Racial Studies, 25*(3), 390–414.

Lane, C. M. (2011). *A company of one: Insecurity, independence, and the new world of white-collar unemployment.* Ithaca, NY: Cornell University Press.

Newman, K. S. (1988). *Falling from grace.* New York, NY: Free Press.

Padavic, I. (2005). Laboring under uncertainty: Identity renegotiation among contingent workers. *Symbolic Interaction, 28*(1), 111–134.

Parks-Yancy, R. (2004). The impact of social capital on African-American and women survivors of organizational downsizing. *Research in the Sociology of Work, 14,* 87–106.

Pfeffer, J., & Baron, N. (1988). Taking the workers back out. *Research in Organizational Behavior, 10,* 257–303.

Pringle, J., & Mallon, M. (2003). Challenges for the boundaryless career odyssey. *International Journal of Human Resource Management, 14*(5), 839–853.

Pugh, A. J. (2014). *The tumbleweed society.* New York, NY: Oxford University Press.

Rodrigues, R. A., & Guest, D. (2010). Have careers become boundaryless? *Human Relations, 63*(8), 1157–1175.

Rodrigues, R., Guest, D., & Budjanovcanin, A. (2015). Bounded or boundaryless? An empirical investigation of career boundaries and boundary crossing. *Work, Employment, & Society, 30*(4), 669–686.

Saxenian, A. (1996). Beyond boundaries: Open labor markets and learning in Silicon Valley. In M. B. Arthur & D. M. Rousseau (Eds.), *The boundaryless career: A new employment principle for a new organizational era* (pp. 22–39). Oxford: Oxford University Press.

Schmidt, S. R. (1999). Long-run trends in workers' beliefs about their own job security: Evidence from the General Social Survey. *Journal of Labor Economics, 17*(4), S127–S141.

Sennett, R. (1998). *The corrosion of character: The transformation of work in modern capitalism.* New York, NY: Norton Company.

Sennett, R. (2007). *The culture of the new capitalism.* New Haven, CT: Yale University Press.

Smith, V. (2002). *Crossing the great divide: Worker risk and opportunity in the new economy.* Ithaca, NY: Cornell University Press.

Snorradottir, A., Tomasson, K., Vilhjalmsson, R., & Rafnsdottir, G. L. (2015). The health and well-being of bankers following downsizing: A comparison of stayers and leavers. *Work, Employment & Society, 29*(5), 738–756.

Tempest, S., McKinlay, A., & Starkey, K. (2004). Careering alone: Careers and social capital in the financial services and television industries. *Human Relations, 57*(12), 1523–1545.

Tomaskovic-Devey, D., & Lin, K. (2011). Income dynamic, economic rents, and the financialization of the US economy. *American Sociological Review, 76*(4), 538–559.

Turco, C. (2010). Cultural foundations of tokenism: Evidence from the leveraged buyout industry. *American Sociological Review, 75*(6), 894–913.

Turner, R. J., Keegan, A., & Crawford, L. (2000). *Learning by experience in the project-based organization.* Erasmus Research Institute of Management Report Series, Research in Management.

Vallas, S., & Prener, C. (2012). Dualism, job polarization, and the social construction of precarious work. *Work and Occupations, 39*(4), 331–353.

Wajcman, J., & Martin, B. (2001). My company or my career: Managerial achievement and loyalty. *The British Journal of Sociology, 52*(4), 559–578.

Weiss, R. S. (1994). *Learning from strangers: The art and method of qualitative interview studies.* New York, NY: Simon and Schuster.

Whyte, W. H. (1956). *The Organization Man.* Philadelphia, PA: University of Pennsylvania Press.

Williams, M., & Gearino, D. (2015). Columbus fares best in recession recovery. *The Columbus Dispatch*, September 13. Retrieved from http://www.dispatch.com/content/stories/business/2015/09/13/columbus-fares-best-in-recession-recovery.html. Accessed on September 19, 2016.

Ydstie, J. (2010). 'Extreme downsizing' may hurt companies later. *Npr.org*, August 9. Retrieved from http://www.npr.org/templates/story/story.php?storyId=129036823. Accessed on March 14, 2016.

Zaloom, C. (2010). *Out of the pits: Traders and technology from Chicago to London*. Chicago, IL: University of Chicago Press.

NEO-NORMATIVE CONTROL AND VALUE DISCRETION IN INTERACTIVE SERVICE WORK: A CASE STUDY

Sarah Jenkins and Rick Delbridge

ABSTRACT

This study addresses the debate regarding employee discretion and neo-normative forms of control within interactive service work. Discretion is central to core and long-standing debates within the sociology of work and organizations such as skill, control and job quality. Yet, despite this, the concept of discretion remains underdeveloped. We contend that changes in the nature of work, specifically in the context of interactive service work, require us to revisit classical theorizations of discretion. The paper elaborates the concept of value discretion; defined as the scope for employees to interpret the meaning of the espoused values of their organization. We illustrate how value discretion provides a foundational basis for further forms of task discretion within a customized service call-centre. The study explores the link between neo-normative forms of control and the labour process by elaborating the concept of value discretion to provide new insights into the relationship between managerial control and employee agency within contemporary service labour processes.

Keywords: Call-centres; interactive service work; neo-normative control; value discretion; service sector

Emerging Conceptions of Work, Management and the Labor Market
Research in the Sociology of Work, Volume 30, 59–85
Copyright © 2017 by Emerald Publishing Limited
ISSN: 0277-2833/doi:10.1108/S0277-283320170000030004

INTRODUCTION

Despite the ubiquity of discretion as a concept in how researchers of work and organizations discuss themes such as the changing quality of jobs, skill levels and the nature of control workers exercise, what is meant by discretion is very rarely specified precisely. As a result, Caza's (2011) review concludes that there is not yet a mature and multi-dimensional theory of discretion in organizations. Put succinctly, although we often use the term discretion, the concept itself has not been fully developed in the context of contemporary forms of work, especially with reference to interactive service work. Part of the explanation for this rests on the history of the concept; discretion first emerged from studies of industrialized work wherein Taylorist management practices were implemented to limit the latitude workers could exercise, separating conception from the work itself. As such, a large part of our understanding of discretion emanates from the way employee autonomy is often restricted within the tasks which workers perform (Braverman, 1974). As Braverman signalled in his 'degradation of work thesis', there is a direct link between the nature of the labour process and the skills and effort which employees exercise within managerial control regimes. As labour process theory (LPT) has matured overtime we witness a more nuanced depiction of the range and complexity of labour processes and ensuing degrees of employee discretion that vary according to different managerial strategies (Edwards, 1979; Friedman, 1977; Fleming & Sturdy, 2011) and phases of capital accumulation (Godard, 2004; Thompson, 2003). But the conception of discretion has remained relatively underdeveloped.

The dominance of Taylorist regimes reported in research on call-centres has added evidence of a trend towards low discretionary interactive service work (Taylor & Bain, 1999). These studies highlight how workers' discretion is limited by the rigours of efficiency targets imposed through bureaucratic and technological controls which require limited use of workers' knowledgeability (Taylor & Bain, 1999). For Taylor and Bain (2007, p. 359), the phenomenon of the call-centre demonstrates the linkages between wider capitalist restructuring, including spatial and technological dimensions, with a distinctive type of labour process that emerged in the context of intensified competition. However, as call-centre studies have burgeoned, research has highlighted the differentiated nature of this sector in relation to control regimes and varying skill levels (Batt, 2000; Frenkel, 2005; Korczynski, 2001; Smith et al., 2008; van den Broek, 2008); categorizations include Frenkel's (2005, p. 358) distinction between mass-services and mass-customized services. The former has an emphasis on cost reduction, standardization and direct controls while the latter adopts a value-added approach by emphasizing quality customer service which affords greater discretion to service workers within normative forms of regulation. Other examples include Korczynski (2005) who identifies the principles of a customer-oriented bureaucracy, and Kinnie, Hutchinson, and Purcell (2000) who contrasted repetitive, tightly controlled, 'transactional' work with 'relational' customer interaction where employee discretion and variation predominate.

As service work becomes increasingly demarcated, it is argued that the nature of control evolves as some corporations search for 'authenticity' in the delivery of 'quality services' (Fleming, 2009; Leidner, 1993). Modern interactive service organizations do not just seek automatons to repeat scripts but want 'real' people to engage in 'authentic' interactions to project an image of a humanized organization. Consequently, employees are recruited because of their 'natural personalities' (Taylor & Tyler, 2000) and sometimes even their zany and edgy characteristics (Fleming, 2005). These developments have prompted debates regarding how employees' identities are managed and controlled to deliver the 'authenticity' sought by some organizations. For instance, Fleming and Sturdy (2011) and Sturdy, Fleming, and Delbridge (2010) suggest that these developments represent a subtle move from pure normative to neo-normative forms of control where workers exercise the discretion to 'be themselves'. Workers bring their identities to work rather than these identities being manipulated by organizational 'thought police' through corporate enculturation programmes. However, the prevailing effect is that while workers may have the 'freedom to be themselves' there is not a corresponding freedom over the labour process (Fleming & Study, 2011).

Examining the diversity of call-centre sector work and the nature of management regimes within these has stimulated a number of questions which this paper seeks to address. These questions are apposite in the context of debates regarding new forms of normative controls in customized interactive service work where organizations seek to capitalize on workers' identities to deliver an 'authentic' customer experience. Our study makes a contribution to these debates by examining a mass-customized call-centre. There is a lacuna in our understanding of how neo-normative forms of control impact on the labour process, specifically in relation to the exercise of discretion in such workplaces. Our research findings show the significance of 'value discretion', defined as the scope for employees to interpret the meaning of the espoused values of their organization. This was particularly important as employees used discretion in interpreting the organization's values and how to translate these into authentic action in delivering the service. We thus contribute to an empirically under-researched and conceptually underdeveloped feature of contemporary work by exploring the links between neo-normative control and various forms of employee discretion. To do this we extend understanding of discretion in interactive service work and consider the place of value discretion in the assessment of discretion within contemporary service work. The study informs current debates about the degree of employee agency exercised within neo-normative control regimes in customer service settings.

The paper proceeds with an overview of the concept of discretion and its relationship to neo-normative control before introducing the case study. The findings are then discussed before the key points of the paper are summarized in a concluding section.

CONTROL AND DISCRETION AT WORK

Starting with F. W. Taylor, job design and employee discretion have been central to long-standing sociological debates about control and core to discussions about the changing nature of work amongst labour process theorists (Braverman, 1974). The concept of discretion is also significant in assessments of management's labour strategies as captured by Friedman's (1977) dual strategy of control which established a continuum of potential approaches to the management of labour from direct control evident in Taylorist low-trust regimes to responsible autonomy which sought to 'harness the adaptability of labour power by giving workers leeway and status, autonomy and responsibility'. In most cases, following the early writings of organizational theorists (Blauner, 1964; Jacques, 1956), the understanding of discretion derives from how tasks are organized. Task discretion focuses on the degree of discretion and personal influence that workers exercise to undertake their duties without restrictive formal rules and overt controls over their actions. Such an understanding of the freedom workers have to determine the pace, order and range of tasks they undertake is also central to measures of job design (Hackman & Oldham, 1976) and more recently assessments of job quality (Findlay, Kalleberg, & Warhurst, 2013). However, as Green and James (2003, p. 65) observe, despite the centrality of the concept of discretion to core sociological debates on control and empowerment, involvement, cooperation, satisfaction and commitment: 'the extent of personal influence over what tasks to perform and how much effort to expend on them is rarely defined precisely'. Caza (2011) defines discretion as 'latitude of action or control over how one does their work' but asserts that there is not yet a mature and multidimensional theory of discretion in organizations.

As noted earlier, the extent to which employees are able to use their discretion is linked to the type of managerial regimes within which they are situated, specifically the degree of trust employees are afforded (Fox, 1974). For example, employees might be able to decide the order of tasks: some tasks may be left to employees' decisions, while others may be closely controlled by managers. For Green (2008, p. 25), 'the key axis for understanding discretion is the fundamental post-Fordist trade-off between the positive effects of discretion on potential output per employee and the negative effects of greater leeway on work effort'. We contend that this trade-off is particularly pertinent to interactive service work because management may seek to promote positive divergences from Taylorized scripted interactions so that the customer enjoys a more 'authentic' form of interaction whilst at the same time attempting to limit the negative divergences which would decrease efficiency. This 'double-edged' sword of discretion was richly depicted in Taylor and Tyler's (2000) study of emotional labour and call-centre work wherein women workers were recruited because of their sociability and required to use their personality in interactions with customers while at the same time required to desist from overly lengthy social interactions which would result in lower call handling times. Hence, there is evidence of the market conditioning of call-centres in the mass service markets actively limiting worker discretion and constraining the potential for both skill development and work meaningfulness (Taylor & Bain, 1999; Taylor et al., 2002).

As service economies have advanced, researchers (Batt, 2000; Frenkel, 2005; Korczynski, 2001) have categorized the diversity of managerial regimes and HR practices within call-centres. These discussions have drawn attention to the way market strategies and product positioning influence the types of control and the degree of employee discretion in call-centre work. For example, Frenkel (2005, p. 358) distinguishes between mass-services and mass-customized services – with the former having an emphasis on cost reduction, standardization and tight controls and the latter prioritizing quality and value adding service, discretion and normative regulation. He acknowledges that generally mass-customized services firms adopt a value-approach by emphasizing quality customer service which affords greater discretion to service workers. Despite attempts to reflect diversity within the sector, there have been few empirical studies of interactive work within 'middle-range' mass-customized regimes and the potential for employee discretion. For example, Korczynski (2005, p. 8) comments, 'A key question, not properly addressed in studies so far is, how far discretion has risen in the original "service offer", rather than in the service recovery aspect of the job'. As such, a missing element in existing studies is to detail the nature and degree of employee discretion afforded to mass-customized employment regimes.

Debates have focused primarily on the development of management controls over interactive service workers, centring on the ways in which informal, normative forms of control require employees to identify with the ideals of customer service or to match and mirror the corporate 'brand'. The work of colleagues within the field of emotional (Hochschild, 1983) and aesthetic labour (Warhurst & Nickson, 2007) has extended an analysis of the ways in which organizations use recruitment to hire employees with the 'right attitude' (Callaghan & Thompson, 2002), personality and/or 'look' to correspond with corporate branding. Within these types of work arrangements managerial regimes are not simply a matter of supervisory direct control and bureaucracy but also integrate normative dimensions as employees are recruited in order to reflect and reinforce corporate values. As Leidner's (1993, p. 87) study reveals, faced with the inescapable element of discretion in the agents' work, Combined Insurance tried to exert control by shaping their employees' characters and habits of thought. Thus, the focus on managing workers' identities and feelings to ensure they behave in an appropriate way in exchanges with customers has prompted further discussions about the scope of control over interactive service work. More recently Sallaz's (2015, p. 26) rich ethnographic examination of normative control in a US call-centre has signalled the 'autonomous learning game' practised by employees which relied on informal norms to regulate the labour process.

As service work becomes increasingly differentiated and customers require more 'authentic' service encounters, the nature of control has also evolved. For example, Fleming and Sturdy (2011) and Sturdy et al. (2010, p. 117) suggest the extension to a hybrid form of control − to neo-normative − because 'neo-normative control works to create and sustain a corporate identity drawn from externally derived values and identities to which employees are expected to subscribe'. This is similar to normative control in the focus on instilling corporate norms to create a sense of shared identity, but differs because under neo-normative control employees' values are formed extra-organizationally. Consequently, under neo-normative control, Sturdy et al. (2010, p. 117) state that the manager plays a 'channelling role' − so that workers' values already present are 'liberated' or 'unleashed'. It is argued that this conceptualization of control addresses some of the 'thorny problems' associated with normative control, particularly that of securing internalization through the displacement of employees' pre-existing social identities and values by corporate norms. Sturdy et al. (2010) note that employees' non-work norms and the expression of employees' emotions and personalities can be utilized by the firm in terms of motivation and task execution. In this sense 'the manager is not explicitly aiming to inculcate and socialize the worker to become a corporate clone, but to promote values from outside the firm in a manner that resonate with organizational objectives' (Sturdy et al., 2010, p. 118).

Recent studies of normative and neo-normative control have explored how the dynamics of control have been developing. They have been relatively silent on how labour is utilized within the context of such call-centre control regimes. For Fleming and Sturdy (2011, p. 190), the freedom to 'just be yourself' within their case study was constrained; 'it did not free workers *from* the call-centre's control, but introduced freedom *around* control'. This is a 'freedom' applied to the expression of the self at work rather than the degree of discretion and participation in the labour process. In this regard, their study corroborates other studies of normative and neo-normative controls in call-centres (Bolton & Houlihan, 2009; Kinnie et al., 2000) which find such regimes are used to engender a fun culture, deployed by managers as a distraction to nullify the impact of low discretion work in a monotonous labour process rather than enhancing employee autonomy. As such, in most cases, normative controls generally coexist with rather than replace traditional forms such as bureaucratic controls (Alvesson & Karreman, 2004). Therefore, these studies focus on the types of managerial regime which restrict rather than facilitate employee discretion.

The study reported in this paper is different because the case organization used neo-normative controls to deliver more 'authentic' and higher levels of customer service that were founded on employees' discretion. As such, workers were encouraged to 'be yourself' in the way they delivered customer service, thereby valorizing workers' extra-organizational identities through the delivery of the service. To interrogate how the process of valorization operates, we need to conceptualize the nature and degree of employee discretion within such work organizations. Assessing how discretion is enacted is fundamental to evaluations of interactive service work (Fleming & Sturdy, 2011; Leidner, 1993; Sallaz, 2015; Thompson & van den Broek, 2010). There are two main reasons for this. Firstly, because of the indeterminacy of labour and the difficulties of appropriating value from service work, organizations seek to harness employee knowledge so that they may utilize their discretion to offer an authentic service encounter. Leidner (1993, p. 178) represents this as a paradox at the heart of interactive service work – organizations want to treat customers as interchangeable units, but also want to make them feel they are receiving a personal service. The second reason is that the interaction between customers and workers presents problems for managers as they seek to exercise control without detrimentally affecting the nature of the customer service relationship (Korczynski, 2009). Consequently, indirect forms of normative control which rely on a range of norms (that can be internal or external to the organization) have evolved to ensure workers use discretion within circumscribed boundaries. For example, Sallaz (2015) details how external norms relating to being a competent conversationalist were used to regulate the labour process at CallCo.

Similarly, professional norms guide how professionals use discretion in interactions with their clients. Indeed, within the literature on public sector professionals, the concept of 'value discretion' emerged as Taylor and Kelly (2006) built on Lipsky's (1980) conception of 'street level bureaucrats'. In these cases, actions are said to be determined by notions of fairness and justice, involving professional codes of ethics or organizational codes of conduct. There is the expectation that professionals can be trusted to abide by established or normative professional practice and exercise their judgement on the basis of their training, knowledge and experience such that normative influences provide both the space for discretion and the necessarily constraining boundaries within which that discretion is expected to be conceived and enacted. We build on these insights *to define value discretion as the scope for employees to interpret the meaning of the espoused values of their organization.* Employees' perceptions of this opportunity for discretion are informed both by management and their own existing value system. Although this is similar to the discretion developed in professional work, in our case the value discretion exercised by receptionists is context-specific, that is informed by organizational rather than professional values. Value discretion provides the underpinning basis for discretion in how workers act in their jobs. It can be understood as having interactional effects with other aspects of discretion that inform the nature of task discretion since this itself stems from how employees act in relation to espoused organizational norms. How these are enacted by managers and employees in specific organizational circumstances will reflect both the extent of value discretion and the processes leading to local socially produced outcomes.

This paper is based on a study of a mass-customized call-centre which sought to manage employees through neo-normative controls. We examine the nature of discretion within such regimes by asking: how is labour utilized and what are the implications for discretion under neo-normative forms of control? For instance, if organizations seek to gain from hiring workers' authentic selves then how is this harnessed by organizations? How are organizational values interpreted and encoded by employees within customer interactions? To address these questions, we further the concept of *value discretion* as the scope for employees to interpret for themselves the meaning of the espoused values of their organization. This provides a foundational basis for further discretion in how workers act in their jobs in relation to task discretion. The evidence reported shows how interactions between managers, employees and clients and employees result in workers willing to go beyond the expectations of their managers in delivering *their own* interpretation of corporate values.

CASE STUDY AND METHODS

The data presented are taken from an in-depth qualitative case study of VoiceTel (a pseudonym), a multi-client call-centre which provides out-sourced answering, message and reception services to businesses across the United Kingdom. VoiceTel is a privately owned family company, founded and managed by a brother and sister (Laura and Tim). The company has grown rapidly from just four receptionists in 2000 to 97 in 2007 (the time of the research). The owners developed innovative technology which allows clients' customer calls to be re-routed through their call-centre. When a call is received, the receptionist's screen displays a range of information so they know for whom they are taking the call, who is available to take calls and other relevant information. All receptionists had approximately 20–40 clients and work was organized into teams of four. Calls were ideally to be answered by the dedicated receptionist, but if this was not possible, they were handled by other team members. Consequently, receptionists develop a sense of responsibility for their 'own' clients such that they become 'normatively enlisted'. Receptionists then re-direct the call or take a message and e-mail or text it to the client. As a result of the investment in technology and the focus on providing high-quality customer service, VoiceTel became a market leader in high-quality virtual reception services. As such, VoiceTel exhibits key characteristics of Frenkel's (2005) depiction of a 'mass-customized' call-centre which emphasized high value-added customer service and where employees exercised discretion.

We sought access to study this organization after the company came to our attention for winning a number of small business awards for its employment practices. Our case study design integrates a range of data collection methods, including observation, interviews and secondary data which allow a holistic and contextualized account of the organization (Yin, 2003). Observation of the workplace provided valuable insights into the labour process and the workplace culture. Before starting field-work, one of the research team 'shadowed' a receptionist for the day to gain an insight into the work process and the research team also spent some time observing how receptionists handled calls prior to commencing interviews. These periods of observation helped to inform the themes explored in the interviews relating to the nature of work, skills, discretion and control. Additionally, focused observation of the recruitment assessment day provided an insight into the selection process and the discussions which led to the hiring of successful candidates. Semi-structured interviews were the primary method of data collection. These were conducted with 66 respondents (75 per cent of the workforce): 3 senior managers (including the owners), 48 receptionists and 15 support staff. All of the receptionists are female, two senior managers are male and one female and all the support staff are female apart from two male IT managers. The average length of interview with receptionists was 49 minutes, all were digitally recorded and transcribed. The interview sought to reflect a wide range of themes addressing the experience, content and management of work, emotional work and skills. As is often the case in organizational research, the managers sought volunteers to take part in the study and so we did not have any control over the sample. However, it was evident from the number of employees (three-quarters of the workforce) who wanted to take part that employees were comfortable to discuss their working experiences. All interviews were conducted in the workplace in a meeting room and all employees were informed of the aims and objectives of the research and that we would be reporting back our broad findings to the employers. Informed consent was an important feature of the ethical framework of the study and employees were given the opportunity to withdraw from the study at any time. None chose to do so and they appeared confident in the way they expressed their views about their work and their employer.

The data from the interviews were coded and broad themes were developed inductively to produce a thematic map of the main issues. From this, more specific categories of data were developed and analysed in relation to the nature and extent of control and discretion. Further reading and coding sought to identify the range of ways in which receptionists exercised their judgement in work and this extended to task discretion as well as the way they interpreted the values of the organization and these were coded as value discretion. As such, the concept of value discretion was developed inductively in order to capture the nature and extent of discretion within this work.

NEO-NORMATIVE CONTROL

The business model pursued by the owners focused on providing bespoke, discrete, high-quality reception services for a variety of client-organizations. Each receptionist worked for approximately 30–40 client-organizations, work involved relaying messages and having a cursory knowledge of the business, the employees who worked within and to customer answer inquiries. Significantly, due to the diversity of the client-organizations receptionists had to be adaptable to respond to varied service requirements. In such cases, rather than normative controls which tend to impose a unified value system, the organization sought to exhort employees to 'be themselves' and use their 'authentic' personalities as part of the service offer. In this section, we illustrate how employees were managed primarily based on neo-normative forms of control. This entailed drawing on and valorizing workers' extra-organizational identities to use as part of the customer service interaction. In organizations like VoiceTel which offer customized services, the emphasis is for employees to be flexible and adaptable and this entailed using their knowledgeability and discretion to provide the personalized services required by the varied client-organizations.

The next section illustrates how neo-normative control was exercised through recruitment and selection and the wider management approach.

Recruitment and Selection

The emphasis on customer service was central to the recruitment and selection process and, as other studies of normative control (Callaghan & Thompson, 2002; Grugulis, Dundon, & Wilkinson, 2000) have illustrated, employees were hired on their personality and value congruence. As Laura, the co-owner of the organization noted,

> They [employees] are the first impression of the company, by nature they have to be cheery, bubbly, professional and very accommodating of our clients' customers' requests.

Workers were hired for their general value orientation based on customer service and this gendered and classed the types of employees who applied and those who were selected. For the owners Laura and Tim, who had never previously employed staff, the success of the organization was based on ensuring they had highly committed and satisfied employees who would care for their clients,

> When we set up the business all we knew was how to be a client, we didn't know anything about anything and we just had very, very strong ideas about customer service ... there was an inherent belief that it would be the quality of our people that would deliver the service and that therefore the company had to be somewhere that people would want to work and progress in and the work had to be enjoyable. (Laura)

Hence, the employers had a clear idea of what qualities made a VoiceTel employee. Sonia's description of a receptionist was representative,

Open and honest, informal, passionate, caring ... top customer service, just the customer always comes first, and it is just going that extra mile.

Recruitment was predominantly through word-of-mouth recommendations; the organization hadn't advertised positions for over two years and employees who recommended someone earned a bonus of £250 bonus. As Laura stated,

That is quite a big incentive for people. But also they are not recommending people that they wouldn't want to work with ... so it's got its own sort of quality control.

One feature of this form of recruitment practice was that it ensured that prospective employees were aware of the nature and type of work required. The owners sought to recruit people with a strong service orientation, seeking evidence that recruits will 'go the extra mile' and engage in discretionary effort. The receptionist workforce was entirely female, although there was a degree of heterogeneity employees in terms of age and personality type, as Leila noted,

Well it is a fantastic place to work because everybody is relaxed there is a friendly atmosphere. Everybody gets on, there is no bitchiness ... everybody has got different personalities.

Within neo-normative regimes, employees are hired for their extra-organizational identities which can then be harnessed by the organization. Rather than moulding employees to a specific type, VoiceTel recruited employees who were 'themselves', as Kirsty details,

Yeah, I can come in and wear whatever I want, and be myself ... and they are employing me for being me. They have, if you know what I mean, cos you can go into some organisations and they try and change you, and mould you to what they want you to try and be, and it is not like that at all here. They say to you, 'Be who you are', like when you are on the telephone, they don't try and mould you to try and be anything else, yeah. Like you answer the telephone like you would want to answer it, and if that is how they like you doing that, then that is why they are employing you, you know.

Receptionists reported how they brought values from outside the workplace when interpreting the meaning of customer service,

I think people like to hear someone on the end of the phone who is going to put them at ease ... I think if you get through to somebody who is quite boring and isn't very helpful ... I always think about how I would like to be treated if I phoned someone and you get companies you know insurance companies and things and you phone them and you just have no hope in them at all and you just think they just haven't got a clue themselves. (Trudy)

In this case, the extra-organizational identities related to gendered and classed identities in terms of employees' interpretations of delivering good customer service. At VoiceTel, these identities were harnessed and fostered by the organization to deliver business success. As such, the recruitment process enabled a synchronicity between the values of the organization and those of the individual receptionists as working-class women. These centre on a potent combination of trust, care and providing a high-quality customer service; this was something which workers could relate to and valued highly.

Management Approach

Once employees were recruited for their service orientation, the organization sought to develop a 'happy' work environment in which they would use these skills and extend their discretionary effort (Jenkins & Delbridge, 2014). Hence, developing and sustaining a strong organizational culture was, from the outset, conceived as core to achieving a committed, professional and caring workforce,

> We have to create that environment but at a higher level in our own business. So very high team spirit ... Everybody knows that if we're forecasting six inches of snow tomorrow, we want people to actually come in rucksacks and walking boots to get here. And we had some-one last year when it snowed like hell, she walked three miles to get here, you know, and you just don't get that in another company ... It's that kind of culture that we have or we have to maintain and manage. (Laura)

The culture had a strong resonance to paternalism; it was based on the values of care and trust, and to this end, extolled the virtues of reciprocity. This was also aided by the owners being a brother and sister partnership and a sense of 'family' was strongly invoked in the organization. Part of the induction process involved the owners taking new recruits to lunch where they would ask about their families, hobbies etc. and get to know the receptionists. In interviews, the receptionists commented on the way the owners remembered these details and would inquire into their families. The familial culture was also evident in the practice of the owners who crafted a relaxed work environment and often brought their children to the workplace. Loyalty and commitment to the owners was also enhanced because of the ways these values translated into how they managed the receptionists. For example, some reported that if they had a health emergency they would be instructed to leave work because their family was more important than the job. Additionally, Liz recalled how her manager had remembered her husband was working in Japan when an earthquake had been reported,

> We are a big family and that is the way that we work, and there was an earthquake in Japan last week, and Chris [manager] shot in the morning straight to me and was like, 'Is Ian OK?' And that is how personal it is, he knows my husband is Ian, they've met once. My family is important to them, not just me ... and you genuinely get that sense of belief that it is.

The aim of engendering a spirit of reciprocity was to communicate to employees that they were valued and cared for so they in turn would reciprocate these values in their interactions with their clients, which would ultimately benefit the organization. As Libby explained,

> They [VoiceTel] provide a good service. They care for the clients and also the way they care for us. I have never known a company like it.

The organization offered above average pay and holiday provisions, there is a private healthcare plan and staff can obtain interest-free loans. Informal practices were also developed which included one-off bonus payments – in one example, £50 notes were attached to the underside of receptionists' chairs – employees are given Easter eggs, Valentine's and Christmas presents, birthdays are celebrated by the whole workforce and the annual company parties are notorious for their generosity.

Significantly, the degree of trust was also transmitted via the managerial regime through the creation of a high-trust (Fox, 1974) workplace which reflected features of Friedman's (1977) responsible autonomy. For the owner, trust was central to her business strategy,

> To have good people doing this job, the job has to have responsibility and accountability cos otherwise people would see it as a really tedious job if you didn't have that relationship with your clients. I mean if we're trusting people to look after our clients' calls, we should be able to trust them. (Laura)

Consequently, the espoused values of trust and care permeated the labour process and specifically management's approach to control. The owners created the space for their employees to use their discretion and knowledge. There were no overt performance measures; no formal call handling times or targets. Although the technology was surveillance-capable, the owners made a conscious decision that this degree of performance management would contradict the values of trust and care. The physical space also helped to convey a relaxed and trusting company. It is open-plan, with high ceilings, light and airy. All offices are glass fronted and the owners and managers operate an open-door policy. The atmosphere was very friendly and relaxed; receptionists dressed how they liked and decorated their desks with personal effects. During quiet periods receptionists could read magazines or browse the Internet. There is a kitchen on each floor where the company provides free tea and coffee.

This management approach had the desired effect; trust was reported as a central feature of the day-to-day experience of work by receptionists. April commented, when asked about the break system,

> If someone from your team was not at their desk then you wouldn't get up to go ... But ... it is not a company that is strict on things, I mean they don't want you to abuse it, but they are very happy ... if you have just had a bad few minutes then you can just get up and go away from your desk or go and grab a coffee.

That said, the informality with which each individual is able to take impromptu coffee breaks or to use the computer to surf the web is facilitated by the fact that a team leader works alongside each team and is able to see who is doing (and saying) what when. This provides the senior managers with reassurance that any poor performance or inappropriate behaviour would be identified and brought to their attention. It also promotes self-disciplining by team members. As Reed (2001) observes, reciprocity balances features of trust and control; and trust and control are different sides of the same analytical coin. Reciprocity promotes responsibility and trust but also obligations and these were conveyed through normative controls. Overwhelmingly, employees' reported that they felt appreciated and cared for by the company,

> You kind of think you belong and you are so well looked after and appreciated, that's the main thing. That's why people stay. You are appreciated for what you do. (Renee)

> It's just little things that they do to show that they do care ... A lot of companies you are just a number or a name, you are not a person, but I feel that here you are a person, you are an individual and you are appreciated for what you do. (Andrea)

Nathalie spoke for many of the receptionists when she described her feelings,

> Because it is not just a company, you feel a part of a family ... because they [the owners] are always very approachable ... they always have an open-door policy ... People generally are proud to work here, cos it is genuinely a good company to work for.

The case thus displays characteristics that are commonly reported in examples of neo-normative control. Recruitment and selection was central to ensuring the right type of personality was recruited but crucially the organization sought extra-organizational identities to deliver a high-quality and authentic service delivery. The management regime demonstrated to employees that they were trusted and in turn this reinforced a cycle of obligation to the employer and informed how employees interacted with their clients. The significance of our study, for example, in contrast to Fleming and Sturdy's (2011) research where workers' expressions of self-identity did not impact directly on their labour process, was that VoiceTel sought to capitalize on women's gendered and classed identities to link directly to the nature of work. In this way, these skills were part of the process of valorization and to meet this end, employees were afforded high degrees of discretion in their interactions with their clients. To evaluate how neo-normative control impacts on the nature of work the following sections set out an integrated assessment of the different forms of discretion at work.

DISCRETION AT VOICETEL

The client-organizations were located throughout the United Kingdom and were highly differentiated; ranging from professional legal, property and health organizations to large and small commercial organizations from all sectors. The client base meant that receptionists had to interact with a wide variety of client-organizations and their customers. Employees had to be flexible and adaptable to use their discretion to interact appropriately depending on the client-organization's requests. In Leidner's (1993) study, some service workers (the insurance agents) used higher levels of discretion than others (McDonald's servers) because flexibility and customer responsiveness were more important than efficient service in the context of their work. More recently, Sallaz (2015, p. 12) depicts how a multi-client call centre in the US dealing with a range of client requests required employees to be adaptable and use 'flexible problem-solving' to handle the wide variety of inquiries. In these contexts Taylorized standardization is rendered useless. The situation is similar in VoiceTel, where the different client-organizations required the deployment of different types of emotional performances depending on the nature of the service (Jenkins, Delbridge, & Roberts, 2010). As such, employees were provided with the space to use their judgement in the deployment of their service by interpreting how best to communicate the values required by the each of the client-organizations within the overall value infrastructure established by VoiceTel of high-quality customer service. It is our argument that this involved using 'value discretion'.

Value Discretion

Under neo-normative control, employees are hired for their extra-organizational identities which are then reinforced within the organization through practices that communicate and promote acceptable behaviour. At VoiceTel, the requirement for employees who demonstrated strong service orientations meant that the organization capitalized on gendered and classed identities. Whilst managers at VoiceTel set parameters to establish how receptionists were to behave, employees are then provided with the space to engage in value discretion by interpreting how best to deploy their judgement in interactions with their various client-organizations. We define *value discretion* as the scope for employees to interpret the meaning of the espoused values of their organization in their interactions. VoiceTel both sets the boundaries for behaviour but also creates the space for employees to determine how they would personally bring the organization's values to life in their specific interactions with customers. How has the company achieved this?

Once employees are hired for their service orientation, they have six weeks of training. In particular, this involves observing and listening to more experienced employees answering calls and interacting with client-organizations and their customers. During this time, the values of VoiceTel are transmitted through both the formal and informal socialization processes as new hires familiarize themselves with the varied norms of interaction required by different client-organizations. We would argue therefore that value discretion operates within organizational boundaries; receptionists are not 'free' to behave as they like in interactions with client-organizations and their customers. Yet, within neo-normative regimes, workers have the latitude to engage in behaviours which they interpret as synonymous with the values of the organization. Employees draw on their own judgement, their training and experience acquired outwith as well as within the organization.

Receptionists were trusted to convey the values of the organization in the way they delivered the service and so essentially the organization communicated that they were 'trusted' to be themselves in ways that materially impacted on how they undertook their roles. As Kirsty notes,

> I feel like I can be myself, you do to a certain extent put on a little bit of an act ... you get the key clients when they pop up and you have to pretend as if you know them, and you don't know them, you haven't got a clue who they are, you don't know what they do, but you just know them because you have been told that they are a key client to the client that you are taking the calls for, so you pretend that you know who they are, but you don't, so in that respect, that is an act, but as far as I am concerned, this is me, what you see is what you get, and that is what I am like at work, when I am on the phones, when I leave.

Echoing Fleming and Sturdy's (2011) study, employees reported being recruited because of who they were. Phoebe drew favourable comparison with her previous employer,

> It's very nice to be yourself, and obviously you had your personality in the bank, but you didn't really show it, whereas here you are you! And that is why you are here ... I think right from assessment you realize that you were picked because of who you are as opposed to the person that they can make you.

Amy also supported the view that employees are enabled to use their judgement,

> You are allowed to be an individual and that is the whole point really. And because the way that you are trained isn't standard, your strengths are allowed to sort of, flourish.

This opportunity to exercise value discretion was particularly evident in the way receptionists negotiated the 'service offer' (Korzcynski, 2005) with their different client-organizations. Receptionists undertook a 'welcome call' with each of their new clients and this interaction established the nature of the service that was to be delivered. The welcome call was based on receptionists 'getting to know' their clients and then discussing the kinds of service they required. In preparation, receptionists read about the company profile and searched their website to learn more about the organization. The training and pre-briefing of receptionists is confined to the observation of other more experienced receptionists. There are no formal scripts nor is there an explicit list of values or principles which the organization required to be enacted. Instead, receptionists are trusted with the latitude to interpret VoiceTel's service values in these interactions and to develop rapport with the client-organizations they were placed with, as Ruth details,

> You are given a client, obviously and you try and read up on what they do on their website, and then you go into one of the quiet offices and then you phone them up and say, 'Hi. I am Ruth I am hopefully going to be your new receptionist, is it ok to talk, have you got time to

talk?' And then you go through the details, how they want their phones answered, what they want me to say, when they are going to divert the calls, so you just get a general idea of what kind of set up they have got. A lot of clients work from home, that is why they have got an answering service, and you find out all of that sometimes, they'll say, 'Oh I have got two little boys', and you get friendly, but you know who those are within minutes, and then you get some that are hard work, you know efficient and very stilted, I find most of the men like that, the women are easy going.

As Ruth noted above, these interactions draw heavily on employees' sense of accepted behaviour in how to talk to customers and in this way, drew on gendered and classed norms of interactions. Receptionists have to be able to use their judgement in knowing how best to interact with the different kinds of service requirements from the varied client-organizations. As highlighted below by Ruby,

> You don't feel like someone is on your back all the while, obviously, you are all being monitored but you know nobody is standing over you.... They [owners] leave you to develop a friendship, a relationship with your clients and I think that is one of the things that makes us quite unique. Like we are not a call-centre just going blahhh.

The interactions are informed by the expectations of individual clients and the judgments of the receptionist. As Esther describes, the welcome call involves gauging the level of service to anticipate the type of performance clients' require,

> You have to judge the client ... you can get some clients who ... don't want to have a relationship with us, they don't want to, but you have got to judge that when you do a welcome call. So if they are happy and bubbly and asking you about your personal life, then they want to be friends and they want to know more about you and they want you to be more involved in their business, but if you do the welcome-call and they are very straight like, 'This is how our business works, this is what I want you to do', they don't want that relationship with you. They just basically want it is on a business level and that is how they want you to act, I have got clients that know more about me than my friends do, but I have got other clients who know absolutely nothing about me and they don't want to know anything about me.

The approach receptionists adopt in the welcome call is subject to considerable discretion, both in terms of the how each employee approaches the call as well as how they interpret the organization's service ethos. Employees were afforded the discretion to interpret the meaning of, and how best to deliver, VoiceTel's espoused commitment to a quality personalized service with their clients. The receptionists acknowledged that in some cases client-organizations provided clear guidance on how they would like their calls managed and the performance they expect from receptionists, whereas, in other cases, the clients' needs would be implied because of the nature of the organization, as Letitia indicates,

> Again it would vary on the clients, I mean some people would actually, specifically say, 'When you answer the phone, I want you to answer it in this way, I want you to answer it is that way', now if that's a certain way we would make a note on the screen 'always be bubbly when you answer call to this caller'. So if they request anything you can make notes on the

screen, if they didn't specifically request anything, it would be down to the receptionist's initiative. I think the situations where it is like that type of company, I think that the receptionist would automatically be ... more sympathetic towards them, rather than it saying on the screen 'please be sympathetic to callers who have lost a loved one.'

In other cases, the performance relied on anticipating how best to deliver a service rather than following explicit instructions, as Chloe stated this required judgement of the receptionist,

> It varies really ... everyone is different and you just speak to them and a lot of the time they will give you the information just by the way that they speak, so you pick things up, you don't have to ask them every question.

Following the preliminary discussion of the client's service requirements, the value-discretionary nature of the work is maintained through the individual receptionist's ongoing interpretations of the 'performance' of a high-quality and personalized service. As Grace details, receptionists exercise their judgement in relation to the way different professional service firms would likely prefer to have their calls answered, even though this hadn't been explicitly communicated. Grace indicates that you use your knowledge to best anticipate the type of service required,

> Some clients say, um ... when you answer the phone could you be like really bubbly and that kind of thing, other clients don't want it. I inherited a group of solicitors in London and they didn't want that [she laughs], because they were getting that with the previous team, they just said 'we want to know who it is and put them through'. And we have had e-mails back saying ...'you are doing a great job, it is nice to get our calls through without all this chit chat [she laughs]. So, you have to assess the company as well, you know that a group of solicitors in London isn't going to want to know what you did on the weekend'. [She laughs]

The varied personalities used by the receptionists was noted by Joan who stated how she used her more reserved manner to best deliver a service to professional firms,

> Well, I would say that I am not too over the top, you know, some people are like really chatty and really bubbly, I don't know, I think that I am kind of middle of the road [she laughs]. I think it depends on the type of company that has come through. And obviously ... I mean we have got one client who is a will writing company, so if the call comes through, obviously, you have got to be a bit more like reserved, yeah, and serious, and then we have got ones that do things like duck herding, so obviously with that type of activity you are like more bubbly.

In conjunction with the social values which women brought to the workplace and that were reinforced by the espoused organizational value system, notions of quality service were also collectively developed and informed by peer relations within the team. This collectively created understanding of what is expected shapes how receptionists act on behalf of clients.

The service offered by receptionists embodies many facets of 'emotional management' (Bolton, 2005; Jenkins et al., 2010). Some client-organizations required receptionists to be 'bubbly', 'chatty' and have an enthusiastic telephone manner, whereas other clients such as solicitors and accountants, required a more sober, reserved and mature manner. Some clients engaged in counselling and personal advice and desired receptionists to be caring and empathetic in their interactions. In this sense, as Bolton's (2005) framework of emotional management elucidates, service employees draw on varied sources to enact different performances; organizational norms, professional codes of behaviour as well as social norms. Crucially, she highlights that the enactment of emotion work is not always prescribed by organizations but can involve a high degree of agency in the way employees draw on accepted social conventions and norms of interaction. We suggest that in so doing, service workers are undertaking value discretion by applying their interpretation of organizational values.

Task Discretion

Receptionists have the space to interpret the type of service offer in negotiation with their different clients and this also informs the range of tasks performed for their clients. The receptionists' ability to exercise value discretion informs how organizational values are interpreted and, as a consequence, how the receptionists undertake tasks for each of their clients. In reflecting the different types of relationships negotiated, the nature and range of tasks undertaken depended on the relationship developed with the client-organization. As Esther details,

> I have clients that I do a lot more than I do for others ... I have got two clients and I know their businesses inside out, I know their style, I know how they work, I know how they use us to do it, everything about their business really. But then I have got other clients that don't want time to get involved in that side of it, they just want me to take their calls.

The freedom to develop different types of relationships meant that receptionists were able to determine the depth of the relations with the different client-organizations,

> I am quite close to some of my clients, so I see them as friends ... I feel like I am letting them down if I don't give them a good service ... I am very protective of my clients, and if I am away for the day, I know that maybe they wouldn't get the service that I gave them, that would make me feel a bit uneasy. (Caitlin)

Gendered relations were significant as receptionists used maternal and familial terms to describe their feelings towards their clients,

> They [the clients) are your babies! And that's a maternal instinct, that's what you do think that it is ... I mean we are very personal with the clients, we send them cards when they are getting married, or when they are ill and all that. (Elsie)

Value discretion thus underpins task discretion, both in terms of how receptionists were able to determine how to organize their time by prioritizing tasks, as well as the nature of their interactions with the client-organization's customer. In other words receptionists take responsibility for both what they do and what they say,

> You have to use your initiative. If your client sends you updates, you have to take that on yourself, to organize everything ... faxes and certain things like that come through it is up to you ... you don't get watched or anything like that. (Grace)

As we have seen, the variety of clients meant that the work itself varied. Receptionists had a degree of freedom to develop different relationships with clients and, in some cases, they were then able to undertake additional tasks beyond the norm (and beyond those sanctioned and expected by the company). The next section details the two domains in which task discretion was evident.

Range and Degree of Service Offered
The interpretation of the values of trust and care had led some receptionists to advise their clients on ways to avoid additional costs, resulting in a reduction in revenue to VoiceTel. Although this could be conceived as transgressing the values (and certainly the immediate interests) of their organization, it was interpreted instead by the receptionists as providing a high-quality service to clients.

> One thing that we normally say to people, instead of an SMS and an email which charges you twice for every message, 'Why don't you have your message by SMS, and then you can check your messages at VoiceTel online?' ... So, a lot of clients do that and they then get charged only the one time ... So, then they think, 'That's great, VoiceTel providing the extra service, and they are trying to save me money by not charging me extra'. (Esther)

Value discretion also helps explain the extra services which the receptionists provide for some of their clients; they are interpreting the values of a quality professional service and then acting *outwith* VoiceTel's expectations,

> One of my clients asked me to send leaflets out for him, like for every new enquiry that comes in to send out like a leaflet, so he had to send me up some ... I went the extra mile with that client, and at the end of the day I go through the lists of people that we have had calling in, and I get their addresses and then I send them out a leaflet, so obviously that does take time away from my other clients, so that client does get a bit extra from me. (Naomi)

Caitlin also described how the relationship developed with one of her clients meant that she engaged in considerable work for her whilst she was on maternity leave,

> he left me in charge, she put my name on her website, she put my name on her mobile, her answer phone, and yeah, I had all of her e-mails sent to me as well, so that is more of the personal.

Neither of these practices was expected by the managers of VoiceTel and they would not have been sanctioned had they known about them.

Another area where employees showed discretion was in handling money for clients. VoiceTel is not set up to receive money from the customers of their clients nor to take online bookings. However, the close working relationships which are built with their clients means that receptionists have to deal with these requests and decide how far to go beyond what is sanctioned by the organization. In one case, a receptionist had been receiving cheques on behalf of one of her clients and was banking them in her lunch hour until the company put a stop to it. Others undertook activities such as booking flights for their clients which were beyond the service provided. The space to interpret the corporate values creates agential spaces for individual receptionists to decide how they should act. In these circumstances, VoiceTel managers have been forced to restrict their employees' commitment to customer service and to protect their employees from engaging in too much discretionary effort,

> There has been a couple of instances where I have tried to do extra stuff for my clients, and I have been told that I am not to do it. (Fiona)

Range and Degree of Performance Offered

Another facet of the task discretion was the extent to which receptionists engaged in a performance to not disclose to the customers of their client-organizations that they were not physically located on their premises (Jenkins & Delbridge, 2017). As Ruby describes,

> You have got to sort of pretend that you are in their [the client's] office, that's what they like, they like us to pretend, so if someone says 'oh I am down the road from you, where are you?', you have got to say 'oh I am new to the area', that is my famous line, but to give the initial caller the actual feeling that you are a part of the office and you are giving a good customer service to them.

Part of the task discretion involved the depth of performance which receptions were prepared to engage in to not disclose that this was a virtual reception service. Alice explained that situations arise which cause dilemmas for receptionists so that they tried not to relay that they are physically based elsewhere,

> We get clients saying, 'I have got an appointment with him at 2 o'clock, where is he?' And you are like, 'oh don't know' and they are like, 'well can't you let me in?' and you are like, 'umm'.

The willingness to engage in these performances rested on the nature and depth of the social relations developed between receptionists and their clients. As Kirsty describes,

> The clients that you tend to know the best, or say if you have met them or something, then you tend to feel more comfortable lying for them

Interviewer: So what sort of stuff would you say?

> Oh, well 'he has just popped away from his desk at the minute, he has gone to make a cup of tea', and things like that.

In all of these cases, discretion over tasks revolved around the extent to which workers used the scope of their latitude depending on the client-organization.

VoiceTel's workplace regime provides a context where receptionists' understanding of their role involves multiple considerations: the espoused values of trust and care as a high-quality customer service provider, their own interpretation of how these values should be translated in interactions and a sense of what their clients would expect. These are aspects of what Korczynski (2005) has described as the hidden (and unrealized) value of the service offer. The scope for discretion over both the tasks to be undertaken and the underpinning values of the company in how those tasks were conducted was a source of considerable satisfaction for many receptionists. It also provided a sense of connection for employees between their workplace and private selves.

DISCUSSION AND CONCLUSION

Although discretion is fundamental to contemporary debates on control, the concept remains underdeveloped (Caza, 2011). This paper seeks to paint a more nuanced picture of neo-normative controls and the nature of the interactive labour process by examining the various forms employee discretion takes in customized service settings. Our study addressed questions relating to how a neo-normative management regime translated to the labour process; specifically, how control was experienced and discretion was enacted. We examined how an organization which extols workers 'to be themselves' valorized workers' extra-organizational identities, in this case gendered and classed identities. In short, this study attempted to clarify the connections between a neo-normative regime and the nature of work, in particular the type of discretion employees are afforded in order to deliver an authentic service. To address these questions, we have elaborated the concept of value discretion and applied it in an empirical setting to depict the nature of discretion enacted by employees. Examining value discretion and its interactional effects on task discretion focuses attention on how employees act in relation to espoused organizational norms. The evidence shows how these interactions resulted in employees going beyond the expectations of their managers to deliver *their own* interpretation of corporate values. As such, while there is individual discretion, the organization's values are socially constructed; not imposed by management nor interpreted freely by receptionists. Management establish parameters but employees work within them, and sometimes beyond them. There are normative influences that are seen to provide both the space for discretion and the necessarily constraining boundaries within which that discretion is expected to be conceived and enacted. Thus, employees' perceptions of this discretion are informed both by management and their own existing value system.

As indicated above, an important feature of this study is the valorization process which harnessed and developed the gendered and classed skills of the workforce directly in interactions with customers. Like Fleming and Sturdy's (2011) study, employees were encouraged to 'just be yourself', however, in contrast, our case demonstrates that the organization sought to realize the value of employees' identities directly in the labour process by creating the space for employees to use their discretion in the nature of the service offer and delivery. As such, the elaboration of the concept of *value discretion* acknowledges how the organization's success depended on employees' gendered and classed identities such that surplus value was extracted from their embodied skills. Receptionists in this setting used their skills and knowledge in the way they enacted value discretion to negotiate the service offer through the 'welcome call' with client-organizations and in how they interpreted the range and diversity of their client's needs – some of which were made explicit whilst others relied on implicit assumptions about how to deliver good service. In turn, value discretion provided the opportunity for further task discretion – as the social relations between receptionists and their client-organizations influenced the range and scope of services and performances offered. Hence, the organization sought to gain value from the identities of the workforce in the way services were provided to their clients. Providing employees with the space for value discretion to be enacted enabled the organization to deliver a customized and 'authentic' service to a diverse range of clients. In this sense, the study elaborates research which examines how the process of valorization can occur. Sallaz (2015, p. 29) highlights a similar process in a call-centre where the labour process is strategically organized to harness external normative orders to its own ends, by relying 'on the hidden order of everyday talk (i.e., the agent's need to experience herself as a competent conversation participant) to motivate workers'. This echoes some of the themes from Janssens and Zanoni's (2005) study of diversity management which showed how diversity strategies are linked to the organization of work. For instance, their study of a call-centre highlighted how, socio-demographic differences were valued because they represented competences which directly contribute to the nature of the service such that, 'Employees are hired *in virtue of* their difference, which is at the core of the service' (Janssens & Zanoni, 2005, p. 332). This was described as an 'open' approach to diversity management because it allowed employees' active participation in the organization on their own terms and the development of a sense of own worth and self-confidence in their job. Thus enabling more space for micro-emancipation (Janssens & Zanoni, 2005, p. 337).

Linked to the points above, a further important feature of our conceptualization of discretion under neo-normative control is the emphasis on employee agency. Workers do not enter the workplace as 'blank slates' (Marks & Thompson, 2010) upon which management may inscribe their corporate-values; they bring their own values and past experiences to bear in interpreting what is appropriate. As Leidner's (1993) examination of routinization in interactive service work argues, we need to take seriously issues of identity, authenticity and individuality; examinations of worker subjectivity should assess how employers' seek to shape workers' consciousness and also workers' agency in providing justifications and interpretations of their experiences. Value discretion represents the space to think and make meaning *outwith* the organization's *espoused* norms and values. Within this conceptualization there is an explicit focus on employees as agents capable of making informed decisions about how they interact with different customers and the degree of discretionary effort they choose to afford in the labour process. But it is important to remember that these actions take place in an organizational context that is also marked by power asymmetries and regulated by management. As Edwards and Collinson (2002, p. 274) rightly note, 'empowerment is not the absence of control but an effort to generate disciplined autonomy within a clearly understood set of expectations and priorities'. Our focus on agency and discretion is not intended to gloss over the power relations central to the employment relationship, but it does support a view of employees as knowledgeable and capable actors. As active agents, the receptionists collectively constructed norms and values as part of the ongoing re-creation of the organizational context rather than as relatively reactive 'recipients' of job designs and managerial controls. Their personal values, identities and histories inform their approach to their jobs and their interpretations of their employers' espoused values.

The degree of value discretion identified in VoiceTel is perhaps unusual but, as an exceptional case, the research emphasizes the potential importance of the concept in understanding interactive service work within mass-customized settings. The nature of discretion was aligned to the market position of VoiceTel as a leader in high-quality, virtual reception services. Consequently, the management regime could be typified as a form of 'responsible autonomy' akin to that outlined by Friedman (1977) rather than the direct controls usually associated with mass-service call-centres. Our study therefore supports Green's (2008) arguments regarding how the 'potential for discretion' varies within and between managerial regimes. The case study therefore highlights the importance of locating employees in both their organizational and wider socio-economic contexts. There are significant contextual features in understanding the relationship between control and discretion in this particular case. VoiceTel was a privately owned company, it had achieved a leading market position and was financially successful and growing, its pay and conditions were above average. Its relatively recent establishment meant that management could recruit employees for value congruence in a local context of poor quality jobs for working-class women. External factors relating to employees' past working experiences, their perceptions of service as customers, and their identities as working women were also significant in understanding their positive responses.

While this is a specific case study and hence limited in terms of empirical generalizability, we would also suggest that there are features of our study which correspond to interactive service work more broadly within the 'missing' middle-range of mass-customized settings, that is service organizations which promote more 'authentic' service interactions. As Leidner's (1993) study of insurance sales indicates and Janssens and Zanoni's (2005) study of diversity management in a call-centre elucidates, many service organizations gain value from utilizing the knowledgeability of workers in the way they deliver interactive service. In this way, value discretion offers the potential of a mediating concept which helps to explain the process of valorization; that is how value is realized through employee interactions in service work. We would also suggest that there is the potential for analytical generalizability because of the way in which modern organizations increasingly rely on and gain value from employee discretion in a range of work contexts, specifically as the concept of value discretion emanates from studies of discretion within the work of public professionals.

In our view, the concept of value discretion could be usefully applied to a range of work settings where employees' interpret the values of their organizations including, but not limited to, in the way they interact with a range of service users where normative and neo-normative controls are exercised. VoiceTel was unusual in that there was a high degree of synchronicity between the values of the workers and that of the organization — this is partly explained because the owners recruited workers on the basis of value congruence. However, workers have the space to base their judgements on various norms and values which can emanate from the organization, professional codes of behaviour as well as everyday norms of social interaction. Therefore, we anticipate that future research could usefully assess how, in more complex work settings, employees experience tensions between different norms and values and how these are navigated to interpret and enact value discretion. And in such settings, how employees' interpretations of their employers' values impact upon how they do their jobs. In this way, the concept of value discretion could also shine a light on the opportunities and spaces for resistance in organizations.

FUNDING

The research was funded by the ESRC/EPSRC Advanced Institute of Management Research, ESRC Grant Number RES-331-25-0014. Thanks to Ashley Roberts for research assistance on the project.

ACKNOWLEDGEMENTS

We thank Steven Vallas and the three reviewers for their insightful and constructive comments on the paper. We would like to thank Ashley Roberts for his help with the data collection.

REFERENCES

Alvesson, M., & Karreman, D. (2004). Cages in tandem: Management control, social identity, and identification in a knowledge-intensive firm. *Organization, 11*(1), 149–175.

Batt, R. (2000). Strategic segmentation in front-line services: Matching customers, employees and Human Resource Systems. *International Journal of Human Resource Management, 11*(3), 540–561.

Blauner, R. (1964). *Alienation and freedom*. Chicago, IL: Chicago University Press.

Bolton, S. (2005). *Emotion management in the workplace*. Basingstoke: Palgrave.

Bolton, S., & Houlihan, M. (2009). 'Are we having fun yet?' A consideration of workplace fun and engagement. *Employee Relations, 31*(6), 556–568.

Braverman, H. (1974). *Labour and monopoly capital*. New York, NY: Monthly Review Press.

Callaghan, G., & Thompson, P. (2002). We recruit attitude: The selection and shaping of routine call-centre work. *Journal of Management Studies, 39*(2), 233–254.

Caza, A. (2011). Typology of the eight domains of discretion in organizations. *Journal of Management Studies, 49*(1), 144–177.

Edwards, R. (1979). *Contested Terrain*. New York, NY: Basic Books.

Edwards, P., & Collinson, M. (2002). Empowerment and managerial labour strategies: Pragmatism regained. *Work and Occupations, 29*, 272–299.

Findlay, P., Kalleberg, A., & Warhurst, C. (2013). The challenge of job quality. *Human Relations, 66*(4), 441–451.

Fleming, P. (2005). 'Workers' playtime? boundaries and cynicism in a 'culture of fun' program. *Journal of Applied Behavioural Sciences, 41*(3), 285–303.

Fleming, P. (2009). *Authenticity and the cultural politics of work: New forms of informal control*. Oxford: Oxford University Press.

Fleming, P., & Sturdy, A. (2011). "Being yourself" in the electronic sweatshop: New forms of normative control. *Human Relations, 62*(2), 177–200.

Fox, A. (1974). *Beyond contract: Work, power and trust relations*. London: Faber & Faber.

Frenkel, S. (2005). Service workers in search of decent work. In S. Ackroyd, R. Batt, T. Thompson, & P. Tolbert (Eds.), *The Oxford handbook of work and organization* (pp. 356–375). Oxford: Oxford University Press.

Friedman, A. (1977). Responsible autonomy versus direct control over the labour process. *Capital & Class, 1*(1), 43–57.

Godard, J. (2004). A critical assessment of the high-performance paradigm. *British Journal of Industrial Relations, 42*(2), 349–378.

Green, F. (2008). Leeway for the loyal: A model of employee discretion. *British Journal of Industrial Relations, 46*(1), 1–32.

Green, F., & James, D. (2003). Assessing skills and autonomy: The job holder versus the line manager. *Human Resource Management Journal, 13*(1), 63–77.

Grugulis, I., Dundon, T., & Wilkinson, A. (2000). Cultural control and the 'culture manager': Employment practices in a consultancy. *Work, Employment and Society, 14*(1), 97–116.

Hackman, J. R., & Oldham, G. R. (1976). Motivation through the design of work: Test of a theory. *Organizational Behavior and Human Performance, 16*(2), 250–279.

Hochschild, A. R. (1983). *The managed heart: Commercialization of human feeling*. Berkeley, CA: University of California Press.

Houlihan, M. (2002). Tensions and variations in call-centre management strategies. *Human Resource Management Journal, 12*(4), 67–85.

Jacques, A. (1956). *Measurement of responsibility*. London: Tavistock.

Janssens, M., & Zanoni, P. (2005). Many diversities for many services: Theorizing diversity management in service companies. *Human Relations, 58*(3), 311–340.

Jenkins, S., & Delbridge, R. (2014). In pursuit of happiness: A sociological examination of employee identifications amongst a 'happy' call-centre workforce. *Organization, 21*(6), 867–887.

Jenkins, S., & Delbridge, R. (2017). Trusted to deceive: A case study of 'strategic deception' and the normalization of lying at work. *Organization Studies, 38*(1), 53–76.

Jenkins, S., Delbridge, R., & Roberts, A. (2010). Emotional management in a mass customized call-centre: Examining skill and knowledgeability in interactive service work. *Work, Employment and Society, 24*(3), 1–19.

Kinnie, N., Hutchinson, S., & Purcell, J. (2000). 'Fun and surveillance': The paradox of high commitment management in call-centres. *International Journal of Human Resource Management, 11*(5), 967–985.

Korczynski, M. (2001). The contradictions of service work: Call centre as customer-oriented bureaucracy. In A. Sturdy, I. Grugulis, & H. Willmott (Eds.), *Customer service: empowerment and entrapment* (pp. 79–101). Basingstoke: Palgrave.

Korczynski, M. (2005). Skills in service work: An overview. *Human Resource Management Journal, 15*(2), 3–14.

Korczynski, M. (2009). The mystery customer: Continuing absences in the sociology of service work. *Sociology, 43*(5), 952–967.

Leidner, R. (1993). *Fast food, fast talk: Service work and the routinization of everyday life*. Berkeley, CA: University of California Press.

Lipsky, M. (1980). *Street level bureaucracy*. New York, NY: Russell Sage Foundation.

Marks, A., & Thompson, P. (2010). Beyond the blank slate: Identities and interests at work. In P. Thompson & C. Smith (Eds.), *Working life: Renewing labour process analysis* (pp. 316–338). Basingstoke: Palgrave.

Reed, M. (2001). Organization, trust and control: A realist analysis. *Organization Studies, 22*(2), 201–228.

Sallaz, J. (2015). Permanent pedagogy: How post-Fordist regimes generate effort but not consent. *Work and Occupations, 42*(1), 3–34.

Smith, C., Valsecchi, R., Mueller, F., & Gabe, J. (2008). Knowledge and the discourse of labour process transformation: Nurses and the case of NHS Direct for England. *Work, Employment and Society, 22*(4), 581–599.

Sturdy, A., Fleming, P., & Delbridge, R. (2010). Normative control and beyond in contemporary capitalism. In P. Thompson & C. Smith (Eds.), *Working life: Renewing labour process analysis* (pp. 113–135). Basingstoke: Palgrave.

Taylor, I., & Kelly, J. (2006). Professionals, discretion and public sector reform in the UK: Re-visiting Lipsky. *International Journal of Public Sector Management, 19*(7), 629–642.

Taylor, P., & Bain, P. (1999). 'An assembly line in the head': Work and employee relations in the call-centre. *Industrial Relations Journal, 30*(2), 101–117.

Taylor, P., & Bain, P. (2007). Reflections on the call centre—A reply to Glucksmann. *Work, Employment and Society, 21*(2), 349–362.

Taylor, P., Mulvey, G., Hyman, J., & Bain, P. (2002). Work organization, control and the experience of work in call-centres. *Work, Employment & Society, 16*(1), 133–150.

Taylor, S., & Tyler, M. (2000). Emotional labour and sexual difference in the airline industry. *Work, Employment and Society, 14*(1), 77–95.

Thompson, P. (2003). Disconnected capitalism: Or why employers can't keep their side of the bargain. *Work, Employment and Society, 17*(2), 359–378.

Thompson, P., & van den Broek, D. (2010). Managerial control and workplace regimes: An introduction. *Work, Employment and Society, 24*(3), 1–12.

Van den Broek, D., (2008). 'Doing things right', or 'doing the right things'? Call centre migrations and dimensions of knowledge. *Work, Employment and Society, 22*(4), 601–613.

Warhurst, C., & Nickson, D. (2007). Employee experience of aesthetic labour in retail and hospitality. *Work, Employment & Society, 21*(1), 103–120.

Yin, R. (2003). *Case study research: Design and methods*. Thousand Oaks, CA: Sage.

ENGINEERING MEDICINE: THE DEPLOYMENT OF LEAN PRODUCTION IN HEALTHCARE

William Attwood-Charles and Sarah Babb

ABSTRACT

Originally developed by the Japanese firm Toyota in the 1950s, the core innovation of lean production is to reorient all organizational activity around continuous improvement and the elimination of waste. We use the case of lean production in two healthcare organizations to explore the process of translating management models into new environments (Czarniawska & Sevón, 1996; Mohr, 1998). We draw on insights from organizational sociology and social movement theory to understand the strategies of actors as they attempt to overcome opposition to model transfer (Battilana, Leca, & Boxenbaum, 2009; Friedland & Alford, 1991; Snow, Rochford, Worden, & Benford, 1986). We examine two attempts to export lean production to healthcare organizations: Riverside Hospital, a research and teaching institution, and Lakeview Associations, a managed health provider. We use these cases to illustrate two ways that management models can get lost in the process of institutional translation: model attenuation, and model decoupling.

Keywords: Healthcare; organizations; management; lean production; continuous improvement

Emerging Conceptions of Work, Management and the Labor Market
Research in the Sociology of Work, Volume 30, 87–115
Copyright © 2017 by Emerald Publishing Limited
All rights of reproduction in any form reserved
ISSN: 0277-2833/doi:10.1108/S0277-283320170000030005

INTRODUCTION

Healthcare in the United States is widely recognized as the most costly in the world, with total per capita expenditures being double that of many European (World Bank, 2015). Indeed, there is a growing consensus that U.S. healthcare is approaching a moment of crisis, as evidenced by articles in the popular media on runaway costs, poor patient outcomes, and the challenges facing the system due to growing demand and an aging population. In response, healthcare administrators and consultants have explored a variety of management innovations purported to make organizations more efficient while improving quality of care (Arthur, 2011; Black & Revere, 2006; Kaluzny, McLaughlin, & Simpson, 1992; Shah & Pathak, 2014).

One particularly popular innovation has been "lean production." Originally developed by the Japanese automobile firm Toyota in the 1950s, the core innovation of lean production is to reorient all organizational activity around continuous improvement and the elimination of waste, thereby adding value for the consumer (Womack, 1990). Unlike Taylorist and Fordist systems, lean production emphasizes flattening managerial hierarchies in order to encourage knowledge sharing and improve working conditions (Vidal, 2006, 2007; Womack, 1996). By adopting lean, its proponents argue that healthcare organizations can both save money by becoming more efficient, while delivering better – and nonetheless personalized – patient-centered care (Jimmerson, Weber, & Sobek, 2005; Kim, Spahlinger, Kin, & Billi, 2006; Koning, Verver, Heuvel, Bisgaard, & Does, 2006; Nelson-Peterson & Leppa, 2007). Indeed, a major component of lean production is its emphasis on improving quality, which could potentially yield savings insofar as it reduces medical malpractice (Chalice, 2007; Dean, 2013; Grunden, 2008; Wellman, Hagan, & Jeffries, 2011). As one leading proponent recently asserted, "[A] different kind of healthcare is possible – care that is patient-focused, with less waste and cost and better medical outcomes. Using the improvement model popularized by the Toyota Production System, we have arrived at *lean healthcare* and three organizing principles – focus on patients, value, and time – that are built upon a foundation of continuous improvement and respect for people" (Toussaint, 2010, p. 3).

In this paper, we use the case of lean production in healthcare to explore how management models get lost in the process of institutional translation. While models of management are continuously flowing across countries and sectors, their translation is not always successful (Milkman, 1997; Vallas, 2003). Powerful groups may have a vested interest in the institutional status quo, and managers attempting to implement change may settle for outcomes that are "good enough" (Vidal, 2006, 2016). The new environment may also be characterized by identities, norms, and meaning systems that are difficult to reconcile with proposed changes.

Extending a concept from new institutionalist sociology, we refer to the agents of change in our account as "model entrepreneurs," a group that includes management consultants, management academics, and management practitioners seeking to implement lean production in healthcare organizations. Model entrepreneurs are a particular variety of institutional entrepreneurs, actors who attempt to initiate divergent changes in a field of activity (Battilana, Leca, & Boxenbaum, 2009; Dimaggio, 1988). Our story traces the efforts of model entrepreneurs to implement lean production in two healthcare organizations, which we refer to as Riverside Hospital and Lakeview Associates. Both are large healthcare providers in a major metropolitan region. Whereas Riverside is a prestigious teaching and research institution, Lakeview Associates is a multi-specialty group practice dedicated exclusively to outpatient care.

Even under ideal conditions, translating models of management requires a delicate process of disembedding and reembedding (Czarniawska & Sevón, 1996), as model entrepreneurs attempt to redefine interests, norms, and practices. In particular, those who seek to import new models of management to healthcare organizations must secure the cooperation of groups that possess considerable power to either block or enable change. For example, physicians have been observed to use status-based countertactics to block initiatives that they believe run contrary to their identity and interests (Kellogg, 2009, 2012). To secure buy-in from empowered organizational actors, model entrepreneurs may engage in frame alignment – that is to say, in translating features of the new model to emphasize its compatibility with the norms and interests of these actors (Battilana, 2006; Battilana et al., 2009; Snow, Rochford, Worden, & Benford, 1986, p. 464). We also show that the intended audience of such framing efforts may include not only healthcare providers, but also healthcare managers, who represent key potential allies in any process of model transfer.

Given these challenges, it is not surprising that model translations do not always succeed. We argue that there are at least two ways that models of management can get lost in translation. The first is model attenuation: a watering-down so radical that the results bear little resemblance to the original model. The second is decoupling (Meyer & Rowan, 1977), in which managers allow the model to be buffered from the organization's core activities. Riverside Hospital provides an example of how entrepreneurs may, in the process of reframing, attenuate a model out of existence. It was dominated by the norms of academic medicine, and administered by managers who wielded little coercive power over physicians, and who were physicians themselves. In this context, model entrepreneurs focused on framing the model as compatible with the norms and interests of academic medicine; they were eventually able to rhetorically align lean with the new environment, but at the expense of the model itself. In contrast, at Lakeview Associates, a more traditionally managerial group of administrators deployed lean in their respective jurisdictions. However, these managers soon became alienated by the approach of external consultants, who were perceived as rigid, authoritarian, and lacking in respect for local knowledge and norms. Unable to engage collaboratively with model entrepreneurs to adapt lean to local circumstances, managers also increasingly perceived lean as time-consuming, inefficient, and a distraction from the real work of the practice. As a consequence, they resisted covertly, resulting in a lean office that was decoupled from the work of the organization. In both cases, the model failed to significantly alter organizational practices in the ways that were originally intended.

LEAN MEDICINE

Lean production is not new to the healthcare field. As early as 2005 lean consultants and medical administrators, in an attempt to control rising healthcare costs and improve quality of services, began adapting lean methods to the context of healthcare work (Black & Revere, 2006; Jimmerson et al., 2005; Kim et al., 2006; Koning et al., 2006; Womack & Miller, 2005). In many ways, healthcare is an ideal receiving environment for lean production. Unlike previous managerial initiatives that emphasized a rigid division of labor and direct supervision over the labor process (Gilbreth, 1914, 1916; Taylor, 1911), lean production's primary innovation is flexible specialization and worker self-supervision (Womack, 1990). Proponents of lean production also tend to have a broader understanding of "value" than their stopwatch wielding Taylorist counterparts, one that would take into consideration qualitative aspects of service delivery (Chalice, 2007; Dahlgaard, Pettersen, & Dahlgaard-Park, 2011). The deployment of lean production in healthcare also coincides with the widespread adoption of patient-centered principles, which encourage the active role of patients in the decision-making process (Barry & Edgman-Levitan, 2012; Davidson et al., 2007).

While lean principles have sometimes been successfully applied in many healthcare organizations, it has often led to mixed and unclear results (Mazzocato, Savage, Brommels, Aronsson, & Thor, 2010; Vest & Gamm, 2009). There are considerable methodological limitations to existing studies on the effectiveness of lean and whether or not successes can be sustained over any length of time (Holden, 2011; Poksinska, 2010; Radnor, Holweg, & Waring, 2012). There is also evidence that lean production exacerbates preexisting tensions between classes of healthcare workers and managers (Waring & Bishop, 2010). This is not to suggest that lean production is inherently incompatible with healthcare work, but that its translation — like many cases of translation — is potentially fraught.

MODELS OF MANAGEMENT AND DIVERGENT CHANGE

Lean production is a "model of management" – a collection of techniques, authority relations, and organizational ideologies that implies a particular way of organizing work (Guillén, 1994). When management models are transported into new institutional contexts, they may evolve in unexpected ways. For example, Guillén (1994) shows how German firms adopted the trappings of U.S.-style Scientific Management in the early 20th century, but gutted it of one of its defining features: deskilling. Similarly, in the 1990s many U.S. automakers imported Japanese management techniques, but sometimes in ways that were more cosmetic than profound (Milkman, 1997). In the process of institutional translation, aspects of the model's previous use that could potentially be perceived by an audience as illegitimate are often removed or recontextualized (Czarniawska & Sevón, 1996; Mohr, 1998). Thus, some features of management models may be lost in translation, and others acquired as the characteristics of the original model interact with those of the adopter (Ansari, Fiss, & Zajac, 2010).

Institutional entrepreneurs are individuals or groups who attempt to initiate "divergent changes" that "break the institutional status quo in a field of activity" (Battilana et al., 2009, p. 68). To do so, they need to mobilize resources and allies to their cause, and thereby legitimate their institutional projects. There are at least two overlapping barriers institutional entrepreneurs may encounter on the road to divergent change. The first is the agency of empowered actors to resist institutions they view as illegitimate (see DiMaggio, 1988, p. 13). The second barrier is normative constraints – that is to say, the means by which actors can legitimately pursue their interests (Friedland & Alford, 1991, p. 251). For example, norms around caregiving (Hochschild, 1983; Lopez, 2006) in the healthcare field could be, at least superficially, in conflict with the interest of organizational efficiency. Whether or not a new model is inherently incompatible with existing norms, these norms can be used as resources by empowered actors to resist a model's implementation.

One recurring theme in the literature on institutional transformation is that the success of institutional entrepreneurs in mobilizing resources depends on their skill in manipulating discourse to bring actors' interests and norms into alignment with those of the new logic (Garud, Hardy, & Maguire, 2007; Garud, Jain, & Kumaraswamy, 2002; Greenwood, Hinings, & Suddaby, 2002; Maguire, Hardy, & Lawrence, 2004; Thornton & Ocasio, 2008; Zilber, 2007). In this sense, the task of the institutional entrepreneur is to engage in "frame alignment" similar to that described in literature on social movements in political sociology, or the "linkage of individual and [social movement organization] interpretive orientations, such that some set of individual interests, values and beliefs and [social movement] activities, goals, and ideology are congruent and complementary" (see Battilana, 2006; Battilana et al., 2009; King & Soule, 2007; Levy & Scully, 2007; Snow et al., 1986, p. 464).

Regardless of the charisma and rhetorical giftedness of an institutional entre-preneur, she may encounter inhospitable environments. Indeed, the deployment of lean production in American healthcare presents an ideal arena for exploring difficulties around model translation between institutional fields. U.S. healthcare organizations operate in highly institutionalized professional environments, and have only in recent decades been penetrated by managerialist ideologies (Scott, 2000). They are also saturated with potentially non-compliant empowered actors. Historically, hospitals and other healthcare organizations were domi-nated by physicians and their professional associations, which acted as gate-keepers, requiring extensive socialization in order to impart not only skills, but also norms and values (Abbott, 1988; Freidson, 1970; Larson, 1977; Ouchi, 1979; Starr, 1982).

In the healthcare field, physicians are the most obvious group of empowered actors that must be mobilized to support a new model of management. In some cases, these powerful actors can be persuaded to go along using a combination of ideological and managerial controls (Reich, 2014a, 2014b). In other cases, however, they can present a powerful front of resistance. As Kellogg (2012) finds, physicians socialized into a hierarchical, professional culture may use status-based countertactics to block managerial initiatives, which they regard as a threat to their identity. Moreover, managers themselves may also stand in the way of successful model deployment. Managers have multiple commitments, as well as potentially their own distinct set of interests and norms, and because of this may satisfice (Vidal, 2006, 2016) or even deliberately subvert an institu-tional change project. Translating lean production into the context of health-care thus relies on successfully framing change to at least two empowered audiences: physicians and managers.

CASES AND METHODS

We chose cases that exemplified the two dominant organizational forms in U.S. healthcare: the hospital and the health maintenance organization. In both Riverside Hospital and Lakeview Associates, top management saw lean pro-duction as a tool for addressing perceived inefficiencies and growing fiscal pro-blems. Both deployed lean around the same time and made use of many of the same resources (consulting groups, think tanks, and management texts) in their implementation of the model.

Riverside Hospital is a teaching and research institution that possessed a decentralized authority structure and a relatively incoherent bureaucratic hier-archy. It was founded with a charitable mission, but later expanded as federal teaching and research funds were made available (and even today receives a considerable amount of research funding from the National Institute of Health). As a result of this legacy, while Riverside is a private, non-profit entity, it possesses a strong ethos of public service. Divisions are often headed by lay, physician-managers, who came to their position as a consequence of their academic and scientific merits.

Lakeview Associates is a multi-specialty group practice dedicated exclusively to outpatient care. Founded as a health maintenance organization, Lakeview possessed a centralized authority structure and a clearly defined bureaucratic hierarchy. While Lakeview Associates is also a non-profit, it has a distinctly commercial (and corporate) character in that it does not rely upon lay managers – as in the case of Riverside Hospital – and officially espouses efficiency in healthcare provision as a value. Managers at Lakeview Associates often had some experience in caregiving – usually as a nurse or medical assistant – but also professional managerial training.

To explore lean deployment in our two cases we draw on a variety of qualitative sources. We conducted a total of 125 hours of fieldwork at Riverside and Lakeview over the span of two years. Fieldwork included shadowing model entrepreneurs and consultants as they met with healthcare workers, attending lean training sessions and seminars, sitting in on management meetings where lean protocols were being designed, and observing team huddles and workers go about their daily routines. We also conducted 36 semi-structured interviews with organizational actors who were responsible for managing the deployment of lean production. These participants included external consultants, internal consultants, lean engineers, vice presidents, division heads, administrators, office managers, clinic managers, and medical assistants responsible for overseeing teams of care workers. In addition to field notes and semi-structured interviews (including periodic follow-up interviews), we draw on internal organizational publications, press releases, news reports, training manuals, Power Point presentations, forms and spreadsheets, and other documentation provided by internal consultants. Taken in combination, these experiences allowed us to compare the rhetoric of lean against the reality of its implementation (Edwards & Collinson, 2002; Zbaracki, 1998), but also how the reality of lean changed in the process of the model's deployment and how that related to the actions of particular actors.

Of the 36 interview participants, 14 were from Riverside Hospital, 21 were from members of Lakeview Associates, and one participant was from an external consulting agency. The composition of the 35 interviews with members of Riverside Hospital and Lakeside Associates is broken down in Table 1 by managerial level.

In conducting our analysis, we looked for instances where actors invoked frames, contested frames, or attempted to transform frames. We focused in particular on the justificatory devices actors used to legitimize or delegitimize a frame, as well as the efforts to bring particular frames in alignment with other frames. Because frames are checked against the lived reality of actors, we also looked for instances where practices would potentially lend support for or ammunition against particular frames. We also focused on instances where

Table 1. Informants by Managerial Level and Organization.

	Riverside Hospital N = 14	Lakeview Associates N = 21
Upper level management N = 18	8 Emma, Samantha, Sophia, Jacob, Isabelle, Ethan, James, Aubrey	10 Stewart, Grace, Sheryl, Kelly, Riley, Austin, Millie, Phoebe, Holly, Evelyn
Mid and lower level N = 17	6 Olivia, Ava, Emily, Addison, Abigail, Mia	11 Jack, Owen, Luke, Tamara, Madison, Lucy, Charlotte, Claire, Zoe, Darcy, Victoria

Table 2. Lean Deployment in Two Cases: Context, Strategy, and Results.

	Riverside Hospital	Lakeview Associates
Type of organization	Academic medical center	Managed care organization
Model entrepreneurs	Office of Lean Transformation (local), external consultants	Care Management Office (local), external consultants
Empowered actors	Division chiefs Physicians	Practice managers Physicians
Dominant norms	Professionalism, science	Care, managerialism, professionalism
Initial obstacles	Lack of buy-in from division chiefs and physicians, around norms of professionalism	Lack of buy-in from physicians
Framing strategies	Lean as scientific practice	Lean as efficient
Emerging obstacles	Attenuation of lean model to get buy-in from division administrators and physicians	Increasing resistance from practice managers, around norms of efficiency and caregiving; managerial satisficing
Translation failure	Model attenuation	Model decoupling

actors attempted to reconcile seemingly disconfirming evidence with either their own framing of events or the frames provided by others. In the following sections, we narrate our findings, which are summarized in Table 2.

RIVERSIDE HOSPITAL

At Riverside Hospital, model entrepreneurs faced considerable structural and cultural opposition to their deployment of lean. Model entrepreneurs lacked the authority to enforce compliance, and therefore needed to persuade division chiefs and high-level administrators to go along. Through a process of frame extension and transformation, model entrepreneurs eventually aligned lean with the dominant norms and interests at Riverside. However, while this framing of lean resonated the most with Riverside decision-makers, it discarded much of lean's original framing around the value of efficiency and standardized practices. This made lean palatable to Riverside decision-makers, but at the cost of abandoning the model's core features. Ultimately, this framing of lean proved untenable, as the model's increasingly narrowed use, and failure to deliver concrete performance results, came to be perceived as a form of organizational waste.

Organizing Lean's Deployment

The "Lean Transformation Office" at Riverside Hospital, while small and poorly lit, enjoyed a central location on this teaching hospital's campus just around the corner from the main cafeteria. Lean was introduced at Riverside Hospital by a newly appointed CEO charged with the difficult task of turning around the financially struggling institution. The model was valued by high-level managers for its potential to enhance quality of care, improve organizational efficiency, and serve as the basis for alliances between neighbor healthcare organizations. Samantha, the vice president of Lean Transformation, was a woman in her late 40s with a mischievous sense of humor and, despite her small stature, an imposing figure. As a former information technology officer at Riverside, she was a tireless champion of the model and a well-known figure in the broader lean medicine movement.

With the support of Riverside's newly appointed CEO, Samantha and her office worked to adapt the model to the context of academic medicine at Riverside. While mindful of the need to tailor the model to their particular organizational culture, Samantha also made a concerted effort to staff the newly formed office with young administrators, who were not yet socialized into the traditional culture of the hospital. As she put it, "I was looking for people that were uncontaminated by the old way of doing things." In addition, several "lean engineers" hired from outside the organization were employed to ensure that the innovations proposed by physicians and administrators were in keeping with the tenets of lean. These lean engineers did not have a background in healthcare and came from industries where lean production methods were commonly applied and regarded as legitimate, particularly manufacturing. For the most part, these individuals were full-time hospital employees, occasionally aided by external consultants.

Yet in spite of its title, the Lean Transformation Office had no authority to transform what they viewed as entrenched pathological practices. As a project manager in the Lean Transformation office remarked: "We can't force groups to take on a lean project, but divisions have to send people to get a lean education. Well, I wouldn't even call it an education so much as 'lean awareness ...' " Division chiefs, who headed departments, were almost exclusively physicians who were promoted based upon their academic and research experience. They had a considerable degree of autonomy when determining how work should be structured and performed in their divisions. Model entrepreneurs schooled in the dynamics of industrial manufacturing initially believed once division chiefs were convinced of lean's applicability to healthcare work, they would be able to deploy the model in their divisions by way of decree. However, as one division chief explained, this was an unrealistic expectation considering the nature of authority relationships at Riverside Hospital:

> How is it that you become a professor at Riverside's medical school? It's not by coloring between the lines. You are supposed to be constantly doing things that are outside the mainstream, ignoring authority. It is the nature of how you get promoted. You can't be shy ... So this is not an environment that encourages or is even able to enforce compliance. I'm considered a very important person, a leader in the healthcare information community, but they don't listen to me. At best, all I can do is cajole based off my informal authority.

Moreover, although division chiefs occupied a position of authority in the organization, the nature of authority relationships at Riverside was qualitatively different from the type of "command and control" authority relationships lean consultants were used to in manufacturing. Managers had little ability to issue commands, particularly to physicians, who technically were not even employees of the hospital, but rather members of an affiliated physicians' group. As Samantha said to an engineering audience at a lean event:

> How do you diffuse lean to 10,000 people in an organization when a couple thousands of them are physicians and they don't report to the hospital? All you have is your considerable charm and influence. You literally have nothing else going for you.

Frame Alignment

At Riverside, implementation of lean was for all intents and purposes voluntary. Rather than directly transforming the practices and authority relationships within Riverside, model entrepreneurs were forced to focus their efforts on securing "buy-in" – that is to say, to persuade a range of hospital authorities to change practices within their jurisdictions. These authorities included: division chiefs, administrators, and high-ranking physicians.

To align the framing of lean with Riverside's dominant institutional logic, model entrepreneurs provided training sessions for high-level physicians and administrators describing the virtues of the model, and sponsored pilot projects. The progress of these projects was documented and broadcasted by model entrepreneurs to demonstrate lean's success in the organization. Finally, model entrepreneurs sponsored rituals and events that were meant to transform the way workers understood their activities in the hospital, such as the regular hosting of "lean research-sharing seminars," *gemba* walks in which physicians toured the production floor, and "lean office hours," opportunities for workers to visit with lean engineers for guidance and support.

The Lean Transformation Office slowly began deploying the model by selecting a few high-level administrators and physicians for lean training sessions. These initial sessions were led by outside consultants and conducted on a weekly basis for three months. According to participants who attended early lean training sessions at Riverside, the initial framing focused largely on the technical aspects of lean and its success in manufacturing. Initially, model entrepreneurs did not appear to be particularly attuned to normative environment at Riverside, and presented lean in its unadulterated industrial form to hospital authorities, neglecting to remove context-specific features of lean when framing the model to their audience. For example, they maladroitly amplified rhetorical features of the original model, relying heavily upon orientalist tropes of an exotic, mystic, and Zen-like Other when framing lean management techniques, with terms like *gemba*, *hansei*, and *muda*, to name only a few. These terms were repeatedly the butt of jokes in interviews and rarely would a participant utter them without an accompanying eye roll. One division chief, who took great pride in his surly and irreligious presentation of self, dismissively referred to these as "ninja techniques." In reaction to the orientalist fantasy of lean provided by model entrepreneurs, this participant stated bluntly:

> When they were explaining *kaizen* they said, "in Japan, unlike the West, they have a deep understanding and sense of forgivingness, how to ask for an apology, you know, re-looking at what they do, self-critique, stuff that's really far beyond what we've achieved in Western civilization." I just raised my hand and said, "I'll believe that bullshit when they apologize for the rape of Nanking." [laughs] And that kind of shut her down for a while ...

The frequent use of pseudo-Japanese terminology and folklore only served to invite comparisons between the two societies, further embedding the lean model in a specific industrial as well as cultural context (even if a mythic one). Here we can see how model entrepreneurs, in their initial framing of lean to administrators and division chiefs, saw little need to disembed the model from the context of an industrial regime or align their framing of lean with preexisting logics.

Fewer than six months into lean's deployment, model entrepreneurs realized they would need to take a different approach if they hoped to secure buy-in. Faced with obvious skepticism, lean proponents began to frame the model around ideals likely to resonate with healthcare providers, rhetorically amplifying such values as quality, safety, and patient care. To persuade hospital authorities of the applicability of lean to healthcare, the Lean Transformation Office arranged for a group of prominent division chiefs and administrators to visit Thedacare, a community health system in rural Wisconsin regarded by many in the lean community as an exemplar of lean in medicine. As one member of the Transformation team recalled, "I think a lot of the time people say, 'Lean won't work because you don't understand healthcare.' Thedacare shows that it can work."

However, the trip to Wisconsin actually served to undermine the organization's own strategy of generating buy-in. Two division chiefs we spoke with separately who were on this same trip to Thedacare described the environment there in terms of a slavish devotion to the lean production model. One division chief, Steve, compared Thedacare to a Pentecostal revival meeting, while another compared it to a religious cult:

> We were calling it ThedaCult. It was like Jonestown. They definitely drank the Kool-Aid. So, I wouldn't necessarily recommend going there. They all talk like Sarah Palin, which is really scary. But they did what you really need to do if you want to implement lean correctly.

This division chief grudgingly accepted that they "did what you need to do" to implement the model, only to later remark, "I'm not sure I could stand doing what Thedacare did." Another division chief spoke of Thedacare's ability to produce compliance in terms of a uniquely mid-western orientation toward wanting to please one's employer, something that wasn't true of elite Northeastern medical workers:

> If you go to Thedacare, it is a Stepford community! You have a CEO who says that Thedacare is lean and is *the* management paradigm. Lean is part of *everything*. Everything in the organization is a lean process; literally every manager is holding an A4 [a lean form used for process improvements] in front of you when you get out of bed in the morning. From the perspective of Thedacare, everyone has bought into lean. At Riverside, you have 20,000 people and they don't want to dogmatically follow a process. Give me a break.

Lean proponents had failed to appreciate that Thedacare and Riverside occupied very different positions in the field – and status hierarchy – of medicine. As members of a research hospital affiliated with an elite medical school, Riverside decision-makers considered themselves to be above simplified and standardized processes. Riverside division chiefs depicted Thedacare workers as docile, a quality they related to both being rural and low-status professionals. Furthermore, they argued that workers at the prestigious hospital and medical school were rewarded for the ability to "color outside of the lines." The use of hackneyed terms, apparently without any hint of irony, and what they assumed to be blind acceptance of managerial authority were not regarded as appropriate for Riverside, given its high-status position. As one division chief said of the general mood upon leaving Thedacare, "we realized that – if this is what lean is about – it wouldn't fly back at home." There was a tension between the identity and norms held by division chiefs, particularly around their role as experts, and that of model entrepreneurs. Being confronted with the reality of lean production at Thedacare produced in these division chiefs no small amount of status anxiety. In an effort to draw a boundary between where lean should and should not be applied, one division chief made a distinction between the innovation of experts and lean's formalized method at generating process improvements:

> Lean doesn't innovate. It takes a pre-existing process and finds a way to cut out waste. You have to follow a process [for innovating] and, well, I wouldn't say it goes to the lowest common denominator, but you generally get group opinion or group think. Real innovation comes when people have flashes of brilliance about completely different ways to do stuff. Lean doesn't really allow for that.

This division chief valued norms of innovation and exceptionalism, two values he suggested came into conflict with lean's emphasis on rule following, as well power sharing, which he believed came at the expense of "brilliance."

After a year of attempting to convince decision-makers of lean's applicability to work at Riverside, model entrepreneurs finally attempted to tailor their framing of the model to the specific context of academic medicine. In addition to a series of intensive training courses geared toward senior management, the lean office at Riverside began to schedule "office hours" for physicians to visit with lean engineers and ask questions about the model. Through their appropriation of the academy's rituals and symbols, model entrepreneurs attempted to align their framing of lean with scientific values and identities, in a process of "frame extension" (Snow et al., 1986).

One division chief, "James," an affable man in his late 50s with a gentlemanly disposition, believed he could produce the buy-in of physicians and technicians by relating efforts to gather metrics on medical errors with the task of publishing academic articles. Prior to extending lean's framing, James stated that physicians actively resisted self-reporting errors, as they believed their mistakes would be used against them. Indeed, this chief presented lean as an initiative that could help physicians advance their academic careers. As he put it:

> To get buy in you can't just say, "lean is very important to me as a chief and you all have to do it." That doesn't work ... But if I say, "I want you to publish a paper." It like, "Oh shit!" Then they see the benefits ... [Laughs] I wrote a lean paper for a journal and everyone was like, "oh wow, this is cool. Let's get him to come and give us lectures."

Tellingly, however, this division chief stated that he downplayed references to lean, even while attempting to implement the model in his department:

> They don't like lean. They do not like it at all. And it has backfired in multiple places for me. Whenever I have to go sell lean to the department it's like, "oh here he comes again." I used to do *gemba* walks, I don't do that anymore. So, the less I use the word "lean" the better. It is about, "let's see how we can continuously improve what we do."

This division chief believed he was able to overcome barriers to lean's implementation by no longer framing many of the proposed innovations as "lean." The rituals that characterized the industrial and corporate framing of lean, such as performing *gemba* walks and requiring workers to adhere to standardized protocols, were abandoned, while its compatibility with scientific values and identities, as well as professional interests, were emphasized. In doing so, this division chief went beyond mere frame extension (extending the boundaries of lean), and instead engaged in a process of frame transformation, systematically redefining lean so as to align the model with the dominant norms of Riverside physicians. In other words, if he couldn't impose new practices in his department, he could at least convince actors that lean wasn't too different from what they were already doing and wanted to do. In essence, James was able to claim a victory for lean and his department without having to wrestle with divergent change.

Another attempt to reframe lean to resonate with values and identities characteristic of academic medicine was with the hosting of a monthly "lean research-sharing showcase." Held in a traditional collegiate wood-paneled conference room, these seminars were structured similarly to an academic conference, with presentations of research findings from behind a lectern on projects ranging from the streamlining of the surgical pathology process to the lean standardization of room entry. Notably absent in all of the observed presentations were the use of lean jargon, such as *gemba* walks, *kaizen*, value-added, *mura*, etc. Instead, physicians and nurses presented research findings, emphasizing to the audience that process improvements were being developed not by lean managers or external consultants, but rather internal medical actors – thus, consonant with the identity of healthcare workers. As a team of nurses impressed upon the audience, "It's scary – if you waste ten seconds per room entry, you end up missing patients. This adds up to a total of 26 million seconds per year lost." Around the room, heads shook in mournful disbelief that such harm could be visited upon patients by failing to adhere to standard room entry protocols. Those in attendance participated in a collective ritual of compatibility between the values of lean and that of academic medicine. As Samantha said of the similarity between physicians and herself:

> Physicians come from a scientific background. They can appreciate the science of lean. I'm more like them, I think scientifically. Many physicians feel like management dictums are arbitrary and not really methodical, lean represents a step towards something physicians would do if they were to be put in charge.

Yet, the reach of these lean showcases was limited: apart from the teams presenting research and their immediate supervisors, only a dozen or so workers in an organization with 20,000 employees attended these events – a large portion of them being from the lean office at Riverside.

Implementation

Through a dialectical process of framing and reframing, model entrepreneurs were able to achieve highly limited successes in getting Riverside administrators and professionals to support lean initiatives. The purpose of these framing efforts was ultimately to change practices at Riverside. Ultimately, however, model entrepreneurs could point to only limited successes at changing the way things were done and, even then, these changes did not diverge from preexisting logics, nor were they entirely in keeping with the original premise of lean: promoting organizational efficiency. The most vivid example of a successful lean project comes from Jacob. As Jacob described it:

> We had this problem, when you draw blood sometimes, the blood cells break up, and it's called "hemolysis." .... The solution we came to was simple, just do two separate draws at the same time. And yes, that would mean sticking the patient with a needle twice instead of once, but you got it all done at once, and potentially saved time. But nurses didn't want to do it because they didn't like sticking their patients twice just in case of this eventuality. So, we never got any sort of buy-in. But then we got a new nursing head that wanted this to be a lean project. We said we already knew what the answer was: get the damn nurses to do what we tell them to do. Anyway, she did the project and got the nurses together to talk about it, and they came to the exact same conclusion we came to. But this time it worked, it stuck around, because obviously if people feel ownership of the process, they are going to adhere to it.

In this instance, lean clearly had some success. By getting workers to participate in generating a standard they initially felt was harmful to patients, this department was able to secure buy-in from nurses where the initiative previously had failed.

Such successful examples notwithstanding, several major barriers remained to lean's full implementation. First, many powerful organizational players remained cynical about lean, as described above, and continued to resist it. Second, with every round of reframing, the scope of the model became increasingly narrowed as aspects that diverged from preexisting norms and interests were removed in order to enhance the model's legitimacy. Thus, while model entrepreneurs continuously adjusted their framing of lean to appeal to their audience, lean became more and more diluted even as it became less threatening to decision-makers. Model entrepreneurs were able to secure some buy-in, but it became unclear what exactly actors were buying into. Division chiefs still regarded the divergent features of lean as contrary to their interests, identity, and norms, and therefore elected to discard them. The features of lean that were used in effort to produce buy-in were retained, such as around improving care quality or producing academic research, but as a result lean was adapted more to the preexisting organizational logic at Riverside than the other way around.

Third, model entrepreneurs failed to convince powerful organizational actors that it could deliver on its most important promise: efficiency improvements and financial savings. Lean was perceived by many decision-makers at Riverside as a form of organizational bloat and as a primary source of inefficiency. This perception might have at least partly resulted from the extreme challenges lean faced at Riverside – as noted above, it was both diluted and weighed down by ongoing resistance. Yet whatever the reason, many top administrators were skeptical. For example, the finance department at Riverside ordered a department to cease a process improvement effort they deemed wasteful because it required considerable human resources and would not likely yield much in the way of organizational savings. As the administrator who initiated this process improvement event recalled:

> We wanted to simplify a requisition form because it was being filled out incorrectly half of the time. We had this idea that we could combine everything into a single form. After months of meeting with top hospital brass, the head of finance ended up pulling the plug. We'd poured hundreds of hours into the project, but for nothing.

As a consequence of these barriers, practices at Riverside Hospital overall remained largely unchanged, a far cry from the lean transformation model entrepreneurs hoped for. As one project manager in the Lean Transformation office said:

> Even though we've been doing lean for several years now, I feel like it's just getting started. We are a small group, so the work implementing lean is slow, just one department at a time. But nothing sticks. It's so funny, if you were to pull up management meetings from three years ago, it's like, "oh yeah, we talked about this exact same problem, here it is, it's back again." *laughs*

Even Samantha acknowledged the failure of her office to produce meaningful or sustained organizational change:

> If you are looking for a bunch of actual cases of what lean is and examples of its implementation, you aren't going to find much. I have this feeling of horror every time visiting lean engineers want to go through the hospital and see what changes we've made ... What we've accomplished is more cultural, we are laying the groundwork.

LAKEVIEW ASSOCIATES

At Lakeview Associates, the preexisting managerial structure made it possible for model entrepreneurs to issue directives that they could reasonably expect to be followed. In striking contrast to Riverside, where lean was intensively framed, reframed, and attenuated to get buy-in from key allies, at Lakeview it was imposed from the top down, with little negotiation with practice managers, and by an unpleasant outside consultant. In this context, despite the relatively good fit between preexisting norms and interests and the model being proposed, over time practice managers grew to resent what they believed to be burdensome and inefficient features of the model. Practice managers responded by decoupling the requirements that workers adhere to standard work, collect data, and complete countermeasure forms. They justified their resistance on the grounds that lean was wasteful and poorly suited to the practicalities of healthcare work. Realizing they faced a managerial revolt, model entrepreneurs relaxed their requirements, with the result that lean became even more decoupled from the activities of Lakeview workers.

Organizing Lean's Deployment

The "Care Management Office" at Lakeview Associates was responsible for deploying lean across the organization's 14 practices. Located in a corporate office park, the office inhabited a series of hanger-like buildings connected by a glass dome, giving one the impression of being in a giant, sterile terrarium. However, while geographically scattered across the metro region, organizationally Lakeview Associates was far more centralized than Riverside Hospital, even as Riverside shared a single campus. Sheryl, the vice president of Care Management, was a serious and studious devotee of lean whose placid demeanor would suddenly become animated when discussing the transformative potential of the lean production model. The narrative Sheryl told was one of a "lean journey" spearheaded by a reforming CEO who she described as a "real visionary." After touring several prototypes of lean healthcare, this CEO created the Care Management Office, and hired an external consulting agency to prepare its staff for deploying lean at Lakeview. In addition to working with an outside consulting group, several members of the Care Management Office at Lakeview participated in the same lean think tank that was frequented by members of the Lean Transformation Office at Riverside.

Beyond simply a quest for organizational self-actualization, the impetus for Lakeview's adoption of lean, according to several high-level administrators, was cost reduction. Senior management regarded organizational efficiency as essential to the long-term financial viability of Lakeview. As one administrator said, "We knew reimbursements were going to be declining ... That was really the point ... Find the best way of doing things and save money that way." With the blessing of senior management, the Care Management Office deployed the model at Lakeview by issuing directives down the organizational chain of command, meeting regularly with practice managers, the administrators responsible for overseeing day-to-day operations at Lakeview's 14 sites, to actively implement the model across the entirety of the organization.

Prior to lean's introduction at Lakeview, several practice managers had worked on an initiative to develop and codify guidelines that would then be shared across the organization. Thus, practice managers at Lakeview were already invested in the goal of improving efficiency and quality of care, unlike the Division Chiefs at Riverside. Lean was appealing to both senior management and practice managers because it purported to provide techniques that would allow administrators to objectively test the effectiveness of process improvements. After establishing the Care Management Office, the external consulting agency then began to mentor a handful of Lakeview managers whose job would be to train practice managers across all of Lakeview's sites.

The corporate organizational structure at Lakeview was a legacy of its founding during the "era of managerial control and market mechanisms" (Scott, 2000). From Lakeview Associate's initial conception, it possessed a centralized and rationalized organizational structure, very unlike that of Riverside. This allowed the outside consulting group, working with internal model entrepreneurs, to use a clearly defined hierarchy to pursue their agenda. At Lakeview, senior management wanted lean to make an impact as quickly as possible to produce financial savings for the organization. One of the major goals was to standardize practices across all 14 of Lakeview's practices. Standardization and simplification went hand in hand, making it feasible for model entrepreneurs and practice managers to monitor whether lean was being implemented in the prescribed manner, and if it was producing the intended results.

Frame Alignment

Model entrepreneurs performed far less buy-in work at Lakeview Associates than at Riverside Hospital primarily because it was assumed the primary audience they were addressing at Lakeview was already bought. Practice managers often had medical backgrounds, but came to their positions after attaining business or public health degrees, and saw themselves as career administrators rather than healthcare researchers or care workers. Thus, they shared with model entrepreneurs a managerial identity, as well as similar concern with financial considerations. Moreover, unlike decision-makers at Riverside, who possessed considerable professional autonomy, Lakeview's decision-makers were deeply embedded in a bureaucratic hierarchy that left relatively little scope for overt resistance. Model entrepreneurs could reasonably expect the deployment of lean to be carried out in terms of commands that would cascade down each level of the organization.

Indeed, in Lakeview's practice managers, model entrepreneurs appeared to encounter a willing audience, at least initially. As the manager of one practice said of her first encounter with lean, "My supervisors approached me about adopting lean and of course when they ask you if you'd like to do something you do it. That is our attitude [here]. We say 'Yes.'" Unlike Riverside Hospital, the leadership audiences at Lakeview were receptive to managerial innovations – being as they were representatives of managerial authority themselves. When asked how lean was able to spread so quickly throughout Lakeview with so little overt resistance, one practice manager appeared confused by the premise of the question.

Implementation

In contrast to Riverside, where decision-makers resisted lean from the very beginning, at Lakeview, leaders accepted the model, at least initially – indeed, in Lakeview's hierarchical structure, they had little choice. As one lean process improvement leader recalled, "nobody came to our department and asked 'do you want to be involved with this [lean],' it was kind of a top down directive. There was definitely a feeling that this was something done to us." The results could be seen in changes in the everyday practices of many workers, particularly medical assistants and low-level administrators. At every level of the organization, goals were explicit. For example, when describing the contents of a *hoshin* document (an internal lean tool), Sheryl said:

> Each department has things they are working on to impact the metrics at the practice level, which then impact the metrics at the organizational level. It's not perfect yet, but what we are trying to do is cascade down organizational goals so that every staff in our organization knows what the eleven things are, and how their work impacts the goal.

Unlike Riverside Hospital where lean was implemented either voluntarily or on a project-to-project basis, senior management at Lakeview were able to diffuse the model quite rapidly and uniformly throughout the organization. As Sheryl recalled, "We did this much earlier in the process than typically gets recommended ... we kind of went off the reservation in terms of what the consulting group would've guided us to do. But it was an experiment; we wanted to engage more people." Goals and their particular meanings for workers were communicated (at least ideally) each morning during 10-minute, standardized "team huddles." These huddles were part of an initiative known as "Managing for Excellence" (ME), which took place in front of whiteboards that were gridded off into boxes containing goals, metrics, and information relating to performance improvement. Another central feature of lean at Lakeview was the principle of "standard work" – protocols approved by lean engineers and healthcare workers regarding processes ranging from how to guide a patient into a room to the proper method for laying out surgical instruments on a cart. These processes were posted to an internal database that all workers had access to and were expected to use uniformly.

At Lakeview, lean had some notable successes in changing the everyday practices of workers. To generate standard work protocols, "Improvement" events were held that provided workers an opportunity to meet and discuss potential solutions to everyday problems. As one Care Management administrator recalled of an Improvement event:

> Orthopedic clinicians were getting frustrated that it was taking so long for patients to get an x-ray. So, we got everyone from physicians to secretaries to talk about the problem, and it was really nice because you got to hear different points of views. We ended up doing a few experiments and, come to find out, it was taking so long because physicians were often not putting in orders, or were putting in the wrong orders. One of the chiefs said, "Wow, this is great. I am blaming radiology, when it is really our fault."

Workers genuinely appreciated being able to share their perspectives with other classes of healthcare workers with whom they otherwise would not have been in contact.

Nevertheless, there were pockets of work practices at Lakeview that remained relatively untouched by lean, and in other contexts practice managers allowed lean to be decoupled from everyday practice where it once was deployed. The most obvious area where lean was never applied was in the work of physicians, the highest-status professionals at Lakeview. As at Riverside, doctors were mostly able to use their professional powers to evade and resist the directives of the Care Management Office. Senior management was able to increase the number of patients physicians were expected to see in a day, but was unable to have much impact on their interactions with patients. As one practice manager noted, lean's implementation primarily occurred around the edges of physicians' work.

> If you try to implement something that doesn't touch physicians directly, it is easy to do. When you touch the physicians directly, it is incredibly difficult. As much as they say, "yeah, I'll buy-in," they wouldn't have it. There really was a kind of a complete and utter lack of physician support in internal medicine, there was a little more in pediatrics. But we did a lot around the periphery. It really was like pulling teeth.

We observed 10 team huddles in the course of our research: physicians were present at none. When pointed out to practice administrators and low-level managers, all acknowledged it was rare for a physician to attend. To emphasize this, one administrator claimed that in one instance a medical assistant guided a physician by the hand to a team huddle. That physicians were not required to adhere to the same standard work requirements as medical assistants fostered no small amount of resentment, although not necessarily directed toward management. Rather, in one of the team huddles, jokes were directed toward the high-status position of physicians who deigned to join their lowly ranks. One lean engineer was even confused as to whether physicians worked for Lakeview Associates:

> Ummm ... I think they do. I really should know. They work for Lakeview definitely, but in a lot of ways, it seems that they are more like contractors. You can only push so hard because they could leave and then you are in trouble because they are the ones bringing in the revenue. It is kind of a delicate dance of trying to show them why we need to change without them leaving.

In fact, Lakeview physicians *were* employees of the organization. Nevertheless, neither the Care Management Office nor practice managers possessed the authority to interfere with physicians' professional jurisdiction. While physicians resisted lean from the outset, they did not occupy managerial positions that were crucial to lean's deployment. Nurses and medical assistants reported directly to practice managers, and carried out the bulk of the interactions with patients, whether in person or by phone. Thus, the initial decoupling of lean from the work of physicians, while acknowledged and lamented by model entrepreneurs, was not fatal.

A far greater problem was that over time, the practice managers responsible for implementing lean came increasingly to resent and resist it. Although practice managers shared model entrepreneurs' managerial identity, interests and norms, many came from caregiving backgrounds, and saw responsiveness to the nurses and medical assistants they supervised as an important part of their jobs. Practice managers legitimated their authority not only in terms of their managerial experience, but also in terms of their close proximity to care work. This occasionally resulted in tension, particularly when the outside consultant charged with guiding lean's deployment openly treated the considerations of caregivers as naïve and childish. For example, in a meeting we attended between the outside consultant, a model entrepreneur, and a practice manager, the outside consultant interrupted the practice manager as she relayed a report given to her by the nursing staff. The outside consultant, who was previously listening with look of detached annoyance, suddenly stood up and began pacing around the model entrepreneur and practice manager. He exclaimed loudly, "how do you know what the nurses are telling you is true?" The practice manager calmly took a stab at her salad and said, "I trust them." In a voice laced with disdain the consultant said, "Nurses, they are like my children. When they come back from basketball games, I ask them 'how did you do?' They tell me they did good, but when I ask them the score, they don't even know!"

The outside consultant believed that it was naïve for practice managers to take workers' accounts of their activities at face value: meaningful knowledge could only be generated through appropriate lean methods. Any knowledge generated by practice managers prior to lean's introduction was similarly worthless. While sharing many of the same values and assumptions as the Care Management Office, over time practice managers began to resent having to impose the orders of an outside agent that seemed to have little respect for or understanding of the local context. This undermined model entrepreneurs' framing of lean as a participatory initiative that was designed to mobilize the input of all parties in order to improve the conditions of work and quality of care. In this light, the model was vulnerable to the claims of hypocrisy (Brunsson, 1989).

Feeling disrespected by the outside consulting group, practice managers also began to lose faith in the Care Management Office, which did not appear to be on the side of practice managers, but was rather there to pass on directives from the outside consulting group. One practice manager said of Sheryl, "she used to be in internal med operations management, so she actually has some clinic experience in managing a site, but I think it's been so long."

Practice managers began to question whether lean was, in fact, the participatory, bottom-up initiative that had been sold to them. They felt that the directives provided to them by the Care Management Office were removed from everyday realities of healthcare workers and imposed from the top down.

In contrast to lean's flexible reputation in manufacturing, practice managers began equating lean with rigidity. As one participant noted:

> If you have to tell a patient they have cancer, that isn't a 12-minute visit because lean says the next widget needs to come in after 12 minutes and you need to go because there's someone waiting outside. It is inhumane to say, "I only had 12 minutes with you, you have cancer, and I will have my nurse take care of you now." You probably wouldn't choose to see that doctor ever again. I know I wouldn't.

Practice managers also experienced lean as involving a tremendous amount of busy-work. One practice manager, when asked how lean was deployed in the organization, swiveled around to her computer to print off a *hoshin* chart. She explained that it was a lean tool developed to ensure that directives created at the top of the organizational hierarchy were executed across the organization:

> It's a map and it just goes everywhere, they all have a north, south, east, and west box [containing different data]. It's crazy ... you know, it's ... I have 19 things that I need to keep track of!

This practice manager might not have been so upset by the top down enforcement of lean had it not been so time-consuming, taking her attention away from what she saw as her real job. She increasingly identified herself in opposition to the Care Improvement Office and, by extension, upper-management. As she later said, "I think that as a leader, I should be out in my clinic, I should be out there helping my staff, trying to protect my staff, and to ensure that patient care is good."

The opposition to lean on the part of practice managers was not a rejection of managerial authority as such – or its legitimacy in the context of medicine – but rather a response to what they believed to be inefficiencies in its application. The work involved in collecting data, compiling reports, holding team meetings, following up with workers to see if they had memorized standardized protocols was a job unto itself. This came at a time when practices were not filling vacant positions, making the lean initiative seem even more like an unnecessary imposition. Finally, over time, practice managers became less convinced that lean was actually achieving its intended result – organizational efficiency. As one manager remarked:

> I don't think it actually saves that much money. I really don't. I think our practice saved $10,000 on medical supplies, which is not bad, but the investment, the cost to [Lakeview] for lean is on the order of almost $8 million ... I think it's rigorous, but I think in healthcare it's too mathematical, and at the same time not mathematical enough.

For example, model entrepreneurs insisted that practices create "control rooms," which were often renamed conference and/or break rooms. While the goal was to replicate some of the high-tech features of lean used in manufacturing, these rooms could actually control very little. Instead of arrays of computer monitors with constantly updated metrics, control rooms at Lakeview consisted mostly of printed out spreadsheets (not all of which were up to date) and goals written on dry-erase boards. One practice manager appeared embarrassed giving a tour of what was supposed to be the epicenter of lean at the practice, a sense that was heightened when a subordinate entered the room to microwave a burrito. What became clear was that model entrepreneurs' performance of precision and control did not correspond with their actual ability to measure and control healthcare work.

Another lean innovation that appeared increasingly absurd was gathering data and presenting it on Managing for Excellence (ME) boards. Workers were expected to self-monitor and gather data on their daily practices in order to share information that would allow managers to assess productivity and increase efficiency. Yet as several practice managers related, the practice of self-monitoring and gathering data did not occur in a frictionless manner, but rather often slowed down and - in some cases - impeded the actual work being carried out. Furthermore, it was often unnecessary, as more reliable data could be gathered elsewhere. As one practice manager remarked:

> When patients get discharged from the hospital, if they are over 65, they need to be called within two days. You could track that on a ME board, but that is very time consuming. My feeling is that it wouldn't be very accurate. Because if you didn't remember to call, then why would you document that you forgot? *laughs*

As another practice manager stated:

> At some point people get so burned out with all of the metrics, meetings, and countermeasure forms. You just can't deal with it anymore. My two operations managers almost quit. It felt like all they were doing was lean, and there is still actual work to be done ... There are certain components that work, but the adoption in healthcare has been a really rocky one. And there has been a shift at the senior level in the organization in terms of supporting lean. I think they support parts of it, but not all of it.

The time-consuming nature of self-reporting, in combination with the pressure to increase throughput, was particularly frustrating. For example, supervisors were supposed to continuously quiz workers on their activities, and often complained about the waste of time involved. One practice manager admitted that she was no longer requiring this, as it was thoroughly despised by her staff. Another practice manager remarked, her voice dropping to a whisper so as to not be overheard:

> We need to have less consultants. I think the more that we can become dependent on ourselves, the better. It is hard having a lot of people from outside of the organization consulting, coaching us.

Unlike physicians, who questioned lean's managerial logic, practice administrators justified their opposition on the grounds of managerial authority itself. While outside consultants and model entrepreneurs attempted to present lean as an objective, scientific technique, practice managers justified their resistance in terms of local knowledge and their own managerial experience. Faced with the tradeoff between lean's performance of efficiency and actually being efficient, they chose the latter, leading them to subtly resist the model, and shield areas under their control from its full implementation. For example, one practice manager confessed that she did not expect her workers to conduct team huddles in accordance with official protocols, and that she allowed workers to use ME boards to work on projects of their own choosing, rather than on projects determined by the Care Management Office. To appear as if the practice was conforming to official policies, this practice manager directed her workers to put certain information on ME boards before Care Management administrators visited the practice on their regular rounds. Recalling a meeting between practice managers and Care Management leaders, the same practice manager who decoupled standard work protocols in her practice noted:

> Every administrator has 10 metrics that require countermeasure forms, and there are 14 sites. So, there should be 140 countermeasure forms that senior leaders have to look at every month. When we realized this, another practice manager whispered to me, "I'm not putting in a countermeasure form for everything. Wait and see how long it'll take them to notice." We noticed yesterday that a woman from another practice presented an old countermeasure form. And not one person noticed! I was sitting there thinking, "That's the same one she did two months ago!" And it was. But for the lean people, it was all new!

Another practice manager admitted that countermeasure forms were not always completed as per official protocols, usually because there were no reasonable strategies to counter the failure to meet a specified goal.

Lakeview practice managers' opposition to lean was usually covert, as the examples above suggest. However, the eruption of a scandal at Lakeview allowed practice managers to resist more openly. Only two months into our field research, word came out that lean had cost the organization more than it had saved. With this announcement, a group of practice administrators collectively voiced their opposition to lean and began to dismantle the program in their practices, transferring lean engineers back to the corporate administrative offices for redeployment elsewhere. As one senior administrator described the revelation:

> Several practice managers went to my old boss at the middle of this year and said, "We want lean out of here. We're tired of having lean engineers at our sites, we are spinning and spinning with boards and measurements and all of this stuff and we're not doing what we need to be doing to take care of patients. It's time for them to go." And so they did, they took them [lean consultants] out of those sites.

Practice administrators began to ignore reporting on several key metrics they believed had no sound basis, and also to flout the requirement they complete forms when the practice failed to meet targeted goals. After months of going back and forth with the Care Management Office and the outside consultant attempting to convey what they believed was the absurdity of developing countermeasures in response to meaningless data, a core group of practice managers stopped reporting on certain metrics altogether. These practice managers argued that lean was unnecessarily cumbersome, wasteful, and distracted from more important work they could be doing. They felt disrespected by the outside consultant, and that their experience as managers with local level, contextual knowledge was being ignored. At this point, the external consulting agency, in an attempt to maintain face, suggested that the number of metrics be reduced from 14 to 6. Yet this adaptation came too late for many practice managers, who continued to decouple lean from most day-to-day activities.

CONCLUSION

In this paper, we have examined the process in which model entrepreneurs attempted to translate and deploy a model of management in two healthcare organizations that are characterized by differing authority relationships: professional and managerial (Scott, 2000). Literature from organizational sociology and management studies emphasizes the ability of actors to implement divergent change through discursive framing strategies (Battilana et al., 2009; Garud et al., 2007, 2002; Greenwood et al., 2002; Maguire et al., 2004; Thornton & Ocasio, 2008; Zilber, 2007). Like these authors, we draw on concepts from social movements literature (Snow et al., 1986) to describe how agents of change attempted to translate a model into a new institutional environment through a delicate process of disembedding and reembedding (Czarniawska & Sevón, 1996; Mohr, 1998).

At both Riverside and Lakeview, lean apparently failed to achieve its intended results, but for opposite reasons. At Riverside, model entrepreneurs faced an organization dominated and governed by academic physicians. Through an intensive process of framing and reframing to make the model commensurable with local norms and interests, they were eventually able to secure a certain level of local buy-in. However, the "lean" that was diffused throughout Riverside as a result was a shadow of its former self. In contrast, at Lakeview, model entrepreneurs relied on a strong local managerial hierarchy to deploy the model wholesale, and engaged in little framing, negotiation, or adaptation to local circumstances. This eventually contributed to resistance by local practice managers, justified in local norms of caregiving, but also on the apparent inability of lean to deliver on its promised goal of efficiency. In the end, lean production failed to make a profound impact on the way work was structured and performed at either Riverside or Lakeview.

Based on these cases, we have argued that there are at least two ways that models of management can get lost in translation. The first is the model attenuation: a watering-down so radical that the resulting model bears little resemblance to the original. We might expect attenuation to be more likely to occur in circumstances where proposed changes diverge radically from preexisting norms and interests. To put it another way, not all organizations present an equally favorable "opportunity structure" for model transfer

(Gamson & Meyer, 1996; Meyer & Staggenborg, 1996; Tarrow, 1993). Where an existing institutional logic is profoundly at odds with that of the new model proposed, entrepreneurs may find themselves forced either to abandon their project, or to frame a model out of existence. It may be, for example, that most academic medical centers are simply not congenial environments for the deployment of lean production.

On the other hand, it may be that some environments present so congenial an opportunity structure that model entrepreneurs fail to engage in the necessary framing and translation. Where they can count on a strong managerial hierarchy to follow orders, model entrepreneurs may be tempted to simply force a model, more or less undigested, onto a new organizational context. Yet this approach can lead to decoupling, a second way that a model can get lost in translation (Meyer & Rowan, 1977). Middle managers may lack the capacity to resist overtly, but when antagonized by a model that fails to respect local knowledge and norms, they may fight the model covertly by creating a buffer between the model and organizational activities.

In the end, lean was completely abandoned at Riverside Hospital, while it retained a minimal presence at Lakeview Associates. A year after our final interview with Samantha, she left Riverside to join a nearby lean healthcare think tank. Interviews with Riverside managers confirmed the Lean Transformation Office had been merged with another department that oversaw healthcare quality initiatives. Repeated attempts were made to contact lean engineers at Riverside for status updates, but to no avail. As one respondent stated, "The folks you probably spoke with are no longer here." A similar, sudden departure occurred at Lakeview Associates, as Sheryl and several other model entrepreneurs resigned from the Care Management Office. These exits coincided with a changeover in high-level leadership at Lakeview and a suspicion that lean would no longer be an organizational priority. This was confirmed in our subsequent interviews with administrators a year later, who reported their staff had been halved, and that it mostly served a ceremonial function. In interviews prior to their departure, model entrepreneurs expressed the belief that, even in their personal absence, lean would nonetheless endure as a way of thinking. Yet while model entrepreneurs may possess sophisticated and brilliantly articulated theories of change that address collectively agreed upon problems, if they are unable to alter objective social relations and material practices they have failed: they may have theorized a new world, but the point was to change it.

REFERENCES

Abbott, A. D. (1988). *The system of professions: An essay on the division of expert labor*. Chicago, IL: University of Chicago Press.
Ansari, S. M., Fiss, P. C., & Zajac, E. J. (2010). Made to fit: How practices vary as they diffuse. *Academy of Management Review*, 35(1), 67–92.

Arthur, J. (2011). *Lean six sigma for hospitals: Simple steps to fast, affordable, and flawless health-care.* New York, NY: McGraw-Hill.

Barry, M. J., & Edgman-Levitan, S. (2012). Shared decision making — The pinnacle of patient-centered care. *New England Journal of Medicine, 366*(9), 780–781.

Battilana, J. (2006). Agency and institutions: The enabling role of individuals' social position. *Organization, 13*(5), 653–676.

Battilana, J., Leca, B., & Boxenbaum, E. (2009). How actors change institutions: Towards a theory of institutional entrepreneurship. *The Academy of Management Annals, 3*(1), 65–107.

Black, K., & Revere, L. (2006). Six sigma arises from the ashes of TQM with a twist. *International Journal of Health Care Quality Assurance, 19*(3), 259–266.

Brunsson, N. (1989). *The organization of hypocrisy: Talk, decisions and actions in organizations.* Chichester; New York: Wiley.

Chalice, R. (2007). *Improving healthcare using Toyota lean production methods: 46 Steps for improvement* (2nd ed.). Milwaukee, WI: ASQ Quality Press.

Czarniawska, B., & Sevón, G. (1996). *Translating organizational change.* Berlin; New York: Walter de Gruyter.

Dahlgaard, J. J., Pettersen, J., & Dahlgaard-Park, S. M. (2011). Quality and lean health care: A system for assessing and improving the health of healthcare organisations. *Total Quality Management & Business Excellence, 22*(6), 673–689.

Davidson, J. E., Powers. K., Hedayat, K. M., Tieszen, M., Kon, A. A., Shepard, E., . . . Armstrong, D. (2007). Clinical practice guidelines for support of the family in the patient-centered intensive care unit: American college of critical care medicine task force 2004–2005. *Critical Care Medicine, 35*(2), 605–622.

Dean, M. (2013). *Lean healthcare deployment and sustainability.* New York, NY: McGraw-Hill Education.

DiMaggio, P. J. (1988). Interest and agency in institutional theory. In L. G. Zucker (Ed.), *Institutional patterns and organizations: Culture and environment* (pp. 3–21). Cambridge, MA: Ballinger.

Edwards, P., & Collinson, M. (2002). Empowerment and managerial labor strategies pragmatism regained. *Work and Occupations, 29*(3), 272–299.

Freidson, E. (1970). *Professional dominance: The social structure of medical care* (1st pbk. ed.). New Brunswick, NJ: Aldine Transaction.

Friedland, R., & Alford, R. R. (1991). Bringing society back in: Symbols, practices, and institutional contradictions. In W. W. Powell & P. J. DiMaggio (Eds.), *The new institutionalism in organizational analysis* (pp. 232–266). Chicago, IL: University of Chicago Press.

Gamson, W. A., & Meyer, D. S. (1996). Framing political opportunity. In D. McAdam, J. D. McCarthy, & M. N. Zald (Eds.), *Comparative perspectives on social movements* (pp. 275–290). Cambridge: Cambridge University Press.

Garud, R., Hardy, C., & Maguire, S. (2007). Institutional entrepreneurship as embedded agency: An introduction to the special issue. *Organization Studies, 28*(7), 957–969.

Garud, R., Jain, S., & Kumaraswamy, A. (2002). Institutional entrepreneurship in the sponsorship of common technological standards: The case of sun microsystems and java. *Academy of Management Journal, 45*(1), 196–214.

Gilbreth, F. (1914). Scientific management in the hospital. *Modern Hospital,* (3), 321–324.

Gilbreth, F. (1916). Motion study in surgery. *Canadian Journal of Medicine and Surgery, 40,* 22–31.

Greenwood, R., Hinings, C. R., & Suddaby, R. (2002). Theorizing change: The role of professional associations in the transformation of institutionalized fields. *Academy of Management Journal, 45*(1), 58–80.

Grunden, N. (2008). *The Pittsburgh way to efficient healthcare: Improving patient care using Toyota-based methods.* New York, NY: Healthcare Performance Press.

Guillén, M. F. (1994). *Models of management: Work, authority, and organization in a comparative perspective.* Chicago, IL: University of Chicago Press.

Hochschild, A. R. (1983). *The managed heart commercialization of human feeling*. Berkeley, CA: University of California Press.

Holden, R. J. (2011). Lean thinking in emergency departments: A critical review. *Annals of Emergency Medicine, 57*(3), 265–278.

Jimmerson, C., Weber, D., & Sobek, D. K. (2005). Reducing waste and errors: Piloting lean principles at intermountain healthcare. *Joint Commission Journal on Quality and Patient Safety, 31*(5), 249–257.

Kaluzny, A. D., McLaughlin, C. P., & Simpson, K. (1992). Applying total quality management concepts to public health organizations. *Public Health Reports, 107*(3), 257–264.

Kellogg, K. C. (2009). Operating room: Relational spaces and microinstitutional change in surgery. *American Journal of Sociology, 115*(3), 657–711.

Kellogg, K. C. (2012). Making the cut: Using status-based countertactics to block social movement implementation and microinstitutional change in surgery. *Organization Science, 23*(6), 1546–1570.

Kim, C. S., Spahlinger, D. A., Kin, J. M., & Billi, J. E. (2006). Lean health care: What can hospitals learn from a world-class automaker? *Journal of Hospital Medicine, 1*(3), 191–199.

King, B. G., & Soule, S. A. (2007). Social movements as extra-institutional entrepreneurs: The effect of protests on stock price returns. *Administrative Science Quarterly, 52*(3), 413–442.

Koning, H., Verver, J. P. S., Heuvel, J., Bisgaard, S., & Does, R. J. M. M. (2006). Lean six sigma in healthcare. *Journal for Healthcare Quality, 28*(2), 4–11.

Larson, M. S. (1977). *The rise of professionalism: A sociological analysis*. Berkeley, CA: University of California Press.

Levy, D., & Scully, M. (2007). The institutional entrepreneur as modern prince: The strategic face of power in contested fields. *Organization Studies, 28*(7), 971–991.

Lopez, S. H. (2006). Emotional labor and organized emotional care: Conceptualizing nursing home care work. *Work and Occupations, 33*(2), 133–160.

Maguire, S., Hardy, C., & Lawrence, T. B. (2004). Institutional entrepreneurship in emerging fields: HIV/AIDS treatment advocacy in Canada. *Academy of Management Journal, 47*(5), 657–679.

Mazzocato, P., Savage, C., Brommels, M., Aronsson, H., & Thor, J. (2010). Lean thinking in healthcare: A realist review of the literature. *BMJ Quality & Safety, 19*(5), 376–382.

Meyer, D. S., & Staggenborg, S. (1996). Movements, countermovements, and the structure of political opportunity. *American Journal of Sociology, 101*(6), 1628–1660.

Meyer, J. W., & Rowan, B. (1977). Institutionalized organizations: Formal structure as myth and ceremony. *American Journal of Sociology, 83*(2), 340–363.

Milkman, R. (1997). *Farewell to the factory: Auto workers in the late twentieth century*. Berkeley, CA: University of California Press.

Mohr, J. W. (1998). Narrating the organization: Dramas of institutional identity. *American Journal of Sociology, 104*(1), 277–278.

Nelson-Peterson, D. L., & Leppa, C. J. (2007). Creating an environment for caring using lean principles of the Virginia mason production system. *Journal of Nursing Administration, 37*(6), 287–294.

Ouchi, W. G. (1979). A conceptual framework for the design of organizational control mechanisms. *Management Science, 25*(9), 833–848.

Poksinska, B. (2010). The current state of lean implementation in health care: Literature review. *Quality Management in Healthcare, 19*(4), 319–329.

Radnor, Z. J., Holweg, M., & Waring, J. (2012). Lean in healthcare: The unfilled promise? *Social Science & Medicine, 74*(3), 364–371.

Reich, A. D. (2014a). Contradictions in the commodification of hospital care. *American Journal of Sociology, 119*(6), 1576–1628.

Reich, A. D. (2014b). *Selling our souls: The commodification of hospital care in the United States*. Princeton, NJ: Princeton University Press.

Scott, W. R. (Ed.). (2000). *Institutional change and healthcare organizations: From professional dominance to managed care*. Chicago, IL: University of Chicago Press.

Shah, N. D., & Pathak, J. (2014). Why health care may finally be ready for big data. Harvard Business Review.

Snow, D. A., Rochford, E. B., Worden, S. K., & Benford, R. D. (1986). Frame alignment processes, micromobilization, and movement participation. *American Sociological Review, 51*(4), 464–481.

Starr, P. (1982). *The social transformation of American medicine.* New York, NY: Basic Books.

Tarrow, S. (1993). Social protest and policy reform: May 1968 and the Loi d'Orientation in France. *Comparative Political Studies, 25*(4), 579–607.

Taylor, F. W. (1911). *The principles of scientific management.* Mineola, NY: Dover Publications.

Thornton, P. H., & Ocasio, W. (2008). Institutional logics. In *The Sage handbook of organizational institutionalism* (p. 840). London: SAGE Publications Ltd.

Toussaint, J. (2010). *On the Mend: Revolutionizing healthcare to save lives and transform the industry.* Cambridge, MA: Lean Enterprise Institute.

Vallas, S. P. (2003). Why teamwork fails: Obstacles to workplace change in four manufacturing plants. *American Sociological Review, 68*(2), 223–250.

Vest, J. R., & Gamm, L. D. (2009). A critical review of the research literature on six sigma, lean and StuderGroup's Hardwiring Excellence in the United States: The need to demonstrate and communicate the effectiveness of transformation strategies in healthcare. *Implementation Science, 4*(1), doi:10.1186/1748-5908-4-35

Vidal, M. (2006). Manufacturing empowerment? 'Employee involvement' in the labour process after Fordism. *Socio-Economic Review, 5*(2), 197–232.

Vidal, M. (2007). Lean production, worker empowerment, and job satisfaction: A qualitative analysis and critique. *Critical Sociology, 33*(1), 247–278.

Vidal, M. (2016). *Satisficing and permissive institutionalization in the market: The case of American manufacturing.* Unpublished manuscript.

Waring, J. J., & Bishop, S. (2010). Lean healthcare: Rhetoric, ritual and resistance. *Social Science & Medicine, 71*(7), 1332–1340.

Wellman, J., Hagan, P., & Jeffries, H., (Eds.). (2011). *Leading the lean healthcare journey: Driving culture change to increase value.* New York, NY: Productivity Press, Taylor & Francis Group.

Womack, J. P. (1990). *The machine that changed the world.* Riverside, NJ: Simon & Schuster.

Womack, J. P. (1996). *Lean thinking: Banish waste and create wealth in your corporation* (1st Free Press ed., and updated). New York, NY: Free Press.

Womack, J. P., & Miller, D. (2005). Going lean in health care. In *Calls to action.* Cambridge, MA: Institute for Healthcare Improvement.

World Bank. (2015). *World development indicators.* Washington, DC: World Health Organization. Retrieved from http://wdi.worldbank.org/table/2.15

Zbaracki, M. J. (1998). The rhetoric and reality of total quality management. *Administrative Science Quarterly, 43*(3), 602–636.

Zilber, T. B. (2007). Stories and the discursive dynamics of institutional entrepreneurship: The case of Israeli high-tech after the bubble. *Organization Studies, 28*(7), 1035–1054.

DOING MORE WITH LESS: INTENSIVE CARE AND THE LOGIC OF FLEXIBLE TEAMWORK

Jason Rodriquez

ABSTRACT

This article examines how a profit-centered restructuring of labor relations in an academic medical center undermined team-based care practices in its intensive care unit. The Institute of Medicine has promoted team-based care to improve patient outcomes, and the staff in the intensive care unit researched for this paper had established a set of practices they defined as teamwork. After hospital executives rolled out a public relations campaign to promote its culture of teamwork, they restructured its workforce to enhance numerical and functional flexibility in three key ways: implementing a "service line" managerial structure; cutting a range of staff positions while combining others; and doubling the capacity of its profitable and highly regarded intensive care unit. Hospital executives said the restructuring was necessitated by changes to payment models brought forth by the Affordable Care Act. Based on 300 hours of participant-observation and 35 interviews with hospital staff, findings show that the restructuring lowered staff resources and intensified work, which limited their ability to practice care they defined as teamwork and undermined the unit's collective identity as a team. Findings also show how staff members used teamwork as a sensitizing concept to make sense of what they did at work. The meanings attached to teamwork were anchored to positions in the hospitals' organizational hierarchy.

Emerging Conceptions of Work, Management and the Labor Market
Research in the Sociology of Work, Volume 30, 117−140
ISSN: 0277-2833/doi:10.1108/S0277-283320170000030006

This paper advances our understanding of he flexible work arrangements in the health care industry and their effects on workers.

Keywords: Health care; organizations; flexible working; teamwork; health care industry

INTRODUCTION

A significant amount of sociological research has examined the new arrangements that increasingly characterize work in the post-industrial globalized economy, highlighting how the transition from a manufacturing to a service-oriented economy has also changed the relationship between managers and workers (Crowley & Hodson, 2014; Crowley, Tope, Chamberlain, & Hodson, 2010; Kalleberg, 2001; Smith, 1997). Employers have sought more flexible, profit-centered arrangements in the labor process, redefining the terms of work to exert power and control over employees in new ways that match the shift from the "shop floor" to the "service theater" (Sherman, 2007). For example, flexible work arrangements have led to a sharp increase in non-standard employment relationships, in which workers are hired temporarily or for fixed-terms so employers can more easily control labor costs by quickly hiring and firing employees (Kalleberg, 2013). For those with salaried, standard work arrangements, flexibility has taken functional forms such as team-based work groups, shared governance, and other practices that seemingly empower workers as parties to the decision-making process. While functional flexibility in some ways diminishes the hierarchical system of control that characterizes work in complex organizations, in other ways it also creates new opportunities for employers to exert control over workers at the level of subjectivity (Vallas & Hill, 2012).

The health care industry, which accounts for 17% of the national GDP and a workforce that has swelled to more than 15 million people, is perhaps the ideal sector to examine how flexible arrangements shape the experience of work. In particular, team-based work has become an important component of the rise of a bureaucratic logic in the social organization of medicine, as hospitals have sought to improve value by cutting costs while enhancing patient safety (Reich, 2014; Scott, Richard, Ruef, Caronna, & Mendel, 2000). For example, in his 2011 Harvard Medical School commencement address, the noted surgeon and best-selling author Atul Gawande implored the doctors of tomorrow to recognize that contemporary medicine requires that they learn to work as team members, rather than cling to a bygone era when physicians had the authority to determine all aspects of patient care on their own (Gawande, 2011). In the address, Gawande argued that patient outcomes and worker engagement improve when physicians work collaboratively with others. The imperative to practice medicine as part of a tightly coordinated team, promoted by institutional stakeholders, regulatory agencies, and professional organizations, represents a shift in the organization of work in the health care industry consistent with broader shifts in the economy toward flexible work arrangements.

Calls for teamwork in medicine are supported by some evidence that communication, coordination, and leadership – practices consistent with conventional notions of teamwork – improves patient safety (Blegen et al., 2010; Hicks, Barry, Hobson, Ko, & Wick, 2014; Manser, 2009). Although patient safety has been a concern in medicine since Hippocrates' call to "do no harm," the contemporary call to patient safety was renewed after publication of the Institute of Medicine report *To Err is Human*, which argued that up to 98,000 preventable deaths and up to one million nonfatal injuries occur every year due to medical mistakes (Kohn, Corrigan, & Donaldson, 2000). In its follow-up report, *Crossing the Quality Chasm,* the Institute suggested that medical mistakes were not so much a result of individual mistakes so much as they were a result of organizational level problems that could be improved with better systems, including team-based care (Institute of Medicine, 2001).

Research about effects of teamwork on workers has drawn inconsistent conclusions (Crowley, Payne, & Kennedy, 2014; Kalleberg, Nesheim, & Olsen, 2009). Some studies, for example, have argued that teamwork increases worker satisfaction and a sense of commitment to workplace (Appelbaum, Bailey, Berg, & Kalleberg, 2000; Hodson, 2001), particularly among nurses (Griffin, Patterson, & West, 2001; Kalisch, Curley, & Stefanov, 2007; Kalisch, Lee, & Rochman, 2010). Other scholars, however, have argued that teamwork is little more than a managerial ideology that creates conditions to exacerbate the exploitation of workers and increase work intensity (Barker, 1993; Sewell, 1998). Still a third perspective emphasizes conflict in the labor process, showing that workers resist calls for teamwork (Vallas, 2003a; Vidal, 2007). In this paper, I take a novel approach, showing how teamwork acts as a sensitizing concept; that is, as a cultural frame of reference to help make sense of what people are doing at work (Benford & Snow, 2000; Blumer, 1954). Talk of teams and teamwork in organizations is a sense-making tool workers use to describe ongoing group processes and interpersonal relationships for which no other vocabulary exists. Such an approach changes the focus of study away from whether teamwork regimes are good or bad, and instead examines what teamwork even means given that different groups in different positions on the occupational and organization hierarchy may define it differently. Furthermore, as those definitions become the basis for collective action they also express emergent power inequalities, as certain positions in the hierarchy are more or less able to assert their definitions as a rationale for organizational changes.

Given the high cost of health care in America and its generally mediocre outcomes compared to other industrialized nations, restructuring labor relations to increase flexibility is a primary cost-reduction strategy among hospitals looking to improve value (Aiken, Clarke, & Sloane, 2000) The research presented here is a case study of one such hospital. This paper examines how a significant restructuring in an academic medical center that intended to increase the flexibility of its workforce had the consequence of undermining the very practices ICU staff defined as teamwork. Based on 300 hours of fieldwork collected over 18 months and 35 interviews with hospital staff, data shows that the ICU staff had an established set of practices based on cooperation and helpfulness, which they said was teamwork. Then, a few months after the hospital began a public relations campaign to promote its culture of teamwork, it restructured its workforce in three key ways: administrators implemented a new, more flexible managerial structure based on "service lines"; cut a variety of lower level positions and combined others; and began work on doubling the capacity of its profitable and highly regarded ICU. Hospital executives told staff that changes in payment models related to the passage of the Affordable Care Act necessitated the labor restructuring. This article argues that the restructuring of employment relationships in medicine undermines the efforts hospitals are also making to improve outcomes by organizing care around teamwork. It also shows how different orientations to teamwork between ICU floor staff and hospital executives were anchored to unequal positions in the organizational hierarchy. This study advances current understandings of teamwork in organizations, shows how meaning is attached to social position within organizations, and underscores the unique contributions of ethnographic methods in social-science research about medicine.

MEDICAL AUTHORITY AND THE RISE OF TEAMWORK

Throughout much of the 20th-century, physicians gained substantial authority to direct patient care and more generally control their work arrangements (Freidson, 1970a, 1970b; Starr, 1982). The organization of medicine closely resembled Freidson's ideal type of "professionalism," in which members of an occupation, physicians in this case, control the terms of work by virtue of their specialized knowledge and the belief that such knowledge cannot be standardized or rationalized (Freidson, 2001). Freidson argued that professionalism is the "third logic" of organizing work, alongside Adam Smith's "market" logic in which consumers control the work people do and Weberian "bureaucracy" in which managers are in control (Freidson, 2001). Scholars have pointed out physicians' dominant position of authority has been challenged on a number of fronts, including the increased power of hospital systems (Light & Levine, 1988), the patient autonomy movement (Rothman, 2001), medical reform efforts (Kellogg, 2011), and medical ethicists (Rothman, 2003). Most modern hospitals, including the hospital researched for this paper, are now firmly entrenched in the bureaucratic logic that dominates and uneasily co-exists with a dying out professional logic of medical care (Reich, 2014; Scott et al., 2000).

Since the Institute of Medicine reported that the organization of care work in hospitals caused medical mistakes (Institute of Medicine, 2001; Kohn, Corrigan, & Donaldson, 2000), additional government agencies and key stakeholders have widely promoted medical teamwork. The Federal agency responsible for implementing IOM recommendation, the Agency for Health Care Research And Quality, promote such team-based work practices through sponsored research and training programs, including a fully developed, ready-to-use program called TeamSTEPPS that provides training materials designed to improve communication and teamwork. Other agencies such as the Joint Commission (2012) as well as the Institute for Healthcare Improvement and the Robert Wood Johnson Foundation have sought to transform bedside care with teamwork (Lee, Shannon, Rutherford, & Peck, 2008). The effort to implement teamwork in medicine is a phenomenon that extends beyond the United States, as the World Health Organization discussed teamwork extensively in its most recent Patient Safety Curriculum Guide (2011).

Furthermore, influential professional associations have endorsed teamwork in medicine. The American Hospital Association, for example, in its long range employment outlook titled "Workforce 2015: Strategy Trumps Shortage," said the tight labor market will require the implementation of teamwork to enhance efficiency and improve staff retention (De Felippi et al., 2010). The American Medical Association also has issued policy briefs supporting team-based care (2015). While teamwork is high on the agenda of various agencies and associations invested in the organization of medical care work, it is unclear how these proposals will translate into practices on the hospital floors. Indeed, the notion of teamwork expressed in these statements is not necessarily consistent with how health care workers practice teamwork (Alexanian, Kitto, Rak, & Reeves, 2015). This paper addresses the slippage between the meaning and practice of teamwork, examining how hospital executives and floor staff in an ICU used the rhetoric of teamwork in ways that reflected their own interests and positions in the hospital hierarchy.

THE MEANING(S) OF TEAMWORK

While teamwork can be viewed a distinctive way to organize work, it can also be viewed as a rhetorical device to describe relationships and patterns of interaction for which no better vocabulary exists. Scholars have found that the meanings people give to teamwork convey the expectations they hold about the roles, scope, membership, and objectives of the group they have defined as a team (Gibson & Zellmer-Bruhn, 2001). In research on teamwork in medicine, researchers have closely linked the concept to patient safety and operationalized it in terms of collaboration, communication, and leadership (Xyrichis & Ream, 2008). Perhaps because teamwork feels like a very familiar concept, survey researchers have tended to measure teamwork against idealized, implicit assumptions about what it is and what it does (Paradis et al., 2014). Recent observational studies, however, show that those idealized descriptions of teamwork typically do not match the actual practices of medical professionals in performing complex medical care. For example, most medical care is done in parallel, with physicians, nurses, and other support staff working independently, increasingly in front of computers (Piquette, Reeves, & Leblanc, 2009). Furthermore, research suggests that medical teams are not typically composed of whole units of staff or entire occupations within an organization, but instead are ad hoc groups of people that come together to complete a specific, urgent procedure such as cardiopulmonary resuscitation or an intubation, which then dissolves when the task is finished (Janss, Rispens, Segers, & Jehn, 2012). Along these lines, a recent ethnographic study of teamwork in an intensive care unit found that although the rhetoric of teamwork was used extensively, care practices did not resemble teamwork as much as they resembled complementary concepts such as coordination (Alexanian et al., 2015). Teamwork in the ICU has been recently characterized as "threads of activity" that are tied and untied throughout the day as tasks that require more than two hands are performed (Reeves et al., 2015).

Research has also shown that the meaning of teamwork in organizations is frequently a point of contestation between workers and managers. Management uses the rhetoric of teamwork as an ideology to exert some measure of control over workers (Barker, 1993; Sewell, 1998; Vallas, 2003a, 2003b). A recent hospital ethnography, for example, showed that teamwork represented a contested ideological frame and source of conflict between managers and floor staff, rather than a resource to enhance solidarity (Apesoa-Varano & Varano, 2014). With the data collected for the present paper, Rodriquez showed how this process extended to staff-family interactions, as ICU unit staff used the rhetoric of teamwork to expand and reduce families' role on the team at key moments (2015). Sometimes workers' ignore or resist managerial talk of teamwork (Finn, Learmonth, & Reedy, 2010; Learmonth, 2009). Along these lines, workers sometimes repurpose managers' rhetoric and attempt to turn it toward their own interests (Turco, 2012). Taken together, research on teamwork must account for the role of the power inequities that form the basis of traditional work hierarchies.

Although widespread support for teamwork exists in the health care industry, research has shown that workers differ in their perceptions, evaluations, and definitions of teamwork. For example, physicians tend to rate the quality of teamwork more highly than nurses (O'Leary et al., 2010; Thomas, Sexton, & Helmreich, 2003). This is most likely due to the fact that physicians have more authority than nurses and what physicians interpret as teamwork nurses interpret as following orders (Makary et al., 2006). Although occupations often act as informational silos that shape perceptions in health care (Hall, 2005), variation between physicians and nurses tells only part of the story. In organizations like hospitals, nurses, and physicians are found throughout the organizational hierarchy, from bedside caregivers to top executives. This paper shows how intra-occupational differences in perceptions of teamwork exist across this organizational hierarchy. Furthermore, this study includes the voices of pharmacists, respiratory therapists, dietitians, social workers, clerks, and technicians who labor alongside nurses and physicians.

The meaning of teamwork, like the meaning of all expressions, ultimately depends on the context in which it is deployed (Blumer, 1969; Garfinkel, 1967; Mead, 1934; Rawls, 2008; Williams, 1985). Thus, this paper does not seek to define teamwork so much as it seeks to understand how teamwork is given meaning by actors who occupy different positions along a hierarchy. Such a position is consistent with prior scholarship working within a broadly conceived symbolic interactionist tradition. For example, Howard Becker famously described how he learned what a "crock" was by pursuing the meanings that medical residents attributed to the term (Becker, 1993). Similarly, Zussman's (1992) research analyzed what ICU staff meant when they described futile care as "torture" not just for the patient, but also to describe the emotional pain of providing futile care to patients who would not survive. A more recent analysis showed how talk about "culture" in a hospital frustrated, rather than enhanced, collective action to improve patient safety (Szymczak, 2014). This study builds on this work using a similar analytic strategy to uncover the range of meanings given to teamwork, but takes the analysis one step further to show how organizational hierarchies shape those meanings.

SETTING AND METHODS

This study was conducted in the flagship hospital of an academic medical center in the United States. It included primary care clinics, a range of subspecialties, including neurology and oncology, and a comprehensive trauma center that treated approximately 25,000 patients annually. The ICU I observed treated approximately 20 patients per day, with a range from 12 to 34 over the course of my observations. It specialized in pulmonary care, treating individuals with lung injuries such as acute respiratory distress syndrome (ARDS), influenza, pneumonia, or chronic obstructive pulmonary disorder (COPD), and would take any patients that required active ventilator monitoring. Patients' injuries often included life-threatening kidney failure and sepsis due to complications of an infection. Its staff included about 80 nurses, 10 attending physicians, 6 physician fellows, and 6 medical residents cycled through the unit every month, as well as approximately a dozen others, including pharmacists, respiratory therapists, dietitians, and unit clerks. Supplementing in-house staff, students rotated onto the unit to learn about critical care.

Observations

Approval for this research was obtained from the hospital's local Institutional Review Board (IRB) and the author's affiliated university. Prior to approval, the unit's Director of Nursing consulted with hospital executives and the unit's Shared Governance committee. Both gave permission for this study. I distributed an IRB-approved explanation of the study to the staff. The data in this paper come from observations and interactions with staff members who consented to participate in this research.

Initially, I was paired with a nurse who volunteered to let me shadow her around the unit. I observed as she treated patients, documented care, attended meetings, spoke with coworkers, among other daily tasks. I expanded observations after I understood her work routines and had met others who allowed me to shadow them. I shadowed nurses, physicians, respiratory therapists, pharmacists, dietitians, and clerks as they worked on the unit. I also observed medical procedures such as endotracheal intubations, IV catheter insertions, CT scans, and MRIs. People commonly shadowed staff around the unit, and I blended in as a researcher there to learn about ICU care. I observed informal conversations among staff and between staff and families, as well as a variety of meetings and medical rounds, which were held at the patients' bedside. I conducted about 300 hours of observations, visiting 2−3 times per week in 3−4 hour stretches over an 18-month period. I took notes on a folded piece of paper. Staff members wrote notes to themselves and my note-taking did not appear to be more obtrusive than theirs. I was never asked what or why I took notes, which were shorthand for extensive notes typed after I left the hospital (Emerson, Fretz, & Shaw, 2011).

Interviews

I also conducted 35 formal, semi-structured interviews with staff. I interviewed 18 registered nurses, 9 physicians, and 8 support staff including the unit's respiratory therapist, pharmacist, dietitian, and unit clerk. Eight of the 35 people I interviewed were supervisors with managerial responsibilities. Each interview was audio-recorded and transcribed. I asked staff about their work history, daily workflow, perceptions of teamwork and examples, comparisons between teamwork in the ICU and other units they worked, interactions with coworkers and family members, the transition to palliative care, and caring for dying patients. I practiced responsive interviewing (Holstein & Gubrium, 1995; Rubin &

Rubin, 2011), meaning that interviews were extended conversations, in which the questions and specific issues discussed varied depending on who was being interviewed and their position in the workplace. Interviews began in the middle of fieldwork, after gaining familiarity with staff and building rapport, which allowed for follow-up questions about prior observations (Weiss, 1995).

Analytic Process

Much like Howard Becker described the "detective work" involved in determining how social actors construct meaning, I paid close attention to how staff talked about teamwork and asked staff a lot of questions to clarify and have them explain what they meant by teamwork (Becker, 1993). After field notes and interview transcriptions were uploaded into HyperRESEARCH (ResearchWare, Inc, 2009), a qualitative data analysis program, and Microsoft OneNote, a note-taking application, all data about teamwork were coded for relevant themes. I began with open coding and then created more focused sub-codes as I analyzed the data and refined interpretive judgments (Charmaz, 2014; Lofland, David, Anderson, & Lofland, 2005).

DOING TEAMWORK IN THE ICU

It was a Monday morning and the ICU unit clerk announced, as he had virtually every weekday for the previous 10 years, "It's 9 AM, time for our morning briefing." The unit staff — physicians and nurses of course, but also the dietitian, respiratory therapist, pharmacist, social workers, nurse technicians, and maintenance staff gathered around his desk. The medical Fellow, a physician who had completed a three-year residency and was in the midst of an additional three-year fellowship specializing in critical care, led the briefing. He began by defining the group: "Good morning, Team." Then he called out questions, "Any patients being discharged? Any planned procedures? Who is the most unstable patient?" and more, reading from a set list of questions on a laminated card. As residents called out answers to his queries, the unit's charge nurse put color-coded magnets next to the corresponding patient's name on the big white board behind the clerk's desk. Then, the Fellow asked each service whether they had anything to announce, "Nursing? Dietary? Pharmacy? Social work? Respiratory? Maintenance?." Just before the briefing ended, the Quality Improvement Specialist, a doctoral-level registered nurse, told the assembled group, "You are expected to speak up if you see anything unsafe."

Just hours after this ritual, I observed a member of the maintenance staff walk out of a patient's room to alert a nurse that the patient had "pulled his tube out." The patients' nurse got up from her workstation and walked into the room. She playfully asked the patient, "What did you do?" and then reattached the ventilator tube to the patients' tracheostomy collar. Upon seeing this interaction, which exemplified the type of teamwork unit managers encouraged, the Quality Improvement Specialist said to me: "That's what I like to see," and added approvingly, "that's the whole thing right there." Research has shown that clinicians' silence when they suspect something unsafe is happening contributes to medical mistakes. Micro-level, relational dynamics are crucial to determining whether a subordinate will "speak up" to someone with authority such as a physician (Henriksen & Dayton, 2006; Szymczak, 2016). The Quality Improvement Specialist had hoped staff felt obligated and empowered to speak up, and seeing a member of the maintenance staff validate the significance of her daily reminders, possibly preventing a tragedy, was evidence to her not only of the unit's teamwork, but also of the power of teamwork to enhance patient safety.

About 10 years prior to the start of my observations, the unit began holding a morning briefing after a communication failure led to a critical adverse event. It took some time, I was told, to get the physicians to "buy in" to the briefing, but the unit's medical director at the time allowed the nurse manager to try it and her persistence paid off. Many staff members credited her for embedding the briefing into the unit's daily routine, but also for almost single-handedly changing the culture of the unit from one indifferent to teamwork to one that made teamwork a central component of its collective identity. In our interview, she explained that increasing practices consistent with teamwork was her highest priority. She said, "First was teamwork. We talked about teamwork. I said whether it is teamwork between you and your peers, teamwork with you and your physician, teamwork with myself. We're all on the same page. We're all in this together." She continued, "I think the more we got involved and the more push for patient safety, the more you tend to realize that you have to have it [teamwork]."

Encouraging her employees to act like a team seems to have been effective, as staff members throughout the unit defined themselves as a team and lauded their teamwork. One nurse, for instance, echoed the sentiments of others when she said the best part of working on the unit, "has to be the teamwork," and added, "I've never worked with a group of people that I enjoy coming to work with every day and that will make my life easier working with them, so that makes a world of difference in taking care of such sick patients."

While unit managers associated teamwork with practices that could enhance patient safety, the unit's floor staff was more likely to describe teamwork as a feeling that they could confidently rely on coworkers for help when they needed it. For example, when I asked a nurse for an example of good teamwork, she explained, "Someone's always floating around, 'Do you need help?' if they've got a moment. 'You need me to do this for you?' If you get an admission or a crisis, you're never in there by yourself. You've got a group of people in there helping you immediately." My observations corroborate her interpretation: nurses frequently offered to help each other with both the daily routine tasks like turning patients to prevent pressure ulcers as well as unexpected moments in which urgent care was required to sustain a patients' life. They likewise described bad teamwork to me by recalling stories of working elsewhere and not getting help with such tasks.

In addition to help with hands-on tasks, nurses also described teamwork as instructional assistance with technical details of ICU care work. For example, when I asked one nurse about what good teamwork was, she explained, "I feel like I can always go to an older nurse with more knowledge and whatnot and ask them a question and I'm not judged for it. And our doctors are the same way. I feel like they're approachable so it does work well as a team, in that sense." They similarly described teamwork as emotional support, especially in the aftermath of a patient death. One nurse, for example, said her first patient, "ended up coding during the day and I had nurses in my room for over an hour and a half." She said it meant a lot to her that they helped her clean up the room, which "was a mess" after they failed to revive the patient. Then they showed her how to complete the paperwork and later checked in to see how she was emotionally handling the patient's death.

Nurses were not the only members of floor staff to make close associations between teamwork and getting instrumental, instructional, and emotional assistance from coworkers. The unit clerk, for example, explained, "I can remember back in 2000, there was a lot less cooperation in here. It would be like a nurse would go kind of like beg somebody to help turn a patient or something, and you might even hear, 'You didn't help me the last time I needed it,' or things like that. And I never hear that anymore." A respiratory therapist noted that medical residents "come in with absolutely no hands-on ventilator training at all, and most of them are keenly aware of that, and when they come in this ICU, the first thing they do is try to find someone that will get them up to speed, and often that's me." The Medical Director of the unit, an accomplished physician, also spoke about the need to ask for and give help when needed. He said, "Are the Residents or Fellows able to ask for help when they need it? We let them do things on their own, but when do they ask for help, and are those the right times that one should ask for help? So we watch all that." Help – getting it and giving it – was the hallmark of teamwork among the ICU floor staff.

TEAMWORK AS A CULTURE

The floor staff talked about teamwork as assistance while the unit's managers highlighted teamwork's connection to patient safety. Hospital executives seemed to conceptualize teamwork as a culture. As I began observations, for example, the hospitals patient safety officer encouraged me to observe a teamwork-training program offered by the hospital every three months to all employees. The four-hour teamwork training was taught by a retired Air Force pilot who worked for a consulting group that promoted Crew Resource Management techniques in hospitals. Crew Resource Management is a set of procedures used primarily in the airline industry, designed to promote communication, particularly across occupational boundaries, in order to mitigate the potential of human error in high-risk situations (Helmreich, 2000; Helmreich & Merritt, 2001; Sexton, Thomas, & Helmreich, 2000). Much of the training focused on techniques to promote an environment in which people feel safe to speak up if they suspect someone with more authority is about to make a mistake. The trainer began with parallel stories: the first a detailed account of a 13-year-old girl involved in a terrible car accident and had an unknown latex allergy, who was being airlifted to a trauma center, and the second about the deadliest accident in aviation history, when two 747s collided on a runway on the island of Tenerife, killing 583 people. In the first, a young nurse who happened to know the girl had a latex allergy spoke up to an intimidating surgeon, thus saving the girl from harm. In the second, a cascade of communication errors caused a pilot to erroneously think his plane was cleared for takeoff and nobody stopped him before it was too late.

The trainer used these stories to suggest that organizational cultures can prevent deadly tragedies. He explained, "If you don't have that culture" patients could be harmed, and that "it really is a culture switch and it sounds really really easy but it's really really difficult." During the training a hospital executive stopped in to introduce himself and say that the hospital was looking for a "culture transformation." He added, "We're asking you to make this culture as good as it can be for you, your team, and your patients."

Furthermore, the hospital leadership had recently unveiled a new public relations campaign to rebrand the hospital around a culture of teamwork and togetherness. The campaign seemed to target staff as much or more than patients and the larger community, as the new slogan, "Together we care, deliver, innovate, and serve!" appeared on virtually every computer screensaver and on posters hung in every elevator and hallway throughout the hospital. The image of four jigsaw puzzle pieces, each representing one of the four actions in the slogan, coming together as an interlocking whole.

The symbolic nature of the campaign, as well as the extent to which it was directed at staff members, was underscored when, one day, at the end of the morning briefing the unit clerk stood up and said, "Alright everybody, bring it in!" The unit staff gathered to form a tight circle. With their arms extended toward the center of the circle, the clerk led the staff in a chant of the new slogan, and then threw their hands in the air and let out a collective "Woo!" as if they were a sports team preparing to take the field. The managers thought the hands-in cheer might enhance teamwork, but staff members seemed to find it a little silly. One staff member said, "I thought it was a reasonable thing to do for the first little while but I think eventually it became a joke" and "a smart-alecky thing." Others described it as "over the top," "a little gim-micky," and even "humiliating." After a few months, the managers decided to cut that out of the briefing and they replaced it with reading aloud cards from patients or their family members thanking them for their care. Although the hands-in cheer did not last long, the public relations campaign to highlight the hospital's culture continued throughout the bureaucratic restructuring that soon commenced.

HOSPITAL RESTRUCTURING

The ICU staff had established practices they marked as teamwork, and the meanings they attached to those practices formed the basis of their collective identity as a team. A few months after I started conducting observations, the hospital executives began to implement a significant organizational restructur-ing of the workplace. The restructuring had three components, which a unit manager later described to me as "a triple whammy." The first component was a transition to "service lines," the second involved a range of cuts to labor costs, and the third was doubling the number of beds on the ICU. These changes, which sought to increasingly rationalize and streamline hospital care, had the effect of undermining very practices the ICU staff identified as teamwork.

The hospital executives suggested the Affordable Care Act caused the need to rationalize care. In a meeting I observed, the unit supervisors explained to the floor staff that hospital executives said cuts to Medicare in the ACA, as well as the federal budget sequestration of 2013, and their expectation that the state would not expand its Medicaid eligibility necessitated the organizational restructuring. Although more patients were being treated at the hospital than ever before, as suggested by its newly opened patient care tower, changes to payment models initiated by the ACA led to lower reimbursements per patient. In the email announcing the restructuring to the unit's staff, the nurse manager wrote, "Our health care facility (like all facilities across the country) is receiving less reimbursement from the government for the work we do. This year, for example, [the hospital] received approximately $15 million less for providing care to a larger number of patients than we did last year. It is imperative that we restructure the way we do business in order to continue to grow our busi-ness, provide care with better outcomes, and maintain our business." A unit manager tried to soften the blow when she explained to a group of senior floor nurses, "They won't cut at the bedside, but they will cut around the bedside." An executive put the restructuring even more delicately: "The biggest cost cen-ter on any unit's budget is going to be your staff, so primarily nursing staff. People come to the hospital for nursing care. So what they wanted to look at was how can they maximize everybody's time?"

Service Lines

The first major part of the restructuring to occur was a transition to "service lines" to manage patient care. Service lines are an innovation in hospital management designed to increase value and promote better continuity of care for patients and staff. The patient safety officer explained the service line concept to me with an example, "So let's use cardiology. From outpatient through your inpatient stay and the ease of transition back to outpatient is one service line. So it makes sense to have common individuals who take care or oversee the care of those patients." The service line concept was ostensibly going to streamline care for the organization while providing greater consistency for patients who would be speaking to the same managers and supervisors throughout their stay at the hospital.

As part of this transition, the ICU was told to replace their charge nurses with "service line specialists". The specialists would have management responsibilities, with each focused on one particular aspect of the unit (staffing, continuing education, etc.) but they would also be expected to work on the unit floors providing care. At the same time, the charge nurse position was eliminated. Cutting this position was perhaps the most significant change of the restructuring for the ICU and it represented a challenge to maintaining the practices they defined as teamwork. The charge nurses circulated throughout the unit 24 hours a day 7 days a week and assisted others with a wide range of tasks. Since they were not assigned any patients, their role was to float around the unit and help other nurses with their patients. They also handled a range of other tasks, including greeting family members, organizing patient admissions and discharges, and facilitating meetings between doctors and families.

Days after the service line restructuring was announced, I walked into the unit's conference room a few minutes before the monthly "shared governance" meeting was to begin, and saw one of the unit nurses consoling a charge nurse who was upset because the hospital was eliminating her position. She, as well as the other charge nurses, was told she could apply for one of the service line specialist positions or take a position as a regular unit nurse. The new supervisor position, however, required a Bachelor of Science degree in nursing, something that, having gone to nursing school more than three decades ago, she did not possess. She was unsure what to do. Another charge nurse decided to go back to being a unit shift nurse because she preferred the opportunity to earn overtime pay compared to becoming a salaried supervisor. The hospital's patient safety officer, in assessing the effects of the announced restructuring, admitted, "It's been disruptive. People have been very, very distracted by that and there's been a lot of turmoil. I mean, people have lost positions that they'd been in for a long time. New people have come in and they're trying to figure everything out. So there's still a lot of uncertainty."

Rationalizing Labor

As the transition to service lines was implemented, and while the hospital publicly promoted its culture of teamwork and togetherness, another component of the restructuring began: a series of job cuts that lowered labor costs and intensified work. The first cut announced was the elimination of an incentive program for "weekend warrior" nurses, which was replaced with a program that required participants to work more for less pay. The weekend warrior program had, for decades, offered a generous hourly pay differential for nurses who agreed to work 46 out of 52 weekends a year (and get weekdays off). The new program cut the pay differential substantially and raised the work requirement to 48 out of 52 weekends. It also included a provision that taking a sick day counted as a full weekend "off." Nurses who wished to stay in the weekend warrior program were required to sign a contract stating they agreed to the new terms. After the news broke, one nurse in the program explained her predicament, "I'm going to stay on weekends because that's what works with school. That's what works with my daughter. But it just seems like the people that made these decisions obviously didn't include anyone. It was just dropped on everybody one day and nobody had a clue." She said that she found out in the middle of a shift, when a unit manager, "came up to us, like, 'Oh well, we're gonna be dropping your pay and you're gonna have to sign this contract."

The changes to the weekend program impacted all the nurses on the unit. A nurse explained, "Sure, I'm not going to be one of the people taking a pay cut, but it's just a matter of time until weekday nurses are working weekends too." She was right, shortly after the change to the weekend program was implemented, nurses who typically worked weekdays began being required to work every other weekend.

The hospital made additional staffing cuts. For example, two different positions, unit clerk and nurse technician, were combined into one position titled "Care Team Associate." Unit clerks and nurse technicians had different responsibilities. While the unit clerk organized and coordinated workflow, greeted patients' families, and guarded the locked doors to the unit, the nurse technicians restocked medical equipment and helped with routine care such as turning patients every two hours and sitting with patients who were at risk of self-harm. Furthermore, staff who transported patients around the hospital saw their positions eliminated. This meant that ICU nurses would at times leave the unit to transport their own patients (e.g., from the ICU to the MRI testing area). Fewer staff on the unit to help meant fewer resources to engage in the helping practices that staff defined as teamwork.

The unit's quality improvement specialist also saw her job eliminated. Her managers said they wanted her to transition to a similar position that covered the general medicine floor as well as the ICU. She explained, "the transition process engendered a profound sense of distrust" toward the hospital executives and she sought employment elsewhere.

Further, during my fieldwork all three of the ICU's physician assistants resigned over a work dispute and they were not replaced. Some of the unit's attending physicians wanted the physician assistants to work shifts in another hospital that the medical center had leased, and the physician assistants did not want to do that. Some attending physicians also preferred that medical residents do procedures that physician assistants often did, such as central line catheter placements. In addition to providing valuable training opportunities for the residents, this change allowed the hospital to bill more because physicians were doing procedures formerly done by physician assistants.

All these cuts to staffing had employees worried and upset. One long-time employee lamented, "I've never seen it this bad," and added, "They're only doing this because they know they can get away with it." A nurse explained the staffing cuts "made a mockery" of the idea that they had any role in the "shared governance" that hospital executives claimed to support: "If you're going to make people think they have some kind of a role in the decision-making process and then you're going to just institute something like that without anyone's knowledge, without anyone's input besides upper management, you probably make six figures, don't ever have to work weekends, and aren't directly affected by this."

As these changes were ongoing, the hospital's chief nursing officer came to the unit's "shared governance" meeting to address staff concerns. One nurse noted that they were not allowed to have any drinks on the unit, even water, which posed a problem because the break room was outside the unit and across the hall. She wondered what could be done so they could have drinks on the unit. The chief nursing officer responded that there are complex OSHA laws as well as Joint Commission regulations that make it a difficult policy to change. Another nurse asked about rumor that all nurses would be required to wear the same uniform to be more identifiable for family members. This idea seemed to greatly offend a large number of nurses. The chief nurse executive replied that she had seen nurses wearing inappropriate attire and she hoped a warning about initiating a standard uniform would suffice to change that behavior. Lastly, there were rumors circulating that ICU nurses would soon be asked to work shifts on the general medicine floors and that nurses on the general medicine floors would be asked to work on the ICU. The chief nursing executive explained her position that there should be a "partnership" between the regular hospital floors and the ICU that would allow a "rising star" nurse to gain experience on the ICU, and that ICU nurses should be willing to help other units. During this interaction, one nurse I was sitting near whispered to a nearby colleague that non-ICU nurses did not have the technical expertise to care for ventilated patients. Afterward, she said her skills would be wasted on the regular hospital floors, whose patients are not nearly as sick as the patients in the ICU. Other staff members said the meeting did little to assuage their concerns.

Expanding the ICU

The third component of the restructuring called for doubling the size of the ICU by adding an identical unit on another floor of the hospital. The ICU was often overflowing with patients onto other, less full ICUs in the hospital and from that point of view, expanding the unit was building on the strengths of the hospital while simultaneously filling more of its beds. In the unit manager's email to staff announcing the changes, she wrote, "There are a lot of changes coming to us — many that I think will be exciting and provide us the opportunity to make positive changes. For example, I am really excited for our patients that they will not be spread over 4–5 units in the hospital. They will now be housed on 2 floors and cared for by our staff!" Not everyone shared her excitement for these changes.

The expansion concerned many of the staff members I knew, particularly in light of the ongoing changes to the service lines and labor cuts. Consistent with those changes, while the unit doubled in size, their nursing budget would increase by about 50%. Some of the support positions such as pharmacy did not see an increase in staff at all. The unit manager did all she could to put a positive spin on what was occurring and pushed ahead to form a volunteer committee to figure out logistical details of the expansion. I observed the first of these meetings, and staff members expressed concern for maintaining the unit's collective identity as a team. In this spirit, the unit manager said she wanted to make sure that new staff members were fully included in the culture of the unit. They decided, for example, that all staff members would work on both floors so that the unit would not segregate into "old-timers" on the original floor and newcomers on the second floor.

The second floor of the unit open after I departed from the field site, but I occasionally checked-in with some of the staff members to see how the expansion was going. The unit's nurse manager said that the service line specialists work some shifts on the unit doing tasks consistent with charge nurses duties, but now they were also assigned a patient to take care of too. She added that training dozens of people was a challenge and the turnover rate had ticked up while staff engagement scores on employee surveys had dipped but now had somewhat recovered. A unit nurse said although she did not feel supported by the hospital executives, the unit's teamwork remained "pretty good." Another told me, "We seem to be having a revolving door with staff now" but that "overall things are going OK."

DISCUSSION

Flexible work arrangements are a key component of how businesses are changing the management-labor relationship as the economy shifts from manufacturing-

based to service-based (Kalleberg, 2013; Smith, 1997). There is perhaps no more
prescient area of the economy to look at for evidence of the effects of these
changes than the growing health care industry, which employs more than 15 million people and accounts for approximately 17% of the national GDP. The hospital discussed in this paper restructured its workforce to increase the flexibility
of its non-standard employment workforce by cutting lower level positions and
combining others. It also increased the functional flexibility of its workforce by
adding new salaried positions with job expectations that required managerial
duties as well as duties that were previously done by charge nurses as well as asking its ICU staff to double its capacity without providing a comparable amount
of additional staffing resources. Furthermore, the hospital's stated reasons for
the restructuring were not to enhance patient outcomes; but rather, to cut costs
due to changes made to payment models brought forth by the Affordable Care
Act. While the hospital had more patients due to the new law, it was also getting
lower reimbursements per patient.

Talk of teamwork in medicine appears through the lens of flexible labor
arrangements as little more than a means of rationalizing care and asking
health care workers to do more work with fewer resources. As this study
showed, the profit-centered labor restructuring undermined the very practices
that the ICU defined as teamwork. Teamwork can be used as a rhetorical
resource to describe a set of practices for which no other vocabulary exists, but
teamwork can be more than that. Teamwork is also an ongoing social activity
that depends as much on the resources available to do it as much as it depends
on the shared belief in a collective identity as a team. The decision to restruc-
ture the workforce while also appropriating the language of a culture of teamwork in its public relations campaign undermined teamwork – in symbol and
in deed – in the ICU. If similar processes occur at other hospitals, in which
rationalization campaigns cut against the grain of teamwork, then efforts to
use team systems to address the problem of patient safety may themselves suffer
as a result.

This study contributes to our knowledge about how organizational rhetoric
can be appropriated to take on new meanings that justify the interests of stakeholders with contrasting interests (Benford & Snow, 2000; Blumer, 1954;
Turco, 2012). The ICU floor staff used teamwork as a rhetorical device to
describe ongoing social relationships for which they did not otherwise have a
vocabulary. Teamwork was used to approximate a description of indeterminate
social relations. The staff relations on the ICU were based on an implicit trust,
an "I have-your-back" mentality that was more than just "coworkers" and
teamwork was a ready-made sense-making tool that also happened to resonate
with executives' rhetoric. The hospital executives' public relations campaign
promoting its culture of teamwork was a fairly concrete rhetoric that served as
an ideology of normative control. While it became a tool to elide the consequences of the labor restructuring, it also devalued the knowledge ICU staff
had learned and shared with each other about how to best care for patients.

Much of the existing research on teamwork in medicine has tended to leave implicit the meaning of teamwork and thereby assume a stable and shared understanding among medical care workers (Paradis et al., 2014). This study shows the meaning of teamwork to be anything but stable; rather, multiple meanings circulated throughout the hospital as floor staff and executives used teamwork as a rhetorical resource to assert their own interests in controlling the character of work. The meaning of teamwork, like the boundaries of belonging to a team (Rodriquez, 2015), is a contested and ongoing social process marked by conflict.

This study also highlights the rising power of hospital executives to define not just the meaning of teamwork, but also the character of the labor process in hospitals. Throughout much of the 20th century, physicians held a dominant position of authority in medicine by virtue of their monopoly over knowledge and the belief that such knowledge could not be rationalized. Thus, physicians had substantial authority to control the terms of work (Freidson, 1970a). While a range of forces have decentered physicians' authority in medicine (Light & Levine, 1988; Rothman, 2001, 2003; Zussman, 1992), this study shows how hospital executives' power to define teamwork on their own terms, disregarding the ICU staff's knowledge about how best to care for patients, represented a challenge not just to physicians' authority, but to all care workers in the organization.

From a labor process perspective, teamwork as unit staff defined it was significantly related to its staffing ratios. Simply put, there were typically enough staff members working at any given time to allow for one to offer help to another. The charge nurses played a crucial role here. Researchers who study medical teamwork write a lot about the importance of communication, leadership, and other characteristics that may enhance workers' ability to work together efficiently, but it is important to remember that simply having enough staff on shift is critical to facilitating the practices we refer to as teamwork. Furthermore, it is equally important to note that hospital executives were able to make such dramatic changes to the organizational structure because its labor force was not unionized. If the nurses had a union to defend their interests, the executives could have negotiated with its staff and perhaps achieved a new service line structure that did not show disregard for the ICU staff's professional knowledge and destabilize its method.

This study also shows the unique strengths of ethnographic methods in better understanding the organization of contemporary hospital care. Most previous scholarship on medical teamwork is survey-based and has tended to compare physicians and nurses perceptions of teamwork (Paradis et al., 2014). These studies have prioritized occupational variation and in doing so have largely missed the organizational variation that exists within organizations. Surveys that examine how perceptions of teamwork vary by occupation often aggregate workers across many organizations to get large enough sample sizes for statistical analysis, and in doing so the effects of organizational hierarchies get washed out. It is important to understand how doctors and nurses give meaning to teamwork, but there is a risk of overstating the variation due to occupation. There are occupational differences that are shaped by position within organizations, such as the as nurses on the ICU floor who interpreted teamwork in terms of situated practices while nurse executives interpreted teamwork as a culture of operational efficiency. These differences are visible when looking holistically at an organization rather than by slicing the data along occupational lines. Recent qualitative research has expanded our knowledge of medical teamwork, showing how teamwork reflects and reproduces power relationships in organizations as well as how the practices of teamwork differ from the rhetoric of teamwork (Apesoa-Varano & Varano, 2014). This study reinforces the need to better understand and account for how the rhetoric of teamwork in workplaces varies by organization in addition to how it intersects with occupational variation.

Future research should continue to look at how flexible arrangements may undermine medical care. It should also recognize that the meaning of teamwork is unstable and varies not just by occupation, but also within organizations and very likely between organizations as well. More ethnographic research into health care organizations would enhance our understanding of how power and position within an organization shapes understandings of teamwork. Furthermore, it is quite possible that the rhetoric of teamwork is used differently across hospitals as well as in other spheres such as families, businesses, and in other types of groups. What does the rhetoric of teamwork accomplish? Who uses it, who resists it, and under what conditions? Future research on teamwork should explore these and other related questions.

REFERENCES

Aiken, L. H., Sean, P. C., & Sloane, D. M. (2000). Hospital restructuring: Does it adversely affect care and outcomes? *The Journal of Nursing Administration*, 30(10), 457–465.

Alexanian, J. A., Kitto, S., Rak, K. J., & Reeves, S. (2015). Beyond the team: Understanding interprofessional work in two North American ICUs. *Critical Care Medicine*, 43(9), 1880–1886. Retrieved from http://content.wkhealth.com/linkback/openurl?sid=WKPTLP:landingpage& an=00003246-900000000-97232

American Medical Association. (2015). *Physician-led team-based care, AMA Team-Based Care Series*. Chicago, IL: American Medical Association. Retrieved from https://www.ama-assn. org/sites/default/files/media-browser/public/cms/team-based-leader_0.pdf

Apesoa-Varano, E. C., & Varano, C. S. (2014). *Conflicted health care: Professionalism and caring in an urban hospital* (1st ed.). Nashville, TN: Vanderbilt University Press.

Appelbaum, E., Bailey, T., Berg, P., & Kalleberg, A. L. (2000). *Manufacturing advantage: Why high performance work systems pay off*. Ithaca, NY: ILR Press.

Barker, J. R. (1993). Tightening the iron cage: Concertive control in self-managing teams. *Administrative Science Quarterly*, 38, 408–437. Retrieved from http://www.jstor.org/stable/ 2393374

Becker, H. S. (1993). How I learned what a crock was. *Journal of Contemporary Ethnography*, *22*, 28–35.

Benford, R. D., & Snow, D. A. (2000). Framing processes and social movements: An overview and assessment. *Annual Review of Sociology*, *26*(1), 611–639. doi:10.1146/annurev.soc.26.1.611

Blegen, M. A., Sehgal, N. L., Alldredge, B. K., Gearhart, S., Auerbach, A. A., & Wachter, R. M. (2010). Improving safety culture on adult medical units through multidisciplinary teamwork and communication interventions: The TOPS project. *Quality and Safety in Health Care*, *19*(4), 346–350. Retrieved from http://qualitysafety.bmj.com/content/19/4/346. Accessed on January 3, 2014.

Blumer, H. (1954). What is wrong with social theory? *American Sociological Review*, *19*(1), 3–10. Retrieved from http://www.jstor.org/stable/2088165. Accessed on April 2, 2016.

Blumer, H. (1969). *Symbolic interaction: Perspective and method*. Berkeley, CA: University of California Press.

Charmaz, K. (2014). *Constructing grounded theory*. Thousand Oaks, CA: SAGE.

Crowley, M., & Hodson, R. (2014). Neoliberalism at work. *Social Currents*, *1*(1), 91–108. Retrieved from http://scu.sagepub.com/content/1/1/91

Crowley, M., Julianne, C. P., & Kennedy, E. (2014). Working better together? Empowerment, panopticon and conflict approaches to teamwork. *Economic and Industrial Democracy*, *35*(3), 483–506. Retrieved from http://eid.sagepub.com/content/35/3/483.short

Crowley, M., Tope, D., Chamberlain, L. J., & Hodson, R. (2010). Neo-Taylorism at work: Occupational change in the post-Fordist era. *Social Problems*, *57*(3), 421–447. Retrieved from http://socpro.oxfordjournals.org/cgi; doi:10.1525/sp.2010.57.3.421

de Felippi, R. P., Altschuler, S. M., Colby, R. A., Fontenot, T. G., Greene, A. H., Lincoln, D., ... Zuhlke, D. L. (2010, January). *Workforce 2015: Strategy trumps shortage*. Chicago, IL: American Hospital Association. Retrieved from: http://www.aha.org/content/00-10/workforce2015report.pdf.

Emerson, R. M., Rachel, I. F., & Shaw, L. L. (2011). *Writing ethnographic fieldnotes*. Chicago, IL: The University of Chicago Press.

Finn, R., Learmonth, M., & Reedy, P. (2010). Some unintended effects of teamwork in healthcare. *Social Science & Medicine*, *70*(8), 1148–1154.

Freidson, E. (1970a). *Professional dominance: The social structure of medical care*. New Brunswick, NJ: Aldine Transaction.

Freidson, E. (1970b). *Profession of medicine: A study of the sociology of applied knowledge*. Chicago, IL: University of Chicago Press.

Freidson, E. (2001). *Professionalism, the third logic: On the practice of knowledge*. Chicago, IL: University of Chicago Press.

Garfinkel, H. (1967). *Studies in ethnomethodology*. Upper Saddle River, NJ: Prentice Hall.

Gawande, A. (2011). Cowboys and pit crews. *The New Yorker Blogs*. Retrieved from http://www.newyorker.com/online/blogs/newsdesk/2011/05/atul-gawande-harvard-medical-school-commencement-address.html. Accessed on November 28, 2012.

Gibson, C. B., & Zellmer-Bruhn, M. E. (2001). Metaphors and meaning: An intercultural analysis of the concept of teamwork. *Administrative Science Quarterly*, *46*(2), 274–303. Retrieved from http://www.jstor.org/discover/10.2307/2667088?uid=3739744&uid=2134&uid=2&uid=70&uid=4&uid=3739256&sid=21103461776723

Griffin, M. A., Malcolm, G. P., & West, M. A. (2001). Job satisfaction and teamwork: The role of supervisor support. *Journal of Organizational Behavior*, *22*(5), 537–550. Retrieved from http://wiley.com/; doi:10.1002/job.101

Hall, P. (2005). Interprofessional teamwork: Professional cultures as barriers. *Journal of Interprofessional Care*, *19*(s1), 188–196.

Helmreich, R. L. (2000). On error management: Lessons from aviation. *British Medical Journal*, *320*(7237), 781–785.

Helmreich, R. L., Merritt, A. C. (2001). *Culture at work in aviation and medicine: National, organizational and professional influences*. (2nd ed.). Burlington, VT: Ashgate Pub Ltd.

Henriksen, K., & Dayton, E. (2006). Organizational silence and hidden threats to patient safety. *Health Services Research, 41*(4 Pt 2), 1539–1554. Retrieved from http://www.ncbi.nlm.nih.gov/pmc/articles/PMC1955340/

Hicks, C. W., Barry, M. J., Hobson, D. B., Ko, C., & Wick, E. C. (2014). Improving safety and quality of care with enhanced teamwork through operating room briefings. *JAMA Surgery, 149*(8), 863–868. doi:10.1001/jamasurg.2014.172

Hodson, R. (2001). *Dignity at work.* Cambridge: Cambridge University Press.

Holstein, J., & Gubrium, J. F. (1995). *The active interview* (1st ed.). Thousand Oaks, CA: SAGE.

Institute of Medicine (U.S.). (2001). *Crossing the quality chasm: A new health system for The 21st century.* Washington, DC: National Academy Press. Retrieved from http://www.ncbi.nlm.nih.gov/books/NBK22857/. Accessed on October 20, 2014.

Janss, R., Rispens, S., Segers, M., & Jehn, K. A. (2012). What is happening under the surface? Power, conflict and the performance of medical teams. *Medical Education, 46*(9), 838–849. Retrieved from http://onlinelibrary.wiley.com/; doi:10.1111/j.1365-2923.2012.04322.x

Kalisch, B. J., Curley, M., & Stefanov, S. (2007). An intervention to enhance nursing staff teamwork and engagement. *Journal of Nursing Administration, 37*(2), 77–84. Retrieved from http://journals.lww.com/jonajournal/Abstract/2007/02000/An_Intervention_to_Enhance_Nursing_Staff_Teamwork.10.aspx

Kalisch, B. J., Lee, H., & Rochman, M. (2010). Nursing staff teamwork and job satisfaction: Nursing staff teamwork and job satisfaction. *Journal of Nursing Management, 18*(8), 938–947. Retrieved from http://wiley.com/; doi:10.1111/j.1365-2834.2010.01153.x

Kalleberg, A. L. (2001). Organizing flexibility: The flexible firm in a new century. *British Journal of Industrial Relations, 39*(4), 479–504. Retrieved from http://onlinelibrary.wiley.com/; doi:10.1111/1467-8543.00211/abstract

Kalleberg, A. L. (2013). *Good jobs, bad jobs: The rise of polarized and precarious employment systems in the United States 1970s to 2000s.* New York, NY: Russell Sage Foundation.

Kalleberg, A. L., Nesheim, T., & Olsen, K. M. (2009). Is participation good or bad for workers?: Effects of autonomy, consultation and teamwork on stress among workers in Norway. *Acta Sociologica, 52*(2), 99–116. Retrieved from http://asj.sagepub.com/cgi/; doi:10.1177/0001699309103999

Kellogg, K. C. (2011). *Challenging operations: Medical reform and resistance in surgery.* Chicago, IL: University of Chicago Press.

Kohn, L. T., Corrigan, J. M., & Donaldson, M. S. (Eds.). (2000). *To err is human: Building a safer health system.* Washington, DC: The National Academies Press. Retrieved from http://www.nap.edu/openbook.php?record_id=9728

Learmonth, M. (2009). Rhetoric and evidence: The case of evidence-based management. In D. A. Buchanan & A. Bryman (Eds.), *The SAGE handbook of organizational research methods* (pp. 93–109). London: Sage.

Lee, B., Shannon, D., Rutherford, P., & Peck, C. (2008). *Transforming care at the bedside how-to guide: Optimizing communication and teamwork.*

Light, D., & Levine, S. (1988). The changing character of the medical profession: A theoretical overview. *The Milbank Quarterly, 66*, 10–32. Retrieved from http://www.jstor.org/stable/3349912

Lofland, J., David, A. S., Anderson, L., & Lofland, L. H. (2005). *Analyzing social settings: A guide to qualitative observation and analysis* (4th ed.). Belmont, CA: Cengage Learning.

Makary, M. A., Sexton, J. B., Freischlag, J. A., Holzmueller, C. G., Millman, E. A., Rowen, L., & Pronovost, P. J. (2006). Operating room teamwork among physicians and nurses: Teamwork in the eye of the beholder. *Journal of the American College of Surgeons, 202*(5), 746–752.

Manser, T. (2009). Teamwork and patient safety in dynamic domains of healthcare: A review of the literature. *Acta Anaesthesiologica Scandinavica, 53*(2), 143–151. Retrieved from http://onlinelibrary.wiley.com/. Accessed on November 28, 2012. doi:10.1111/j.1399-6576.2008.01717.x

Mead, G. H. (1934). *Mind, self, and society: From the standpoint of a social behaviorist.* Chicago, IL: University of Chicago Press.

O'Leary, K. J., Ritter, C. J., Wheeler, H., Szekendi, M. K., Brinton, T. S., & Williams, M. V. (2010). Teamwork on inpatient medical units: Assessing attitudes and barriers. *Quality and Safety in Health Care, 19*, 117–121.

Paradis, E. et al. (2014). Delivering interprofessional care in intensive care: A scoping review of ethnographic studies. *American Journal of Critical Care, 23*(3), 230–238. Retrieved from http://ajcc.aacnjournals.org/content/23/3/230

Piquette, D., Reeves, S., & Leblanc, V. R. (2009). Interprofessional intensive care unit team interactions and medical crises: A qualitative study. *Journal of Interprofessional Care, 23*(3), 273–285. Retrieved from http://www.tandfonline.com/; doi:10.1080/13561820802697818

Rawls, A. W. (2008). Harold Garfinkel, ethnomethodology, and workplace studies. *Organization Studies, 29*(5), 701–732.

Reeves, S., McMillan, S. E., Kachan, N., Paradis, E., Leslie, M., & Kitto, S. (2015). Interprofessional collaboration and family member involvement in intensive care units: Emerging themes from a multi-sited ethnography. *Journal of Interprofessional Care, 29*(3), 230–237. Retrieved from http://informahealthcare.com/; doi:10.3109/13561820.2014.955914

Reich, A. D. (2014). *Selling our souls: The commodification of hospital care in the United States.* Princeton, NJ: Princeton University Press.

ResearchWare, Inc (2009). *HyperRESEARCH.* Randolph, MA: ResearchWare, Inc. Retrieved from http://www.researchware.com/

Rodriquez, J. (2015). Who is on the ICU Team?: Shifting the Boundaries of Belonging on the ICU. *Social Science & Medicine, 144*, 112–118.

Rothman, D. J. (2001). The origins and consequences of patient autonomy: A 25-Year retrospective. *Health Care Analysis: HCA: Journal of Health Philosophy and Policy, 9*(3), 255–264.

Rothman, D. J. (2003). *Strangers at the bedside: A history of how law and bioethics transformed medical decision making* (2nd ed.). New York, NY: Aldine Transaction.

Rubin, H. J., & Rubin, I. S. (2011). *Qualitative interviewing: The art of hearing data* (3rd ed.). Thousand Oaks, CA: SAGE.

Scott, W., Richard, M., Ruef, C. A., Caronna, C. A., & Mendel, P. J. (2000). *Institutional change and healthcare organizations: From professional dominance to managed care* (1st ed.). Chicago, IL: University of Chicago Press.

Sewell, G. (1998). The discipline of teams: The control of team-based industrial work through electronic and peer surveillance. *Administrative Science Quarterly, 43*, 397–428. Retrieved from http://www.jstor.org/stable/2393857

Sexton, J. B., Thomas, E. J., Helmreich, R. L. (2000). Error, stress, and teamwork in medicine and aviation: Cross sectional surveys. *British Medical Journal, 320*(7237), 745–749.

Sherman, R. (2007). *Class acts: Service and inequality in luxury hotels.* Berkeley, CA: University of California Press.

Smith, V. (1997). New forms of work organization. Annual Review of Sociology, *23*, 315–339. Retrieved from http://www.jstor.org/stable/2952554. Accessed on November 6, 2016.

Starr, P. (1982). *The social transformation of American medicine.* New York, NY: Basic Books.

Szymczak, J. E. (2014). Seeing risk and allocating responsibility: Talk of culture and its consequences on the work of patient safety. *Social Science & Medicine, 120*, 252–259.

Szymczak, J. E. (2016). Infections and interaction rituals in the organisation: Clinician accounts of speaking up or remaining silent in the face of threats to patient safety. *Sociology of Health & Illness, 38*(2), 325–339. Retrieved from http://wiley.com/; doi:10.1111/1467-9566.12371

The Joint Commission. (2012). *Improving patient and worker safety: Opportunities for synergy, collaboration, and innovation.* Oakbrook Terrace, IL: The Joint Commission.

Thomas, E. J., Bryan Sexton, J., & Helmreich, R. L. (2003). Discrepant attitudes about teamwork among critical care nurses and physicians. *Critical Care Medicine, 31*, 956–959.

Turco, C. (2012). Difficult decoupling: Employee resistance to the commercialization of personal settings. *American Journal of Sociology, 118*(2), 380–419. Retrieved from http://www.jstor.org/stable/10.1086/666505

Vallas, S. P. (2003a). The adventures of managerial hegemony: Teamwork, ideology, and worker resistance. *Social Problems, 50*, 204–225. Retrieved from http://caliber.ucpress.net/; doi:10.1525/sp.2003.50.2.204

Vallas, S. P. (2003b). Why teamwork fails: Obstacles to workplace change in four manufacturing plants. *American Sociological Review, 68*, 223–250. Retrieved from http://www.jstor.org/stable/1519767

Vallas, S. P., & Hill, A. (2012). Conceptualizing power in organizations. In D. Courpasson, D. Golsorkhi, & J. J. Sallaz (Eds.), *Research in the sociology of organizations* (vol. 34, pp. 165–197). Bingley, UK: Emerald Group Publishing Limited. Retrieved from http://www.emeraldinsight.com/. Accessed on November 10, 2016. doi:10.1108/S0733-558X%282012%290000034009

Vidal, M. (2007). Lean production, worker empowerment, and job satisfaction: A qualitative analysis and critique. *Critical Sociology, 33*(1–2), 247–278. Retrieved from http://crs.sagepub.com/content/33/1-2/247. Accessed on August 18, 2016.

Weiss, R. S. (1995). *Learning from strangers: The art and method of qualitative interview studies* (1st ed.). New York, NY: Free Press.

Williams, R. (1985). *Keywords: A vocabulary of culture and society*. (2nd ed.). Oxford: Oxford University Press.

World Health Organization. (2011). *Patient safety curriculum guide: Multi-Professional edition*. Geneva: World Health Organization.

Xyrichis, A., & Ream, E. (2008). Teamwork: A concept analysis. *Journal of Advanced Nursing, 61*(2), 232–241. Retrieved from http://onlinelibrary.wiley.com/; doi:10.1111/j.1365-2648.2007.04496.x/abstract

Zussman, R. (1992). *Intensive care: Medical ethics and the medical profession*. Chicago, IL: University of Chicago Press.

RACE, RECESSION, AND SOCIAL CLOSURE IN THE LOW-WAGE LABOR MARKET: EXPERIMENTAL AND OBSERVATIONAL EVIDENCE

Mike Vuolo, Christopher Uggen and Sarah Lageson

ABSTRACT

This paper tests whether employers responded particularly negatively to African American job applicants during the deep U.S. recession that began in 2007. Theories of labor queuing and social closure posit that members of privileged groups will act to minimize labor market competition in times of economic turbulence, which could advantage Whites relative to African Americans. Although social closure should be weakest in the less desirable, low-wage job market, it may extend downward during recessions, pushing minority groups further down the labor queue and exacerbating racial inequalities in hiring. We consider two complementary data sources: (1) a field experiment with a randomized block design and (2) the nationally representative NLSY97 sample. Contrary to expectations, both analyses reveal a comparable recession-based decline in job prospects for White and African American male applicants, implying that hiring managers did not adapt new forms of social closure and demonstrating the durability of inequality even in times of structural change. Despite this proportionate drop, however, the recession left African Americans in an extremely disadvantaged position. Whites during the recession obtained favorable responses from employers at rates similar to African Americans prior to the recession. The combination

Emerging Conceptions of Work, Management and the Labor Market
Research in the Sociology of Work, Volume 30, 141–183
Copyright © 2017 by Emerald Publishing Limited
All rights of reproduction in any form reserved
ISSN: 0277-2833/doi:10.1108/S0277-283320170000030007

of experimental methods and nationally representative longitudinal data yields strong evidence on how race and recession affect job prospects in the low-wage labor market.

Keywords: Recession; hiring; racial inequality; social closure; labor queues

INTRODUCTION

Evidence abounds that race remains a "master status" (Hughes, 1945, p. 357) in American society, associated with discrimination across a wide range of socioeconomic outcomes (Pager & Shepherd, 2008). Moreover, race often intersects with other factors that exacerbate disadvantage, such as a criminal record (Pager, 2003) and low education (Wilson, Tienda, & Wu, 1995). Racial minorities have also experienced worse job loss rates than whites in the presence of society-wide labor market shifts, such as deindustrialization (Hill & Negrey, 2010), deunionization (Bound & Freeman, 1992), and outsourcing (Johnson, Burthley, & Ghorm, 2008). In light of emerging research on the group-specific effects of the Great Recession (Grusky, Western, & Wimer, 2011), we ask whether turbulent economic times intensify racial discrimination in hiring in the low-wage, unskilled job market. We gain purchase on this question by analyzing both a field experiment in which young African American and White men applied for entry-level jobs before and during a recession and a nationally representative longitudinal survey of young people.

Weber's ([1922] 1968) concept of "social closure" describes processes in which dominant groups safeguard desirable positions by restricting entry to a limited circle of eligible workers (Murphy, 1988; Parkin, 1979; Weeden, 2002). This effect has been documented in cases of race and gender discrimination (Loveman, 1999; Reskin & Roos, 1990; Roscigno, Garcia, & Bobbitt-Zeher, 2007), such that "superordinate groups preserve their advantage by tying access to jobs or other scarce goods to group characteristics" (Tomaskovic-Devey, 1993, p. 9). As jobs become scarcer during a recession, dominant groups may seek to extend social closure to less desirable jobs. If so, recessions would worsen racial inequalities in hiring, such that African Americans would be excluded from a broader range of employment opportunities.

Alternatively, there are also reasons to expect a more proportional decline in hiring behavior during recessions. Weberian closure theory generally concerns the efforts of workers, rather than employers. Although workers in desirable positions may wish to minimize labor market competition, employers and hiring authorities do not share these interests. If employers' preferences remain stable during recessions, then we would expect fewer workers of all groups to be hired during such periods. We will test these ideas by specifying race-by-recession interactions using unique experimental and observational data collected before and during the recession.

In 2007 and 2008, we conducted a field experiment of low-wage, entry-level hiring. The Great Recession began at about the midpoint of our data collection. This economic shift within the field experiment allows us to test whether employers select only racially privileged applicants – those at the very front of the labor queue – from the many available workers during recessionary periods. We then analyze National Longitudinal Survey of Youth 1997 (NLSY97) data to validate the findings in the field experiment, examining weekly employment arrays from the year prior to the recession and the first year of the recession.

In what follows, we first review theory and research on the socioeconomic effects of racial discrimination, particularly in how race interacts with recessions and other sources of disadvantage and develop a set of hypotheses based on this previous work. We then exploit the unanticipated environmental change during our field experiment to estimate the causal effect of applicant race during a major economic decline, formally testing recession-based differences in employer "callbacks" by race. Next, we analyze observational data from the NLSY97 to test for racial differences in job search success before and during the recession. The results will thus demonstrate whether disadvantage in hiring is proportionate or pronounced; that is, whether African American disadvantage is due to the main effects of racial discrimination and the recession or to a heightened deficit resulting from their combination. In contrast, the absence of differential effects on race groups would suggest that inequality operates similarly within different economic contexts, demonstrating the durability and resilience of racial inequality (Tilly, 1999) even in the face of structural change.

THEORETICAL BACKGROUND

To situate our questions and hypotheses, we first consider the literature on racial discrimination and on how economic incidents like recessions affect hiring. We use these literatures to develop hypotheses based on the main effects of both race and recession on hiring outcomes. We then theorize the interaction between these effects, drawing upon theories of labor queues and social closure, developing further hypotheses regarding the interaction of these effects.

Racial Discrimination and Sources of Employment Disadvantage

The persistence of racial discrimination is among the most consistent findings in U.S. sociology, particularly for socioeconomic outcomes. With regard to labor markets, field experiments have consistently documented discrimination in hiring (Bertrand & Mullainathan, 2004; Pager, 2007a; Pager, Western, & Bonikowski, 2009). Observational data show that this discrimination contributes to lower wages (Huffman & Cohen, 2004; Tomaskovic-Devey, Thomas, & Johnson, 2005), decreased home equity (Krivo & Kaufman, 2004), and health inequalities (Nazroo, 2003). We here concentrate on the persistent effects of racial discrimination in employment among younger and less-educated African American men (Pager, 2007a; Holzer, 2009). Hiring discrimination is especially consequential for such workers because it decreases human capital, leading to persistent socioeconomic differentials over the life course (Tomaskovic-Devey et al., 2005).

Human capital differences in education, work experience, and job training only partially explain race differences in employment outcomes (Kaufman, 2002; Moss & Tilly, 2001; Turner, Fix, & Struyk, 1991). Theories of statistical discrimination and labor market queuing help explain these residual differences. Statistical discrimination models posit that employers use race to draw "quick and dirty" assumptions about group differences in productivity and other characteristics, particularly when they lack detailed information about applicants (Arrow, 1973; Bielby & Baron, 1986; Braddock & McPartland, 1987; Moss & Tilly, 1996; Phelps, 1972; Tomaskovic-Devey & Skaggs, 1999). By assuming racial differences in productivity, employers can rapidly categorize workers based on their group membership, giving less attention to personal qualifications (Pager & Shephard, 2008).

In terms of the match of applicants to positions, racial characteristics can thus determine applicants' relative position in a labor queue that reserves better-quality employment for more favored groups (Aigner & Cain, 1977; Kaufman, 2002; Reskin & Roos, 1990). This phenomenon deepens the concentration of African American and White workers in different occupations, reinforcing racial inequalities (see review by Reskin, 2012; Smith, 2002). As race-specific attributes are attached to specific occupations, employers rank applicants based on the match between their race and the presumed racial appropriateness of a specific occupation. Considering them together, statistical discrimination (Arrow, 1973; Phelps, 1972) and labor market queuing theories (Reskin & Roos, 1990) contend that an applicant's position in line is shaped by the combination of their race, the racial characteristics attached to an occupation, and employer stereotypes and observations of race-employment patterning (Kaufman, 2002). This process results in "homosocial reproduction," such that predominantly White employers tend to select predominantly White workforces (Kanter, 1977).

Based upon the strong experimental evidence on racial discrimination in hiring and theories of statistical discrimination and labor queuing, we offer the following hypothesis on the main effect of race on hiring:

Hypothesis 1. Employers will respond less favorably to African American job applicants than to White applicants.

The Varying Effect of the Great Recession on Individuals

During the recent Great Recession, individuals and families experienced higher unemployment, more erratic work patterns, decreased home values, lowered income and net worth, and higher indebtedness and bankruptcy rates (Carruthers & Kim, 2011). By definition (NBER, 2008), economic opportunity declines during recessions. Indeed, the Great Recession affected a host of economic indicators at both the aggregate and individual levels (Carruthers & Kim, 2011; Grusky et al., 2011), leading to the following hypothesis regarding the main effect of the recession:

Hypothesis 2. Employers will respond less favorably to applicants during official recessionary periods than during non-recessionary periods.

The recent economic downturn has had particularly severe consequences for some social groups (Grusky et al., 2011). Some researchers have dubbed it a "mancession," with men facing higher job separation, lower chances of finding positions, and higher unemployment rates, partially due to the concentration of male job loss in particular sectors (Berthoud & Sosa, 2011; Hout, Levanon, & Cumberworth, 2011; Sierminska & Takhtamanova, 2011). Within families, women increasingly shared the burden by entering the labor force or increasing work hours (Mattingly & Smith, 2010). Young adults and those with only a high school education also faced disproportionate economic disadvantage (Berthoud & Sosa, 2011; Hout et al., 2011; Vuolo, Mortimer, & Staff, 2016; Wolff, Owens, & Burak, 2011). These combined effects led to a recession-induced increase in poverty, especially among young, unskilled men (Smeeding, Thompson, Levanon, & Burak, 2011).

African Americans were hit particularly hard from late 2007 to 2009. The foreclosure crisis was highly racialized, with those residing in segregated African American neighborhoods most likely to have received subprime mortgages and to have faced foreclosure (Rugh & Massey, 2010). At the individual level, African Americans experienced greater losses in terms of mortgage delinquencies, home equity, foreclosures, and personal bankruptcies (Wolff et al., 2011). Further, when each of the demographic categories noted above (i.e., gender, education, age) are broken down by race, African Americans are typically worse off in terms of unemployment and assets than their similarly situated counterparts of other races, especially Whites (Jacobsen & Mather, 2011). For males, Black-White disparities in economic outcomes during recessions are particularly pronounced (Sierminska & Takhtamanova, 2011). Based on the main effects of economic contraction and racial discrimination, African Americans are clearly in a disadvantaged position, but it is less clear whether their losses are disproportionate – a critical question for theory and policy.

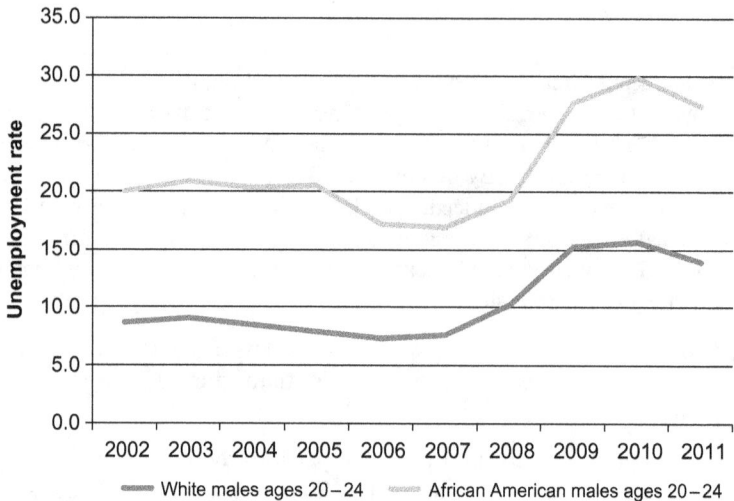

Fig. 1. Unemployment Rates for Males Ages 20−24 by Race. *Source*: U.S. Department of Labor, Current Population Survey, 2002−2011.

Some macro-level evidence can be brought to bear on this question. Fig. 1 shows the U.S. unemployment rate for males aged 20−24 by race. Although there is a distinct difference in levels, the trends for Whites and African Americans are quite similar. Using the difference between 2006 (the year before the recession began) and the 2010 peak, the White unemployment rate increased by a factor of 2.2 (from 7.3% to 15.7%). For African Americans, the rate increased by a factor of 1.7 (from 17.2% to 29.8%). Thus, the unemployment rate did not increase disproportionately for African Americans, although in absolute terms African American unemployment rose 12.6 percentage points compared to 8.4 percentage points for Whites.[1] Moreover, this measure obscures those who drop out of the labor force, which itself exhibits race differences (U.S. Bureau of Labor Statistics, 2012). Job loss, however, does not speak to individual-level *hiring* discrimination, a critical site for testing theories of labor queues and social closure.

Disproportionate Disadvantage: Labor Queues and Social Closure

The statistical discrimination literature suggests some characteristics that are particularly likely to interact with race. When combined with race, these stigmatizing characteristics push applicants even farther back in the labor queue by signaling individual differences in presumed productivity (Spence, 1973). For example, racial disparities are compounded by other bases of discrimination, such as criminal records (Pager, 2007b; Pager et al., 2009) and gender (Greenman & Xie, 2008; Holzer, 2009), underscoring how disadvantage in other domains disproportionately affects African Americans. Yet, these individual-level characteristics do not speak to how recessions would affect labor queues.

Theories of social closure have been advanced to explain how members of a privileged group use categorical distinctions, such as race, to minimize the pool of potential rivals they must face (Reskin, 1988; Tilly, 1999; Tomaskovic-Devey, 1993; Weber, 1968). For example, there is considerable evidence that supervisory and management positions are dominated by Whites (Stainback & Tomaskovic-Devey, 2009), that White women are the dominant beneficiaries of diversity programs (Kalev, Kelly, & Dobbin, 2006), and that African Americans are relegated to the lowest-level supervisory positions, where the workforce is predominantly African American (Elliott & Smith, 2001; Stainback & Tomaskovic-Devey, 2009). While social closure has thus been applied largely to the professional and managerial job market, as well as those requiring proven vocational skills (Bol & Weeden, 2015), there is also reason to apply this logic to the unskilled, low-wage labor market, particularly when jobs are in short supply.

In the less desirable unskilled, low-wage labor market where racial integration has been highest (Tomaskovic-Devey et al., 2006), closure may operate differently (Reskin & Roos, 1990). Pressures for exclusion are weaker for less desirable positions, where Whites may not always gain preference over African Americans. In fact, in this segment of the job market, African Americans exhibit strong personal networks from which they can gain job referrals, though this does not always translate into hiring (Fernandez & Fernandez-Mateo, 2006; McDonald, Lin, & Ao, 2009). Even when Whites and African Americans are successful at gaining employment, job channeling can produce inequalities. In the unskilled job market, Whites are more likely to be channeled upward to a higher position than is advertised, while African Americans are more likely to be channeled downward (Pager et al., 2009).

How do recessions affect social closure? Social closure is both a conscious and unconscious process (Roscigno, 2007; Stainback, 2008; Weber, 1968), and active closure is strongest when status or class advantages are challenged (Chamberlain, Crowley, Tope, & Hodson, 2008; Hodson, Roscigno, & Lopez, 2006; Roscigno, Lopez & Hodson, 2009; Stainback, Tomaskovic-Devey, & Skaggs, 2010; Uggen & Blackstone, 2004). Some research finds that employment segregation declines as demand for workers rises (Szafran, 1982, 1984; see Reskin, 1993). Correspondingly, when many workers are available for few positions, employers will select only those most-preferred applicants at the front of the queue. By this logic, in a labor market flush with jobseekers, the combined effects of human capital and race may further displace younger and less-educated African American males while simultaneously extending White applicants' privileged position in the labor queue as they also begin to seek low-wage (or any) labor. Following Weber (1968), if the dominant status group clings more tightly to the available positions during recessions, they will reserve even the least desirable jobs for in-group members. While "individualistic" characteristics such as educational credentials, trade union membership, and professional licensure can be used for social closure in the professional and skilled job market (Weeden, 2002), if employment becomes scarce even in the unskilled labor market, easily ascertained ascribed characteristics (such as race) may become a de facto differentiator for superordinate groups (Weber, 1968). In such a scenario, we expect that African American disadvantage in hiring will be further compounded during a recession as Whites displace African Americans in the low-wage labor queue (Reskin & Roos, 1990). This scenario leads to the following hypothesis:

Hypothesis 3$_A$. Race differences in hiring outcomes will be significantly greater during recessions than in non-recessionary periods.

Social closure usually considers *workers'* actions to exclude out-group members, but this hypothesis suggests that employers and managers would similarly act to exclude African American applicants as the labor market slackens. That is, the current regime of social closure would shift during recessions from reserving more desirable positions to reserving *all* positions for in-group members, but only if hiring authorities participate in this shift. If not, we would expect proportional losses during the recession.

Proportionate Disadvantage: Durability of Inequality

Broad structural changes, such as deindustrialization, deunionization, and outsourcing, often specifically disadvantage African Americans (Bound & Freeman, 1992; Hill & Negrey, 2010; Johnson et al., 2008; McKee, 2008; Sugrue, 2005). Phenomena such as these may bear little on statistical discrimination as they carry no signal regarding worker productivity, though they clearly affect the length of labor queues and the size of the labor pool. More generally, societywide phenomena (like economic recessions) should be less stigmatizing than individual-level characteristics, such as criminal records and the lack of educational credentials.

Whether the Great Recession of 2007–2009 systematically disadvantaged African Americans remains an open question. Because researchers cannot foresee and manipulate recessions, the extant research has emphasized historical and observational analysis of job loss, greatly complicating efforts to draw causal inferences about racial discrimination in hiring. Beyond methodological barriers to studying structural changes like recessions, it may also be true that the "resilient nature of inequality" across time and various structural contexts will result in similar hiring trends by race in recessionary periods (Tilly, 1999; Wilson, Roscigno, & Huffman, 2015).

Indeed, Tilly's (1999) work on durable inequality provides theoretical expectations for a similar pattern of hiring during recessionary periods. Theories of social closure draw heavily on the actions of workers, rather than managers, to restrict outsiders to privileged positions through processes such as licensures. Tilly states, however, that these wider institutionalized forms of social closure legitimate staffing practices for organizations and their hiring managers. That is, organizational isomorphism results from widely disseminated routines and models. In fact, organizations would prefer to avoid costs that may result from experimenting with and developing new hiring structures that would require re-legitimation. Thus, even in the face of a recession, hiring managers would still default to their typical hiring practices regarding the likelihood of hiring those from subordinate subpopulations. If inequality remains durable regardless of the structural conditions due to prior legitimized hiring practices (Tilly, 1999), we expect African Americans to receive a proportionate amount of employment opportunities in the low-wage labor market both prior to and during a recession.

Indeed, there is no evidence in studies of past recessions that African Americans are the last hired in the queue of available positions (Couch & Fairlie, 2010). This would suggest equivalent losses for Whites and African Americans based on societal shifts (such as recessions) and disproportionately worse losses for racial minorities with individual-level stigmatizing characteristics (such as criminal records). This leads to the following null hypothesis:

Hypothesis 3_0. Race differences in hiring outcomes will not differ significantly during recessions relative to non-recessionary periods.

We offered hypotheses regarding three effects on hiring behavior: the main effect of race, the main effect of recession, and the interaction effect between race and recession. The latter, also known as a difference-in-difference (because it measures the difference between race categories in the recession-induced drop in hiring), considers whether race effects are more pronounced during a recessionary period. We note that the combined effects of Hypotheses 1 and 2 would result in considerable disadvantage for African American applicants during a recession. It is unknown, however, whether the recession would further disadvantage African American applicants beyond these main effects; that is, whether there is a significant difference-in-difference.

In line with our hypotheses, we next examine two specific interactions of race and the recession: (1) the likelihood that applicants receive employer callbacks in a field experiment; and, (2) the likelihood that unemployed jobseekers find work in a nationally representative survey. The field experiment examines high school educated young men applying to unskilled entry-level positions in a single metropolitan area, thus holding other potential sources of disadvantage during the recession constant (male, unskilled, non-college youth). Because it straddled the official start of the recession, this study adds new experimental evidence to a literature that has thus far relied solely on observational analysis

of survey data. We test the robustness of our experimental findings using the
NLSY97 survey, analyzing the odds that unemployed high school educated
young men gain employment. We take advantage of weekly employment arrays
to assess job acquisition in the year before the recession and first year of the
recession, mirroring our experiment to as great a degree as possible, while
adjusting for the varying qualifications of respondents. Consistent findings in
both analyses would lend greater support to our hypothesis tests.

METHODS

Field Experiment

From August 2007 to June 2008, we conducted a field experiment on the effect
of low-level criminal records and race on receiving a callback for entry-level
positions from employers in the Minneapolis-St. Paul-Bloomington metropolitan area. The Great Recession officially began during the course of the study,
providing a rare opportunity to experimentally assess race differentials in recession effects. In the original study design, pairs of applicant "testers" of the
same race were sent to job sites to apply for employment, with one presenting a
fabricated criminal record. For this study, we use only the applicant in the pair
that presented no criminal record, so that our design conforms to a randomized
complete block design (Cox, 1958). That is, race of the applicant, as the experimental treatment, is randomly assigned to each employer in our sample.
Because the recession cannot be experimentally manipulated and there is random assignment of race to employers pre-recession and during the recession,
the recession effect represents a "block."[2]

As in our original design, many field experiments on racial discrimination
employ a "matched" approach (Pager, 2007a), which we now lack. The matched
approach, however, is not necessary unless one wishes to account for employer
effects (e.g., by including employer-specific intercepts for employers who call
back both or neither testers (see Vuolo, Uggen, & Lageson, 2016; Agresti, 2002,
pp. 410–411, 467–468, 493–501)).[3] Such approaches are preferable when race
cannot be randomly assigned (Pager, 2007a, p. 123), as is the case when the unit
of analysis is applicants. With the employer as the unit of analysis, however,
race is randomly assigned to the *employer being sampled*.[4] In this randomized
complete block design, as in other experimental approaches, the randomization
process should ensure no systematic bias in that assignment (Cox, 1958).[5]

Sampling and Experimental Procedures
Our experimental unit (to which applicant race is randomly assigned) is the
employer, with effects blocked by the recession. The research team directed

testers to apply to positions, based on available job postings. Each Sunday, the job classifieds from five print sources (*Minneapolis Star Tribune, St. Paul Pioneer Press, Employment News, Employment Guide*, and *JobDig*) and one online source (*Craigslist*) were reviewed. All entry-level advertisements were included in the sample, as long as they had no special skill requirements (such as a specialized license to operate machinery), instructed applicants to apply in-person, and were located in the seven-county, Twin Cities metropolitan area.[6] Eight male college students in their early twenties were selected as testers.[7] We fabricated tester biographies to be similar in every regard, except for race iden-tifiers (for instance, African American resumes indicated participation in African American student groups, helping to convey race to employers). These biographies presented similar working-class education, employment, and per-sonal backgrounds.[8] Simple randomization was used to allocate the jobs among eight applicant testers, each of whom applied for an average of seven jobs per week. Upon arriving at the application site, testers completed applications, sub-mitted their resumes, and attempted to maximize personal contact by asking to speak to the manager. The latter further ensured that the race of the tester was conveyed to the hiring authority. Our total sample includes 605 employers, with each of the eight testers completing approximately 75 tests.

Variables: Dependent (Callback), Experimental (Race), and
Blocking Effects (Recession)
The primary dependent variable in our experimental analysis is an employer "callback." A callback represents a tangible positive response from an employer: an on-site job offer, an on-site offer for an interview, a job offer through voice-mail, an offer for an interview through voicemail, or a call from an employer for something beyond a reference or request for basic information. Callbacks were tracked for four weeks after each tester left the field.

Our main experimental treatment is the randomly assigned race of the appli-cant. For the recession block, we constructed an indicator variable for the block in which the test occurred. According to the U.S. National Bureau of Economic Research (the official arbiter of U.S. recessions), the Great Recession began in December 2007 (NBER, 2008) and lasted until June 2009 (NBER, 2010). Formally, NBER defines a recession as "a significant decline in the eco-nomic activity spread across the economy, lasting more than a few months, normally visible in production, employment, real income, and other indicators" (2008, p. 1). For our purposes, all tests that occurred from August 2007 to November 2007 were coded as pre-recession, and all tests from December 2007 to June 2008 were coded as occurring during the recession.

Though the precise timing of the recession varied to some extent across regions, Fig. 2 shows that Minnesota generally tracked the nation in entering the recession (Grunewald & Madden, 2009). After a long period of relative pros-perity, unemployment began rising at the start of the recession in December

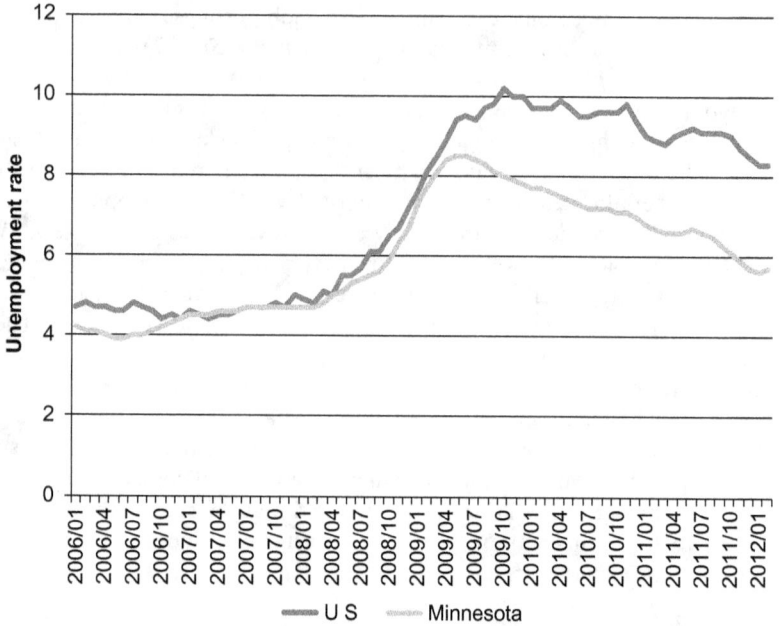

Fig. 2. Unemployment Rate in Minnesota and the United States, 2006–2012. *Source*: Minnesota Department of Employment and Economic Development, 2006–2012.

2007, in the midst of our experiment. Minnesota and its Federal Reserve District may have recovered more quickly than other areas (Grunewald & Madden, 2009), although Minnesota followed national trends through at least mid-2009.

For a randomized complete block experimental design, the method of analysis is typically analysis of variance and linear regression. Because our outcome is dichotomous, we instead use standard logistic regression models. We employ several alternative coding schemes for race and recession effects in order to assess the magnitude and significance of both difference-in-differences and between-group differences. We present models with control variables to adjust for the possibility of incomplete randomization and to assess the strength of the treatment and block effects. These include the source of the advertisement (online vs. paper), whether the test occurred in Minneapolis-St. Paul or a suburb, the industry, whether testers made contact with a hiring authority, and whether they observed persons of color working in the establishment. Our randomization procedure leads us to expect no relationship between the control variables and the experimental and blocking effects.

Survey Data: National Longitudinal Survey of Youth 1997 (NLSY97)

The NLSY97 is a nationally representative survey of U.S. residents born from 1980 to 1984; that is, ages 12–16 in 1997 (U.S. Department of Labor, 2003). Conducted by the U.S. Bureau of Labor Statistics, the survey's primary goal is to collect information on labor market behavior and educational experiences. The survey began in 1997 with a sample of 8,984 respondents. We examine weekly and monthly arrays and individual questions from the annual surveys taken before and during the Great Recession (from 2005 to 2008). Across those survey years, retention rates varied from 81.8% to 83.3%. In 2007, the year the recession began, respondents were between the ages of 21 and 26. We selected a subset of respondents to closely resemble the biographies presented by our testers in the field experiment. Thus, our analyses included only those unemployed in either the pre-recession or recession periods, males, Whites and African Americans, and those with no more than a high school education.[9]

Given our interest in the two periods, we reorganized the data as a two-observation panel data structure. To track unemployment[10] and job acquisition, we use the NLSY97's weekly arrays of employment data. We define the pre-recessionary period as the 52-week array occurring prior to December 2007, with the subsequent 52-week array defined as during the recession.[11] Within our subset, there are 772 unique individuals and 976 observations.[12]

Variables and Statistical Analyses
The dependent variable in the NLSY97 analysis is job acquisition. A respondent was coded as acquiring a job if they were coded in the employment array as unemployed in a given week and then coded as having a job in a subsequent week in the period. Unlike our experiment, survey respondents apply for jobs with widely varying work histories, many of which are related to both race and recession. We therefore include control variables, such as the weeks worked in the year prior to the start of each period, again based on the weekly employment arrays. Given the non-normal and non-uniform distribution of this predictor, we use four categories evenly dividing the 52-week period. We also adjust for the industry and occupation of the last job held, using the socioeconomic index (SEI) for males developed by Hauser and Warren (1997),[13] reported income in the preceding year,[14] receipt of unemployment insurance, and two measures of educational performance and participation. For the latter, these include self-reported high school academic performance[15] and a dummy variable indicating any college attendance.[16] Finally, we include an indicator of whether the respondent reported being convicted of any crime in the last year, which is known to affect job prospects (Pager, 2007b).

Since the effect of the recession varies regionally, we include indicator variables for U.S. Census Region, as well as an indicator for urban location, relative to rural. We also include several life course indicators that may affect gaining employment, including migration to a different county within the last year, parenthood (differentiated by child's residential status), and marital status. As a measure of socioeconomic background of origin, we control for parents' highest education, coded from years of education reported by the parents themselves. Finally, we include age as a control due to the five-year age range included in the NLSY97.

With partially dependent data structured with two observations, we use the "xtgee" procedure in Stata 14.0 to estimate Generalized Estimating Equations (GEE) with a logit link and robust standard errors.[17] We use population averaged models because we wish to compare two like individuals of different races (i.e., an "average" White applicant and an "average" African American applicant). The same logic applies to the recession effect.[18]

FIELD EXPERIMENT RESULTS

Main Effects and Difference-in-Difference

Model 1 in Table 1 shows the main effects of the experimental treatment of race and the block effect of the recession. Both are statistically significant. Consistent with research on racial discrimination in hiring and supporting Hypothesis 1, Whites are 85% more likely to receive an employer callback than African Americans ($p < .01$). Supporting Hypothesis 2, there is also a substantial recession effect; applicants are 53% less likely to receive a callback during the recession than they are in the four months preceding the recession ($p < .001$).

Model 2 shows that these effects are robust to several control measures. The only significant new predictor is contact with the hiring authority. Testers who made contact with the hiring authority were 3.2 times as likely as others to receive a callback.[19] Even with the control measures, however, the magnitude and significance of the race and recession effects are little changed. This stability in the coefficients and standard errors is due to the small amount of covariation between the controls and the race and recession effects, further attesting to successful randomization. Fig. 3 shows the predicted probabilities derived from Model 1, which mirror the raw callback rate. Prior to the recession, Whites received callbacks 44% of the time, compared to 30% for African Americans. During the recession, employers called back Whites 27% of the time, compared to 17% for African Americans. The recession-era White callback rate is thus nearly equivalent to the pre-recession African American rate.

Before explicating these between-group differences, we consider Hypothesis 3, testing whether the declining rate of callbacks during the recession was of greater magnitude for African Americans than for Whites. For African Americans, the callback rate dropped 13 percentage points or 44% (($29.5 - 16.6)/29.5 = 43.7$), relative to a 17 percentage point or 38% decrease

Table 1. Experiment Logistic Regressions for Callback Received Testing Main Effects and Difference-in-Difference.

	Model 1		Model 2		Model 3		Model 4	
	Coefficient (St. Error.)	Odds Ratio	Coefficient (St. Error.)	Odds Ratio	Coefficient (St. Error.)	Odds Ratio	Coefficient (St. Error.)	Odds Ratio
(Intercept)	-0.870***		-1.170***		-0.801**		-1.140***	
	(0.202)		(0.302)		(0.257)		(0.349)	
White (vs. African American)	0.618**	1.854	0.610**	1.841	0.528	1.695	0.573	1.773
	(0.206)		(0.214)		(0.294)		(0.307)	
Recession (vs. pre-recession)	-0.744***	0.475	-0.798***	0.450	-0.845**	0.430	-0.839**	0.432
	(0.203)		(0.219)		(0.312)		(0.327)	
White × recession					0.173	1.189	0.073	1.076
					(0.409)		(0.428)	
Contact with hiring authority			1.124***	3.076			1.123***	3.074
			(0.204)				(0.204)	
Online source (vs. paper)			0.024	1.024			0.023	1.023
			(0.228)				(0.228)	
In MSP (vs. suburbs)			-0.056	0.946			-0.059	0.946
			(0.210)				(0.210)	
Observed minority employees			0.111	1.118			0.110	1.116
			(0.202)				(0.202)	
Industry (vs. restaurant)								
Office work			-0.614	0.541			-0.613	0.542
			(0.475)				(0.475)	
Retail			-0.195	0.823			-0.198	0.820
			(0.280)				(0.280)	

Table 1. (*Continued*)

	Model 1		Model 2		Model 3		Model 4	
	Coefficient (St. Error.)	Odds Ratio	Coefficient (St. Error.)	Odds Ratio	Coefficient (St. Error.)	Odds Ratio	Coefficient (St. Error.)	Odds Ratio
Healthcare			0.569 (0.730)	1.767			0.568 (0.730)	1.764
Warehouse/labor			-0.361 (0.292)	0.697			-0.359 (0.292)	0.698
Hotel			0.176 (0.327)	1.193			0.175 (0.327)	1.191
Driver			0.169 (0.492)	1.182			0.164 (0.493)	1.179
Security			-0.525 (0.814)	0.592			-0.529 (0.814)	0.589
Log-likelihood	-343.42		-343.33				-321.90	
Model χ^2 (df)	39.16*** (2)		39.34*** (3)				81.51*** (13)	

Note: Industry differences are non-significant regardless of baseline.

*p < .05.
**p < .01.
***p < .001.

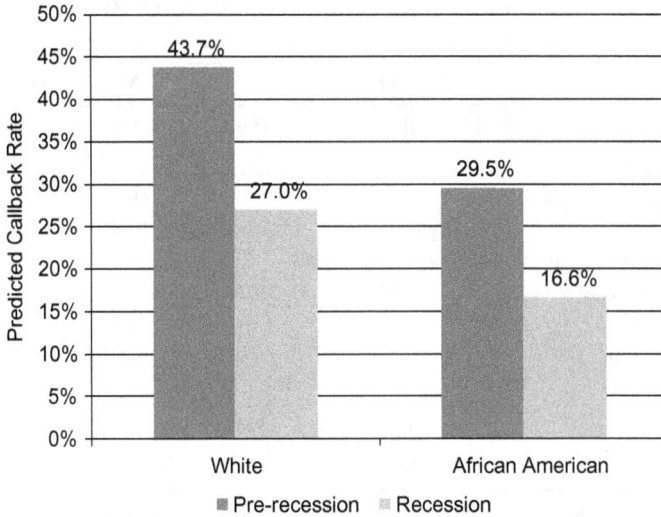

Fig. 3. Experiment Predicted Callback Rate by Race and Recession (Derived from Table 1, Model 1).

for Whites $((43.7 - 27.0)/43.7 = 38.2)$. Model 3 of Table 1 formally tests this difference-in-difference, indicating no significant racial difference in the callback decline between the two periods. We therefore cannot reject the null hypothesis (Hypothesis 3_0) that the recession affected young African American and White men equally, at least in terms of their ability to garner a favorable employer response.[20] Model 4 demonstrates that inclusion of our control measures does not alter this conclusion, with a coefficient for the difference-in-difference close to zero. Of course, the pre-recession starting point was much lower for African Americans than for Whites. We next explore such between-group differences.

Between-Group Differences

In Table 2, we modify the coding of race and recession effects to test whether the differences between each of the four groups in Fig. 3 are statistically significant. Model 5 thus contains the same information as Model 3 in Table 1 (as evidenced by the equivalent log-likelihood and model chi-squared), but uses "simple" coding (see Cohen, 1968) against a new baseline — that of African American testers during the recession period. This model confirms that all other race/recession groups are significantly more likely to receive a callback than are African Americans during the recession. Whites in the recession are twice as likely to receive a callback ($p < .05$); African Americans before the recession are 2.3 times as likely to receive a callback ($p < .01$); and, Whites before the

Table 2. Experiment Logistic Regressions for Callback Received Testing between-Group Differences by Race and Recession.

	Model 5 (No Controls)		Model 6 (Controls)	
	Coefficient (St. Error.)	Odds Ratio	Coefficient (St. Error.)	Odds Ratio
(Intercept)	−1.646***		−1.980***	
	(0.177)		(0.300)	
Race by recession (vs. African American, during recession)				
White, during recession	0.701*	2.016	0.646*	1.908
	(0.286)		(0.298)	
African American, pre-recession	0.845**	2.328	0.839**	2.315
	(0.312)		(0.328)	
White, pre-recession	1.373***	3.946	1.412***	4.105
	(0.228)		(0.245)	

Note: Since these models are only a change in coding of race and recession, the log-likelihood, Model χ^2, and estimates of the controls for Model 6 are the same as Model 4. See Table 1, Model 4 for those values.
*$p < .05$.
**$p < .01$.
***$p < .001$.

recession are almost 4 times as likely to receive a callback ($p < .001$), all relative to African American applicants during the recession. Again, these estimates are little changed by the addition of covariates in Model 6.

Table 3 shows each of the possible comparisons between the groups in our field experiment. The first row is described above. When the baseline is shifted to Whites during the recession, Whites pre-recession are about twice as likely to receive a callback ($p < .05$). As evidenced in Fig. 3, the difference between Whites *during* the recession and African Americans *pre*-recession is small and not statistically significant, indicating near equality in their viability as job candidates. Finally, Whites pre-recession are about 70% more likely to receive a callback than African Americans pre-recession, though this effect is only marginally significant ($p = .07$).[21]

Three main conclusions emerge from the models. First, the recession appears to have had a comparable effect on White and African American applicants, with prospects for young men of both races dimming by approximately equal amounts as would be expected by theories of durable inequality. Both before and during the recession, however, these prospects were much lower for African Americans than for Whites, leading to our second conclusion: that African Americans *prior* to the recession had approximately the same probability of getting a favorable employer response as Whites *during* the recession. Finally, African Americans during the recession are clearly in the most

Table 3.   Odds Ratios for All Between-Group Differences by Race and
Recession from Field Experiment and NLSY97.

	Comparison		
	White, Recession	African American, Pre-recession	White, Pre-recession
A. Field experiment (callbacks)			
Baseline			
African American, recession	2.02*	2.33**	3.95***
White, recession		1.15	1.96*
African American, pre-recession			1.70#
B. NLSY97 Survey (job acquisition)			
Baseline			
African American, recession	1.82*	1.66**	3.23***
White, recession		0.91	1.77*
African American, pre-recession			1.94*

Note: Field experiment odds ratios come from Table 2, Model 5. NLSY97 survey odds ratios come
from Table 5, Model 12.
#$p = .07$.
*$p < .05$.
**$p < .01$.
***$p < .001$.

disadvantaged position due to the main effects of both race and recession.
Compared to all other groups, such applicants have much lower odds of receiving callbacks from employers. Relative to all other race/recession combinations,
African Americans during the recession were 63% less likely to receive a callback ($p < .001$).[22] In short, the estimated recession effect is constant by race.
Nevertheless, racial differences in hiring that are independent of the recession
cause African Americans to be highly disadvantaged during periods of economic contraction.

NLSY97 SURVEY RESULTS

Main Effects and Difference-in Difference

To test the results of our field experiment on a nationally representative sample,
we next analyze NLSY97 data for those unemployed males with only a high
school education seeking employment in the year prior to and during the

recession. Irrespective of race, the percentage acquiring employment is higher in the year prior to the recession (76%) than during the recession (67%). There are, however, considerable differences by race. Prior to the recession, 83% of unemployed Whites gained employment, while only 67% of African Americans did so. During the recession, this number decreases to 77% for Whites and 56% for African Americans. These probabilities mirror those from a logistic regression with no controls, as shown in Model 7 of Table 4. Here, Whites are 2.6 times as likely as African Americans to acquire employment ($p < .001$) and jobseekers during the recession are 33% less likely to find work than those in the pre-recession period ($p < .01$). Model 8 confirms that the difference-in-difference is non-significant. Unlike the field experiment, White and African American applicants, and potentially those applying before and during a recession, present varying qualifications to employers. We therefore use covariate-adjustment to better estimate the difference between White and African American males of similar qualifications, and to better understand the difference-in-difference between the two periods.[23] Indeed, the race effect decreases when controls are added to the model, as some of the unadjusted race effect is due to differences on the controls.

Models 9 and 10 in Table 4 depict the covariate-adjusted models. The results for the main effects of race and recession in Model 9 again lend support to Hypotheses 1 and 2. Net of all controls, White males are 88% more likely to acquire a job than African American males ($p < .01$), while those applying during the recession are 41% less likely to gain employment ($p < .01$). Among the significant control variables, those respondents working more weeks in the previous year are more likely to acquire a job, as are those with higher incomes. Those who migrated in the last year between counties were 76% more likely to get a job, while those convicted of a crime were 54% less likely to find employment.[24]

Fig. 4 shows the predicted probability of job acquisition from Model 9 while holding the control variables constant at their respective means – a comparison of equally qualified candidates of each race in both periods. In the year prior to the recession, unemployed White males acquired a job 85% of the time, compared to 75% for African Americans. During the recession, Whites acquired employment 77% of the time, compared to 64% for African Americans. As with the callback rate in the experiment, rates for Whites during the recession were nearly equivalent to those of African Americans prior to the recession.

Model 10 presents the difference-in-difference. For African Americans, the callback rate dropped 8 percentage points or 15% (($75.0 - 63.8)/75.0 = 15.0$), relative to an 11 percentage point or 10% decrease for Whites (($84.9 - 76.8)/84.9 = 9.6$). The coefficient for the race-by-recession interaction in Model 10 testing this difference-in-difference is not statistically significant and close to zero in magnitude (and in a direction opposite to our hypothesis, as demonstrated by the higher percentage point reduction for Whites). As in the

Table 4. NLSY97 GEE Logit for Acquired Employment Testing Main Effects and Difference-in-Difference with Robust SEs.

	Model 7		Model 8		Model 9		Model 10	
	Coefficient (St. Error.)	Odds Ratio	Coefficient (St. Error.)	Odds Ratio	Coefficient (St. Error.)	Odds Ratio	Coefficient (St. Error.)	Odds Ratio
(Intercept)	0.690*** (0.122)		0.706*** (0.138)		1.331 (1.599)		1.313 (1.606)	
White (vs. African American)	0.963*** (0.153)	2.619	0.923*** (0.217)	2.517	0.630** (0.202)	1.877	0.665* (0.270)	1.944
Recession (vs. pre-recession)	−0.405** (0.144)	0.667	−0.436* (0.189)	0.647	−0.534** (0.181)	0.586	−0.507* (0.229)	0.602
White × recession			0.074 (0.291)	1.077			−0.066 (0.336)	0.936
Weeks worked in previous year (vs. 0–13)								
14–26					0.576* (0.267)	1.779	0.577* (0.267)	1.781
27–39					0.946*** (0.276)	2.575	0.947*** (0.276)	2.577
39–52					0.858*** (0.230)	2.357	0.858*** (0.229)	2.358
Received unemployment insurance					0.654 (0.426)	1.922	0.653 (0.426)	1.921

Table 4. (*Continued*)

	Model 7		Model 8		Model 9		Model 10	
	Coefficient (St. Error.)	Odds Ratio	Coefficient (St. Error.)	Odds Ratio	Coefficient (St. Error.)	Odds Ratio	Coefficient (St. Error.)	Odds Ratio
Industry of last job (vs. none in two years)								
Construction					0.153 (0.414)	1.165	0.154 (0.414)	1.167
Manufacturing					−0.023 (0.413)	0.977	−0.023 (0.413)	0.977
Retail trade					0.063 (0.418)	1.066	0.068 (0.419)	1.070
Transportation and warehousing					0.070 (0.504)	1.072	0.076 (0.504)	1.079
Professional and related services					−0.095 (0.403)	0.909	−0.094 (0.402)	0.910
Entertainment, accommodations, & food services					0.022 (0.380)	1.023	0.023 (0.380)	1.023
Other					0.076 (0.391)	1.079	0.074 (0.392)	1.077
Hauser & Warren SEI Male					0.015 (0.010)	1.015	0.015 (0.010)	1.015
Income (thousands)					0.030*** (0.009)	1.030	0.030*** (0.009)	1.030
High school grades					−0.032 (0.052)	0.969	−0.032 (0.052)	0.969

	b (SE)	Exp(b)	b (SE)	Exp(b)
Ever attended college	0.052 (0.195)	1.053	0.052 (0.195)	1.053
Convicted of crime in last year	−0.778** (0.293)	0.459	−0.779** (0.294)	0.459
Age	−0.085 (0.061)	0.918	−0.085 (0.061)	0.918
Census region (vs. Northeast)				
North Central	0.179 (0.263)	1.196	0.178 (0.263)	1.194
South	0.118 (0.232)	1.126	0.118 (0.232)	1.125
West	0.097 (0.299)	1.101	0.097 (0.300)	1.102
Urban (vs. rural)	0.239 (0.195)	1.270	0.240 (0.195)	1.271
Migrated between counties	0.563* (0.226)	1.756	0.562* (0.226)	1.754
Children (vs. none)				
Non-residential	0.059 (0.195)	1.061	0.061 (0.195)	1.063
Residential	0.343 (0.257)	1.410	0.344 (0.257)	1.410
Married	0.024 (0.245)	1.024	0.023 (0.244)	1.023

Table 4. (*Continued*)

	Model 7		Model 8		Model 9		Model 10	
	Coefficient (St. Error.)	Odds Ratio	Coefficient (St. Error.)	Odds Ratio	Coefficient (St. Error.)	Odds Ratio	Coefficient (St. Error.)	Odds Ratio
Parents' education (vs. HS or less)								
Some college or associates					−0.030	0.970	−0.029	0.971
					(0.197)		(0.197)	
Bachelors or higher					0.303	1.354	0.303	1.353
					(0.280)		(0.280)	
No parent information					0.269	1.309	0.267	1.306
					(0.305)		(0.305)	
Model chi-squared	46.66*** (2)		47.29*** (3)		118.22*** (30)		118.09*** (31)	

*p < .05.
**p < .01.
***p < .001.

experiment, we again cannot reject the null hypothesis (3_0) of an equal reduction in job prospects between the two periods by race.

Between-Group Differences

We again repeated the analyses using simple coding to compare the race by recession groups, as shown in Table 5. We concentrate on the covariate-adjusted estimates in Model 12. Relative to the baseline of African Americans during the recession, Whites during the recession were 82% more likely to find work ($p < .05$). African Americans prior to the recession were 66% more likely to acquire a job compared to their counterparts during the recession ($p < .05$). Finally, Whites before the recession were 3.2 times more likely to find work than African Americans during the recession ($p < .001$).

Table 3 shows all possible NLSY97 race by recession group comparisons. The first row repeats the results of Model 12. The next row changes the baseline to Whites during the recession, showing that pre-recession Whites were 77% more likely to find jobs ($p < .05$). The contrast between recession-period Whites and pre-recession African Americans is not statistically significant, with an odds ratio close to 1. Again, this effect size supports the idea that African

Table 5. NLSY97 GEE Logit for Acquired Employment Testing between-Group Differences with Robust SEs.

	Model 11 (No Controls)		Model 12 (Controls)	
	Coefficient (St. Error.)	Odds Ratio	Coefficient (St. Error.)	Odds Ratio
(Intercept)	0.271*		0.806	
	(0.132)		(1.653)	
Race by recession (vs. African American, during recession)				
White, during recession	0.997***	2.711	0.599*	1.820
	(0.205)		(0.256)	
African American, pre-recession	0.436*	1.546	0.507*	1.661
	(0.189)		(0.229)	
White, pre-recession	1.358***	3.890	1.172***	3.229
	(0.213)		(0.272)	

Note: Since these models are only a change in coding of race and recession, the Model χ^2 and estimates of the controls for Model 12 are the same as Model 10. See Table 4, Model 10 for those values.
*$p < .05$.
**$p < .01$.
***$p < .001$.

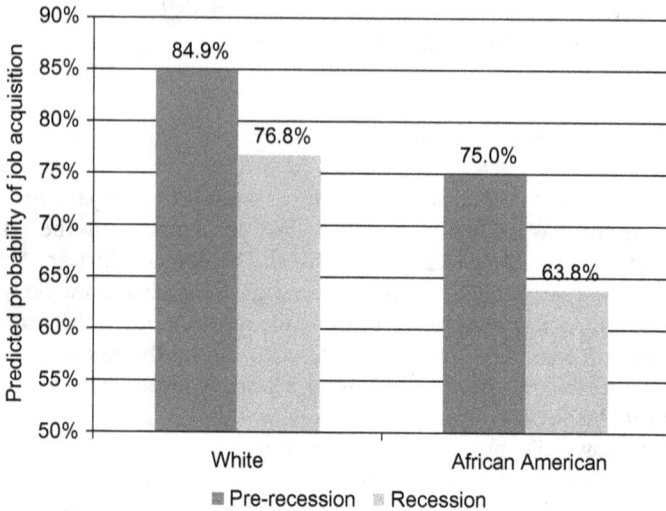

Fig. 4. NLSY97 Predicted Probability of Job Acquisition (Derived from Table 4, Model 9).

American job opportunities in good times approximate those of Whites in hard times. Conversely, in the pre-recession period, Whites were 94% more likely to acquire employment than African Americans ($p < .05$).

All three main experimental findings are thus replicated in the nationally representative survey. First, the prospects of gaining employment decreased during the recession by similar amounts for both White and African American unskilled job applicants. Second, Whites *during* a recession (77%) gain favorable employer responses about as often as African Americans *prior* to a recession (75%). Finally, although the drop across the periods is roughly proportional, the main effects of race and recession combine to put African Americans in the most disadvantaged position. African Americans' lower odds of finding work will likely translate into a diminished socioeconomic future and greater difficulty recovering from the recent deep recession.

LIMITATIONS AND STRENGTHS

This multi-method analysis has limitations that merit discussion, though the limitations of one approach are often the strengths of the other approach. First, we use a simple indicator variable to mark the recession, though recessions represent complex combinations of economic variables over long periods of time (NBER, 2008). Yet, our indicator approach has the advantage of conforming to an established experimental design, which we then mimic in the survey data. People also identify and experience recessions as a qualitative state (yes/no) rather than a continuum and this label has its own implications for behavior, with consequences for employers and applicants. Nevertheless, as shown in Table 6, we obtain similar results when we block on specific months in the experiment rather than the recession dichotomy.

Table 6 shows that the drop in callback rates begins immediately in December with the official start of the recession and remains consistent in magnitude across the recession months. Model comparisons show, however, that the more complex model with month blocks does not fit the data better than the dichotomous recession indicator ($\chi^2 = 6.03$, df $= 9$, $p = 0.74$). By most indicators, the recession deepened throughout 2008 and much of 2009, so a longer observation period may have altered our results, particularly if dominant status groups feel increasingly threatened as the recession progressed and if hiring practices alter to incorporate such social closure. Although Figs. 1 and 2 show the unemployment rate increasing substantially after our experiment ended, we emphasize that unemployment is just one measure of the presence of a recession. We also emphasize that our analyses focus on *hiring outcomes* rather than job loss, which captures the immediate effects of the recession. Indeed, we observed strong and immediate recession effects on hiring, with callback rates dropping precipitously in the first month of December 2007. While we are limited by the end date of our experiment, we tested this idea by analyzing the second year of the recession as a third time point in the NLSY97 panel models, which again supports a proportionate decrease for both White and African American young men.[25]

Second, our experimental findings pertain to a single metropolitan area. Given the high ratio of African American-to-White unemployment in the Twin Cities (Austin, 2011, 2012), however, this area provides an important site for testing racial disproportionality in employment, and the nationally representative survey results affirm the findings of this single location.[26]

Third, our outcomes are not identical in the experiment and the survey. The experiment measured the first step in the hiring process (an employer callback) and the NLSY97 measured actual job acquisition. Survey respondents may have received invitations for interviews and even unrequited job offers (analogous to callbacks in the experiment) while unemployed, but they would not be coded affirmatively on our response variable until they actually accept work. Relatedly, while our testers only used formal means to apply for positions, survey respondents could use any means to acquire employment and were selected on the basis of unemployment, which omits employed jobseekers. While we do not directly address informal job search and networks in gaining entry-level employment, for which a complex race picture emerges (see, e.g., Moss & Tilly, 2001; Fernandez & Fernandez-Mateo, 2006; Stainback, 2008), similar conclusions regarding the low-wage labor queue emerge from both of our methodologies.

Fourth, while we held the other noted sources of disadvantage constant at their lowest levels (young age, high school education, unskilled) in the

Table 6.   Experiment Logistic Regression for Callback Received with Month
Blocks.

	Model 13	
	Coefficient (St. Error.)	Odds Ratio
(Intercept)	−0.642*	
	(0.256)	
White (vs. African American)	0.496*	1.642
	(0.224)	
Month (vs. Pre-recession: October)		
Pre-recession: August	0.369	1.446
	(0.518)	
Pre-recession: September	−0.196	0.822
	(0.295)	
Pre-recession: November	−0.473	0.623
	(0.349)	
Recession: December	−0.779$^{\#}$	0.459
	(0.458)	
Recession: January	−0.885*	0.425
	(0.375)	
Recession: February	−0.713$^{\#}$	0.490
	(0.381)	
Recession: March	−0.886*	0.412
	(0.377)	
Recession: April	−0.880*	0.415
	(0.406)	
Recession: May	−1.661**	0.190
	(0.854)	
Recession: June	−1.204$^{\#}$	0.300
	(0.672)	
Log-likelihood	−340.406	
Model χ^2 (df)	45.18*** (11)	

$^{\#}p < .10.$
$^{*}p < .05.$
$^{**}p < .01.$
$^{***}p < .001.$

experiment, the NLSY97 analysis represents observational data, such that our estimate of the race effect before and during the recession must be adjusted by characteristics that affect candidate viability. While we attempted to control for as many confounders as possible, the estimate may still be subject to omitted variable bias. For example, while our experimental testers were trained for uniform presentation, no such uniformity necessarily exists in observational data and is not easily controlled.

Finally, while losses and disadvantage should be most pronounced among the subset we analyzed, a shared limitation of both the experiment and the survey is that we do not address the experiences of older men, Latinos, women, or more skilled workers. Latinos constitute an increasing percentage of the low-wage labor markets, with Pager et al. (2009) finding that Latino men receive a similar callback rate to Whites, but significantly higher than African Americans. Although an analysis of women could be conducted with the NLSY97,[27] we lack the corresponding experimental data needed for causal inferences. In our view, analysis of gender, race, and recession is an important topic for subsequent research. We are also limited in our ability to draw conclusions about the skilled labor market, given the low numbers of unemployed college-educated men in the NLSY97.[28] In our experiment, we might even expect our applicants to be favored for low-wage positions, as employers might assume skilled workers will leave such positions as soon as they were able. Yet, our applicants still experience the noted decreases in callbacks. Even with these caveats, the comparison examined here is still of critical theoretical and policy concern, even among this specific segment of the low-wage labor market. Through a rigorous field experiment and validation via a nationally representative sample, we can speak confidently to the role of labor queues and social closure in the low-wage labor market for young White and African American men.

DISCUSSION: RACE AND RECESSION

For decades, social scientists have clearly documented racial discrimination in employment opportunities and socioeconomic outcomes (Pager & Shepherd, 2008). In predicting such outcomes, race appears to interact with many other sources of disadvantage or stigma. We here asked whether the recent Great Recession, considered the worst economic downturn since the Great Depression, compounded racial discrimination in employment opportunities, or if racial inequality in the labor market is truly durable and stable throughout recessionary and non-recessionary periods. We examined this question using a field experiment in which the effect of applicant race was varied randomly, with other sources of disadvantage held constant (these include sex, age, education, job skills, and work experience). We then buttressed these findings with an analysis of nationally representative survey data that closely mimicked the experiment. Of course, our results may not be directly comparable to past recessions given historical changes in job prospects and occupational segregation by race. Nevertheless, the processes we identify likely offer generalizable conclusions about employer behavior in times of economic contraction.

Regarding our hypotheses, we found strong support for both the main effect of race (Hypothesis 1) and the recession (Hypothesis 2), but we could not reject the null hypothesis of proportionate disadvantage in hiring during the recession by race (Hypothesis 3_0). Regarding the latter, not only could we not reject the null, but the magnitude of the difference-in-difference in both the experiment and the NLSY97 were both close to zero, indicating that our non-rejection was not simply a function of sample size. After drawing upon theoretical perspectives on labor markets and race (Reskin & Roos, 1990; Tomaskovic-Devey, 1993; Weber, 1968), we did not find that the recession altered the low-wage labor queue disproportionately for White or African American men. Although job opportunities were reduced across racial boundaries, social closure did not appear to extend to the unskilled labor market during the Great Recession. While we cannot speak to supervisory positions, it appears that African Americans still have similar access to less desirable, low-wage positions, albeit at lower rates than Whites. In this segment of the labor market, it appears rates of racial inequality remain similarly disparate.

We did not find support for our alternative hypothesis (3_A) regarding greater social closure in low-wage positions during the recession. Although more advantaged *workers* may wish to close ranks during recessions, it appears these preferences did not extend to employers and managers, whose racial preferences remained stable. Social closure is most likely when worker interests are threatened and status advantages are challenged (see Stainback et al., 2010), so it appears that the recession did not present a *race-based* threat in terms of low-wage, unskilled hiring.

Although our conclusions regarding the unskilled labor market were supported in both experimental and observational analyses, it is possible that social closure increases rather than remains proportional in the *skilled* labor market. We might expect such a result given that social closure is more readily apparent in the skilled labor market and that such positions would be particularly coveted by dominant status groups during difficult economic times. Similarly, the labor market for young, unskilled African American men has continued to deteriorate (Holzer, 2009), such that the recession-era experiences of young women may differ. Thus, we caution that our results are only applicable to the low-wage, unskilled labor market for young White and African American men. Nonetheless, we are confident that our experimental approach, corroborated through nationally representative survey data, validates our basic conclusions for this segment of the labor market.

Why do we find no additional threat to dominant status groups during a recession when other work finds strong race interactions with other characteristics? The other forms of disadvantage examined in field experiments, such as education and criminal records, represent individual characteristics. These are also subject to statistical discrimination (Arrow, 1973), as they signal information on the presumed productivity of workers (Spence, 1973). For example, a felony criminal record may signal secondary characteristics to employers, such as unreliability, lack of trustworthiness, or liability issues. Employers thus use criminal records to make inferences about individual characteristics. Given this interaction (Pager, 2003, 2007b, p. 115), employers not only discriminate against both "felons" and "African Americans," but they combine the characteristics and discriminate even further based upon the label "African American felon." Such an interaction is consistent with processes of social closure. If dominant groups are seeking to maintain status and a source of disadvantage is more prevalent among minority applicants, as is the case for low education and criminal records, hiring authorities can use those disqualifying characteristics to increase social closure in a manner that appears race-neutral.

A deep economic recession, in contrast, is a *structural* rather than an *individual* characteristic, carrying no signal regarding productivity. Hence, employers have no such label on which to further discriminate against African Americans, above and beyond the main effect of racial discrimination; "recession-era African American" is simply a less meaningful and consequential label. That is, unlike low education and criminal records, the presence of a recession is not the sort of applicant-specific characteristic that can be mobilized to increase social closure. As this label carries no particular new threat to the dominant status group, social closure continues to operate during the recession as it did before, as hiring managers have no new information on which to alter long-standing hiring practices. Where we might expect disproportionality, we instead find an effect during the recession that reproduces the inequality in hiring as existed prior to the recession. As theorized by Tilly (1999), inequality is remarkably resilient in the face of structural change, such that hierarchies reproduce themselves across time and contexts. Our results demonstrate this rigidity within these differing economic contexts.

This result suggests further study of race effects in other societal labor market shifts, such as deindustrialization (Hill & Negrey, 2010), deunionization (Bound & Freeman, 1992), and outsourcing (Johnson et al., 2008). Examinations of these phenomena could address the postulate of equivalent losses by race for societal shifts and disproportionate losses by race for individual-level characteristics, though rigorous field experiments of the former would be difficult to execute. Nonetheless, this study adds to the growing literature on the differential effects of the recession. Young unskilled African American men during recessions are greatly disadvantaged in hiring relative to their White counterparts. Even with proportionate recession-based disadvantage, the lower African American baseline implies greater cumulative losses over time (see Oreopoulos, von Wachter, & Heisz, 2012). To the extent that African Americans must wait longer in the labor queue, they sustain heavier losses in human, economic, and social capital (Tomaskovic-Devey et al., 2005). Whites, in contrast, will be hired more quickly than African Americans, but less quickly than Whites prior to the recession. The recovery process thus remains racialized.

Despite the limitations noted above, the evidence presented here is bolstered by the major advantages of an experimental approach. Random assignment of applicant race to employers removes the influence of other factors, allowing for a more precise measurement of the causal effect of race during the recession. While racial discrimination in hiring is well-documented (Bertrand & Mullainathan, 2004; Pager, 2007a; Pager & Shepherd, 2008; Pager et al., 2009), researchers rarely have access to experimental data on the effect of pronounced economic contractions. As we gain greater perspective on the most recent Great Recession, much evidence is establishing differential effects on people in the least advantaged positions, including those subject to racial discrimination (Berthoud & Sosa, 2011; Hout et al., 2011; Sierminska & Takhtamanova, 2011; Wolff et al., 2011). While our difference-in-difference test detected no significant racial differences in the effects of the recession on hiring, African Americans entered and left the recession in a greatly disadvantaged position relative to Whites.

In sum, the odds of positive employer responses are greatly depressed during deep recessions for both Whites and African Americans and we observe a comparable drop in the employment prospects of both groups. Nevertheless, in an absolute sense, African Americans were far more disadvantaged before and during the recession. In noting that "a rising tide lifts all the boats," John F. Kennedy was usually quick to add that "a dropping tide drops all the boats" (Kennedy, 1960). For those in precarious positions already, this drop is especially consequential.

NOTES

1. In Minneapolis-St. Paul, the site of our field experiment, race effects may be particularly pronounced, as the metropolitan area consistently ranks among the highest in terms of the ratio of African American to White unemployment (Austin, 2011, 2012). Within the metropolitan area in the 2010 census, 78.0% of residents identified as non-Hispanic White and 7.7% identified as Black or African American.

2. For an analogy of a randomized complete block design, one can think of two plots of land and two types of seeds for a given plant. One of the two plots of land has been treated with pesticides and one has not. Then each plot is split up into 300 equal squares and one of the two types of seeds is randomly assigned to each square. Thus, each plot is the block and the two types of seeds are the experimental condition being tested. The researcher then measures whether the plant grows to full maturity as the outcome. Even within the two plots of land, each of the 300 blocks might contain subtle differences in the soil that would affect growth to maturity, but randomly assigning the seeds to the squares within each plot should remove any systematic bias that could falsely be attributed to the difference in the seeds. Other sources of bias may be present in social experiments, as we discuss below.

3. In his influential critique of field experiments, Heckman (1998) similarly argues that use of matched pairs is not necessarily preferable to sending random pairs of African Americans and Whites to *different* job sites.

4. While we might have paired one White tester and one African American tester and sent them to the same employers, our interest in the effect of criminal records precluded this approach. We cannot pair on recession, of course, as there is no guarantee that a job will be open during both periods, and we did not foresee whether and when a recession might occur.

5. Because the race of applicants is randomly assigned to employers, systematic differences between employers should be controlled (or rendered ignorable) by the randomization process (Quillian, 2006). To identify significant departures from randomization, we compare the industry and location of job sites by race of applicants in appendix Table A1. Across all categories, there is a great degree of symmetry by race and a chi-squared test of independence is non-significant for both industry ($\chi^2 = 1.65$, df $= 7$, $p = .977$) and suburban or central city location ($\chi^2 = 0.79$, df $= 1$, $p = .373$). As for the block represented by the recession, it is important that the sample within the two blocks (pre-recession and during-recession) differs only by the effect of interest, since exogenous processes may cause a systematic difference that could affect the comparison. For example, the group of employers hiring during a recession may be different to the extent that the recession had unequal effects across industries or locations in the low-wage market within the metropolitan area. Any observed differences in outcomes could thus be due to industry or location effects, rather than race (Heckman, 1998). Appendix Table A1 shows the recession effect by industry and location. Relative to the marginal distribution (we do not have a balanced number of tests within the recession blocks, as 55.4% of tests occurred during the recession), we observe no systematic differences across either industry ($\chi^2 = 2.60$, df $= 7$, $p = .919$) or location ($\chi^2 = 1.45$, df $= 1$, $p = .229$). Despite this symmetry, our models will adjust for the effects of these and other covariates, described below, to attest to the success of the randomization.

6. Advertisements were cross-referenced with a database of completed job sites to ensure that no location was tested more than once.

7. In terms of data quality and tester comparability, 40 hours of tester training was provided to ensure data quality, addressing topics such as research ethics, physical presentation, answering questions concerning work experience, and handling unexpected situations in the field, all compiled in a Tester Training Manual referred to throughout the field experiment. Training also included videotaped mock interviews, in which differences between testers were discussed and addressed, and practice tests at real job sites. Before leaving a job site, testers were instructed to request an extra application to give to a friend or a business card. These were used to document that the testers had in fact applied to the appropriate location. After submitting their applications, testers immediately completed a four-page Tester Response Form detailing their experience, followed by a daily debriefing interview with research staff. Data quality was also ensured through constant contact with research team staff, primarily by mobile phone, with testers calling before and after each test. To ensure that testers were following protocol both before and during the recession, we sent them to apply to sites with research accomplices, who reported on their performance to the research team.

8. More specifically, the resumes reported high school education, steady employment in service industry and labor positions, and no special training or certifications. To construct work records for the biographies, the research team reviewed entry-level job advertisements and compiled a list of all the industries that were represented in the sample. We then created employment histories that touched on the primary job types (e.g., restaurant, hotel, and warehouse work). This ensured that our testers would have relevant work experience that reflected the local and current low-wage job market, maximizing the population of jobs to which they could reasonably apply.

9. Educational attainment is coded within the NLSY97 as attainment at the start of an academic year. We use the attainment at the end of our two periods to limit the sample to those with a high school education.

10. Unemployment in the NLSY97 is coded by survey administrators using the Bureau of Labor Statistics definition: the individual does not have a job, is currently available for work, and has actively looked for work in the prior four weeks (U.S. Department of Labor, 2003). Thus, the final coding as unemployed is a combination of several date-specific questions asked within the survey, including work status, availability, and job search behavior.

11. In each period, we include any respondent who was coded as unemployed in weeks 1–40, leaving the remaining three months to examine whether they secured employment by the end of the period.

12. Therefore, 26.4% of respondents contribute to both periods. Among those only unemployed in one period, 38.5% are in the pre-recession period and 35.1% are in the recession period. Except when derived from more exact survey items based on monthly or weekly arrays as noted, the variables for the pre-recession period and recession period are taken from the 2006 and 2007 annual surveys, respectively. In models with controls, missing data reduces the analytic sample to 725 unique individuals and 916 observations.

13. Given that Hauser and Warren's (1997) calculations were based on the 1990 Census occupation codes, we use the calculations developed by Frederick (2010), which applies Hauser and Warren's formula to the 2002 occupation codes used in the NLSY97. Those lacking employment within the last two years serve as the reference category for the industry variables and are coded at the minimum on SEI.

14. In this relatively low-wage group, the log of income is not necessarily a better choice for inclusion, based upon the distributions of both codings. Either coding produces similar outcomes.

15. The variable includes eight response categories ranging from "Mostly below Ds" to "Mostly As," with higher categories indicating better grades. The NLSY97 also includes GPA from high school transcripts, but this measure contains a considerable amount of missing data such that we chose to include self-reported grades.

16. We also tested a three category college attendance variable to reflect recent attendance, with categories of never attended, attended but prior to preceding year to the given period, and attended within the last year prior to the given period. This coding also did not produce significant results nor alter the results presented.

17. The correlation matrix was defined as unstructured, which imposes no structure on the residual covariance matrix and estimates the variance at each occasion and the covariance between each pair of occasions freely, and is an appropriate choice for few occasions (Rabe-Hesketh & Skrondal, 2012, pp. 298, 332).

18. The alternative subject-specific random effects specification produces nearly identical results. Similarly, if we include only those who are unemployed in a single period (reducing the model to typical logistic regression), we get nearly identical results.

19. We also tested for interaction effects, finding that the effect of contact did not vary by race ($b = 0.056$, $p = 0.889$) or the recession ($b = -0.017$, $p = 0.965$). As essentially no covariation is observed between contact and race or recession due to randomization, this lack of effect should not be surprising.

20. Examination of both marginal and conditional effects leads to the same inferential conclusion.

21. Pager (2007a) argues that careful selection and training can minimize biases due to tester effects, though we recognize that variation in testers could theoretically alter an experiment's conclusions by affecting estimates of *variation*, though not the mean (Heckman, 1998). Returning to the seed analogy of footnote 2, if one of the two seeds has greater variation and more of its distributional tail is above the threshold for growing to maturity, it will surpass the threshold related to the subtle differences in the square

to which it was randomly assigned more often. Thus, it will appear to be a better seed, despite there being no mean differences in the two seeds' actual distributions. Taken to its extremes, this is an argument against all randomized experiments. We remain confident that our testers presented themselves across and within race as uniformly as possible as a result of our careful selection criteria, intensive training, and rigorous quality control. Further, having several testers of the same race should help eliminate any individual-level differences that could be attributed to race. To formally control for possible variation across testers, we further added a random effect for tester to our covariate models in Tables 2 and 3 (similar to the approach in Pager et al., 2009). All results were virtually identical (available upon request).

22. This effect and significance test is obtained using Helmert coding (see Cohen, 1968) for race and recession effects.

23. Appendix Table A2 shows descriptive statistics for each of the variables in our analysis, cross-classified by the recessionary period and race. Among this subset, race is about equally divided in both periods. Among the covariates, there are expected differences observed between Whites and African Americans on several measures (e.g., weeks worked, region, parenthood, income, SEI, college attendance, marriage, parent's education). Although to a much lesser extent, there are also some differences between the pre-recessionary and recessionary period (e.g., weeks worked, income). These differences stress the need for covariate adjustment for our main variables of interest.

24. Unlike in the experiment where randomization eliminates covariation with the controls, it is conceivable that the effects of the covariates vary by race or recession in the survey data. We tested for all such interactions, finding no significant interactions by race. The recession effect, however, varied significantly by urbanicity and marital status. Prior to the recession, there is an advantage for those in urban areas in terms of job acquisition, which disappears during the recession. Married individuals were less likely to acquire employment prior to the recession and more likely to find work during the recession. Importantly, these interactions do not alter the main effect of race, the main effect of year (as estimated through the margins command in the presence of an interaction), and the predicted probabilities for the race and recession combinations. Because they do not affect the results, we exclude them in order to maintain symmetry with the experiment. These models are available upon request.

25. In analogous models that add the subsequent annual employment array (December 2008 to November 2009) when the recession reached its peak ($N = 1,438$; unique individuals $= 961$), we still find no difference-in-difference (both with and without controls). From an analogous model to Table 4, Model 10, the predicted chance of acquiring a job in 2007, 2008, and 2009 is 86%, 77%, and 63%, respectively, for Whites, and 73%, 61%, and 57%, respectively, for African Americans. As with Model 10, the coefficients testing the difference-in-difference, though non-significant, are actually in the opposite direction to our hypothesis. Whites experienced a 22.6 percentage point drop in employment acquisition from 2007 before the recession to its peak in 2009, while African Americans experienced a 16.2 percentage point drop over the same period. Thus, we again find no grounds to reject the null hypothesis of proportionate decreases, but caution that we cannot confirm this result experimentally. With regard to between-group differences, all groups have higher odds of acquiring jobs relative to African Americans during year 2 of the recession, though the comparisons to Whites during year 2 of the recession and African Americans during year 1 of the recession are not statistically significant. Results are available upon request.

26. We also conducted an in-depth analysis of geographic context within the metropolitan area by collecting suburb and neighborhood (for jobs in Minneapolis or St. Paul) information based on the location of each jobsite, totaling 110 unique geographic units in our dataset. Measures examined include the percentage under 18, African American, residing in the same home as a year ago, single-headed households, that speak English

less than very well, with a Bachelor's degree over age 25, below the poverty line, of adults employed, and voting Democrat, as well as the mean household income and Index I crime rate. As with the audit-level covariates discussed above, the race and recession coefficients remain identical when the geographic area characteristics are included (utilizing cluster-corrected standard errors). Thus, our randomization was very robust to location characteristics as well. None of these measures were statistically significant, either singly or as a whole. It would appear, then, that employers are more responsive to the characteristics of the applicant (i.e., race, personality as assessed through contact) than those of the area in which the jobsite is located. Results are available upon request.

27. In an analogous set of models for women, the results again suggest a lack of difference-in-difference (both with and without controls), though the race effect is less straightforward. While the recession effect remains significant in all models, the race effect is marginally significant without controls and non-significant with controls. Alternatively, when considering the between-group effects, all groups are significantly more likely to acquire work relative to recession-era African American women. Thus, unlike the men, the two forms of coding do not produce consistent results in the predicted probabilities (specifically, African American women experience a drop in job acquisition during the recession regardless of coding, while White women's decrease is less dramatic in the simple coding). Without a field experiment where causality is directly addressed, we urge caution in interpreting these results, and urge future research into the experiences of women during the recession by race. Results are available upon request.

28. Among those White or African American men who reported unemployment, very few respondents had achieved either an associate (pre-recession: $n = 28$, or 4.6%; recession: $n = 22$, or 3.9%) or a bachelor degree or higher (pre-recession: $n = 78$, 12.9%; recession: $n = 75$, 13.1%). When cross-classified by race and employment acquisition, the cell counts are too low for meaningful analysis.

ACKNOWLEDGMENTS

This research was supported by the JEHT Foundation and the National Institute of Justice (grant 2007-IJ-CX-0042). We are indebted to the Council on Crime and Justice, as well as Ebony Ruhland and Hilary Whitham, for their integral role in conducting this project. We owe special thanks to Devah Pager for consulting on the original project from which this paper emerged, and Erin Kelly, Suzy McElrath, Heather McLaughlin, Vincent Roscigno, and Kevin Stainback for valuable feedback.

REFERENCES

Agresti, A. (2002). *Categorical data analysis* (2nd ed.). Hoboken, NJ: Wiley.
Aigner, D. J., & Cain, G. G. (1977). Statistical theories of discrimination in labor markets. *Industrial and Labor Relations Review, 30*, 175–187.
Arrow, K. J. (1973). The theory of discrimination. In O. Ashenfelter & A. Rees (Eds.), *Discrimination in labor markets* (pp. 3–33). Princeton, NJ: Princeton University Press.

Austin, A. (2011). High black unemployment widespread across nation's metropolitan areas. In *Economic policy institute, issue brief #315*. October 3, 2011. Washington, DC: Economic Policy Institute.

Austin, A. (2012). Black metropolitan unemployment in 2011. In *Economic policy institute, issue brief #337*. July 2, 2011. Washington, DC: Economic Policy Institute.

Berthoud, R., & Sosa, L. C. (2011). Patterns of employment disadvantage in a recession. *Research in Labor Economics, 32*, 83–113.

Bertrand, M., & Mullainathan, S. (2004). Are Emily and Greg more employable than Lakisha and Jamal? A field experiment on labor market discrimination. *American Economic Review, 94*, 991–1013.

Bielby, W. T., & Baron, J. N. (1986). Men and women at work: Sex segregation and statistical discrimination. *American Journal of Sociology, 91*, 759–799.

Bol, T., & Weeden, K. A. (2015). Occupational closure and wage inequality in Germany and the United Kingdom. *European Sociological Review, 31*, 354–369.

Bound, J., & Freeman, R. B. (1992). What went wrong? The erosion of relative earnings and employment among young black men in the 1980s. *The Quarterly Journal of Economics, 107*, 201–232.

Braddock, J. H., & McPartland, J. M. (1987). How minorities continue to be excluded from equal employment opportunities: Research on labor market and institutional barriers. *Journal of Social Issues, 43*, 5–39.

Carruthers, B. G., & Kim, J.-C. (2011). The sociology of finance. *Annual Review of Sociology, 37*, 239–259.

Chamberlain, L., Crowley, M., Tope, D., & Hodson, R. (2008). Sexual harassment in context: Organizational and occupational foundations of abuse. *Work and Occupations, 35*, 262–295.

Cohen, J. (1968). Multiple regression as a general data-analytic system. *Psychological Bulletin, 70*, 426–443.

Couch, K. A., & Fairlie, R. (2010). Last hired, first fired? Black-white unemployment and the business cycle. *Demography, 47*, 227–247.

Cox, D. R. (1958). *Planning of experiments*. Hoboken, NJ: Wiley.

Elliott James, R., & Smith Ryan, A. (2001). Ethnic matching of supervisors to subordinate work groups: Findings on bottom-up ascription and social closure. *Social Problems, 48*, 258–276.

Fernandez, R. M., & Fernandez-Mateo, I. (2006). Networks, race, and hiring. *American Sociological Review, 71*, 42–71.

Frederick, C. B. (2010). *A crosswalk for using pre-2000 occupational status and prestige codes with post-2000 occupation codes*. Technical Report, Working Paper No. 2010-03. Center for Demography and Ecology, University of Wisconsin-Madison, Madison, WI.

Greenman, E., & Xie, Y. (2008). Double jeopardy? The interaction of gender and race on earnings in the United States. *Social Forces, 86*, 1217–1244.

Grunewald, R., & Madden, T. (2009). Recession persists; modest recovery in view: District economic outlook. *Federal Reserve Bank of Minneapolis fedgazette: Regional Business & Economic Newspaper, 21*(4), 17–18.

Grusky, D. B., Western, B., & Wimer, C. (Eds.). (2011). *The Great Recession*. New York, NY: Russell Sage Foundation.

Hauser, R. M., & Warren, J. R. (1997). Socioeconomic index of occupational status: A review, update, and critique. *Sociological Methodology, 27*, 177–298.

Heckman, J. J. (1998). Detecting discrimination. *The Journal of Economic Perspectives, 12*, 101–116.

Hill, R. C., & Negrey, C. (2010). Deindustrialization and racial minorities in the Great Lakes region, USA. In M. Cross (Ed.), *Ethnic minorities and industrial change in Europe and North America* (pp. 55–76). New York, NY: Cambridge.

Hodson, R., Roscigno, V. J., & Lopez, S. H. (2006). Chaos and the abuse of power: Workplace bullying in organizational and interactional context. *Work and Occupations, 33*, 382–416.

Holzer, H. J. (2009). The labor market and young black men: Updating Moynihan's perspective. *Annals of the American Academy of Political and Social Science, 621*, 47–69.

Hout, M., Levanon, A., & Cumberworth, E. (2011). Job loss and unemployment. In D. B. Grusky, B. Western, & C. Wimer (Eds.), *The Great Recession* (pp. 59–81). New York, NY: Russell Sage.

Huffman, M. L., & Cohen, P. N. (2004). Racial wage inequality: Job segregation and devaluation across U.S. labor markets. *American Journal of Sociology, 109*, 902–936.

Hughes, E. C. (1945). Dilemmas and contradictions of status. *American Journal of Sociology, 50*, 353–359.

Jacobsen, L. A., & Mather, M. (2011). A post-recession update on U.S. social and economic trends. *Population bulletin update*, December 2011.

Johnson, J. H., Burthley, G. C. III, & Ghorm, K. (2008). Economic globalization and the future of black America. *Journal of Black Studies, 38*, 883–899.

Kalev, A., Kelly, E., & Dobbin, F. (2006). Best practices or best guesses? Assessing the efficacy of corporate affirmative action and diversity policies. *American Sociological Review, 71*, 589–617.

Kanter, R. M. (1977). *Men and women of the corporation*. New York, NY: Basic Books.

Kaufman, R. L. (2002). Assessing alternative perspectives on race and sex employment segregation. *American Sociology Review, 67*, 547–572.

Kennedy, J. F. (1960). Remarks of Senator John F. Kennedy, Cheyenne, WY Frontier Park, September 23. *American Presidency Project*, Santa Barbara. Accessed on July 29, 2012.

Krivo, L. J., & Kaufman, R. L. (2004). Housing and wealth inequality: Racial-ethnic differences in home equity in the United States. *Demography, 41*, 585–605.

Loveman, M. (1999). Is 'race' essential? A comment on Bonilla-Silva. *American Sociological Review, 64*, 891–898.

Mattingly, M. J., & Smith, K. E. (2010). Change in wives' employment when husbands stop working: A recession-prosperity comparison. *Family Relations, 59*, 343–357.

McDonald, S., Lin, N., & Ao, D. (2009). Networks of opportunity: Gender, race, and job leads. *Social Problems, 56*, 385–402.

McKee, G. A. (2008). *The problem of jobs: Liberalism, race, and deindustrialization in Philadelphia*. Chicago, IL: University of Chicago Press.

Moss, P., & Tilly, C. (1996). 'Soft' skills and race: An investigation of black men's employment problems. *Work and Occupations, 23*, 252–276.

Moss, P., & Tilly, C. (2001). *Stories employers tell: Race, skill, and hiring in America*. New York, NY: Russell Sage.

Murphy, R. (1988). *Social closure: The theory of monopolization and exclusion*. Oxford: Clarendon Press.

National Bureau of Economic Research. (2008). *Determination of the December 2007 peak in economic activity*. Cambridge, MA: NBER. Retrieved from http://www.nber.org/dec2008.pdf

National Bureau of Economic Research. (2010). *Announcement of June 2009 business cycle trough/end of last recession*. Cambridge, MA: NBER. Retrieved from http://www.nber.org/cycles/sept2010.pdf

Nazroo, J. Y. (2003). The structuring of ethnic inequalities in health: Economic position, racial discrimination, and racism. *American Journal of Public Health, 93*, 277–284.

Oreopoulos, P., Wachter, T. V., & Heisz, A. (2012). Short- and long-term career effects of graduating in a recession. *American Economic Journal: Applied Economics, 4*, 1–29.

Pager, D. (2003). The mark of a criminal record. *American Journal of Sociology, 108*, 937–975.

Pager, D. (2007a). The use of field experiments for studies of employment discrimination: Contributions, critiques, and directions for the future. *The Annals of the American Academy of Political and Social Science, 609*, 104–133.

Pager, D. (2007b). *Marked: Race, crime, and finding work in an era of mass incarceration*. Chicago, IL: University of Chicago Press.

Pager, D., & Shepherd, H. (2008). The sociology of discrimination: Racial discrimination in employment, housing, credit, and consumer markets. *Annual Review of Sociology, 34*, 181–209.

Pager, D., Western, B., & Bonikowski, B. (2009). Discrimination in a low-wage labor market: A field experiment. *American Sociological Review, 74*, 777–799.

Parkin, F. (1979). *Marxism and class theory: A bourgeois critique.* New York, NY: Columbia University Press.

Phelps, E. S. (1972). The statistical theory of racism and sexism. *American Economic Review, 62*, 659–661.

Quillian, L. (2006). New approaches to understanding racial prejudice and discrimination. *Annual Review of Sociology, 32*, 299–328.

Rabe-Hesketh, S., & Skrondal, A. (2012). *Multilevel and longitudinal modeling using Stata* (3rd ed.). College Station, TX: Stata Press.

Reskin, B. F. (1988). Bringing the men back in: Sex differentiation and the devaluation of women's work. *Gender and Society, 2*, 58–81.

Reskin, B. F. (1993). Sex segregation in the workplace. *Annual Review of Sociology, 19*, 241–270.

Reskin, B. F. (2012). The race discrimination system. *Annual Review of Sociology, 38*, 17–35.

Reskin, B. F., & Roos, P. A. (1990). *Job queues, gender queues: Explaining women's inroads into male occupations.* Philadelphia, PA: Temple University Press.

Roscigno, V. J. (2007). *The face of discrimination: How race and gender impact work and home lives.* New York, NY: Rowman & Littlefield.

Roscigno, V. J., Garcia, L. M., & Bobbitt-Zeher, D. (2007). Social closure and processes of race/sex employment discrimination. *Annals of the American Academy of Political and Social Science, 609*, 16–48.

Roscigno, V. J., Lopez, S. H., & Hodson, R. (2009). Supervisor bullying, status inequalities, and organizational context. *Social Forces, 87*, 1561–1589.

Rugh, J. S., & Massey, D. S. (2010). Racial segregation and the American foreclosure crisis. *American Sociological Review, 75*, 629–651.

Sierminska, E., & Takhtamanova, Y. (2011). Job flows, demographics, and the Great Recession. *Research in Labor Economics, 32*, 115–154.

Smeeding, T. M., Thompson, J. P., Levanon, A., & Burak, E. (2011). Poverty and income inequality in the early stages of the Great Recession. In D. B. Grusky, B. Western, & C. Wimer (Eds.), *The Great Recession* (pp. 82–126). New York, NY: Russell Sage.

Smith, R. A. (2002). Race, gender, and authority in the workplace: Theory and research. *Annual Review of Sociology, 28*, 509–542.

Spence, M. (1973). Job market signaling. *Quarterly Journal of Economics, 87*, 355–374.

Stainback, K. (2008). Social contacts and race/ethnic job matching. *Social Forces, 87*, 857–886.

Stainback, K., & Tomaskovic-Devey, D. (2009). Intersections of power and privilege: Long-term trends in managerial representation. *American Sociological Review, 74*, 800–820.

Stainback, K., Tomaskovic-Devey, D., & Skaggs, S. (2010). Organizational approaches to inequality: Inertia, relative power, and environments. *Annual Review of Sociology, 16*, 225–247.

Sugrue, T. J. (2005). *The origins of the urban crisis: Race and inequality in postwar Detroit.* Princeton, NJ: Princeton University Press.

Szafran, R. F. (1982). What kinds of firms hire and promote women and blacks? A review of the literature. *Sociological Quarterly, 23*, 171–190.

Szafran, R. F. (1984). Female and minority employment in banks: A research note. *Work and Occupations, 11*, 55–76.

Tilly, C. (1999). *Durable inequality.* Berkeley, CA: University of California Press.

Tomaskovic-Devey, D. (1993). *Gender and racial inequality at work: The sources and consequences of job segregation.* Ithaca, NY: ILR Press.

Tomaskovic-Devey, D., & Skaggs, S. (1999). An establishment-level test of the statistical discrimination hypothesis. *Work and Occupations, 26*, 422–445.

Tomaskovic-Devey, D., Stainback, K., Taylor, T., Zimmer, C., Robinson, C., & McTague, T. (2006). Documenting desegregation: Segregation in American workplaces by race, ethnicity, and sex, 1966-2003. *American Sociological Review, 71*, 565–588.

Tomaskovic-Devey, D., Thomas, M., & Johnson, K. (2005). Race and the accumulation of human capital across the career: A Theoretical model and fixed-effects application. *American Journal of Sociology, 111*, 58–89.

Turner, M. A., Fix, M., & Struyk, R. J. (1991). *Opportunities denied, opportunities diminished: Racial discrimination in hiring.* Washington, DC: Urban Institute Press.

U.S. Bureau of Labor Statistics. (2012). Employment situation summary. *Economic News Release,* October 5, 2012. Washington, DC: Bureau of Labor Statistics. Accessed on November 1, 2012.

U.S. Department of Labor. (2003). *NLSY97 user's guide.* Washington, DC: Bureau of Labor Statistics, U.S. Department of Labor.

Uggen, C., & Blackstone, A. (2004). Sexual harassment as a gendered expression of power. *American Sociological Review, 69*, 64–92.

Vuolo, M., Mortimer, J. T., & Staff, J. (2016). The value of educational degrees in turbulent economic times: Evidence from the youth development study. *Social Science Research, 57*, 233–252.

Vuolo, M., Uggen, C., & Lageson, S. (2016). Statistical power in experimental audit studies: Cautions and calculations for matched tests with nominal outcomes. *Sociological Methods & Research, 45*, 260–303.

Weber, M. (1968). *Economy and society.* Berkeley, CA: University of California Press.

Weeden, K. A. (2002). Why do some occupations pay more than others? Social closure and earnings inequality in the United States. *American Journal of Sociology, 108*, 55–101.

Wilson, F. D., Tienda, M., & Wu, L. (1995). Race and unemployment: Labor market experiences of black and white men, 1968-1988. *Work and Occupations, 22*, 245–270.

Wilson, G., Roscigno, V. J., & Huffman, M. (2015). Racial income inequality and public sector privatization. *Social Problems, 62*, 163–185.

Wolff, E. N., Owens, L. A., & Burak, E. (2011). How much wealth was destroyed in the Great Recession? In D. B. Grusky, B. Western, & C. Wimer (Eds.), *The Great Recession* (pp. 127–158). New York, NY: Russell Sage.

APPENDIX

Table A1. Experiment Industry and Location of Job Sites by Race and Recession.

	Cases	African American	White	χ^2 (df)	Pre-Recession	During Recession	χ^2 (df)
Industry				1.65 (7)			2.60 (7)
Office work	39	56.4%	43.6%		43.6%	56.4%	
Retail	115	51.3	48.7		41.7	58.3	
Healthcare	9	55.6	44.4		33.3	66.7	
Restaurant	217	55.6	44.4		44.2	55.8	
Warehouse/labor	120	52.5	47.5		45.8	54.2	
Hotel	68	50.0	50.0		51.5	48.5	
Driver	25	52.0	48.0		40.0	60.0	
Security	12	41.7	58.3		50.0	50.0	
Location				0.79 (1)			1.45 (1)
Suburbs	401	51.9	48.1		42.9	57.1	
Minneapolis-St. Paul	204	48.0	52.0		48.0	52.0	
Total	605	50.6	49.4		44.6	55.4	

Table A2. NLSY97 Descriptive Statistics.

	Pre-Recession			Recession		
	Total	White	African American	Total	White	African American
Race						
White	47.5			49.3		
African American	52.5			50.7		
Acquired employment	75.5	83.3	66.8	67.0	77.2	56.4
Weeks worked in previous year						
0–13	23.0	16.7	29.8	25.7	19.5	32.1
14–26	16.2	14.8	17.7	10.5	9.5	11.5
27–39	17.6	17.9	17.2	13.3	14.5	12.0
39–52	43.3	50.6	35.3	50.5	56.4	44.4
Industry of last job						
No report in last two years	7.5	4.9	10.5	8.7	5.0	12.5
Construction	14.1	18.3	9.2	17.2	23.4	10.8
Manufacturing	11.6	12.6	10.5	11.9	11.3	12.5
Retail trade	13.7	11.4	16.2	12.7	15.1	10.3
Transportation and warehousing	5.3	2.3	8.8	4.3	4.2	4.3
Professional and related services	15.3	13.7	17.1	14.0	12.1	16.0
Entertainment, accommodations, and food services	14.9	14.8	14.9	14.7	12.6	16.8
Other	17.7	22.1	12.7	16.6	16.3	16.8
Hauser & Warren SEI Male	24.3 (10.2)	25.8 (10.8)	22.6 (9.1)	23.6 (10.0)	25.2 (9.5)	22.0 (10.3)
Income (thousands)	12.0 (12.2)	14.5 (12.9)	9.2 (10.7)	14.2 (14.7)	18.4 (16.9)	9.9 (10.6)
High school grades (range 1–8)	4.7 (1.6)	4.8 (1.7)	4.5 (1.4)	4.7 (1.6)	4.8 (1.7)	4.6 (1.4)
Ever attended college	31.5	33.8	29.0	32.4	35.3	29.5

Convicted of crime in last year	10.2	9.9	10.5	6.3	5.8	6.8
Received unemployment insurance in last year	5.8	6.5	5.0	7.0	7.5	6.4
Age	23.7 (1.4)	23.6 (1.5)	23.7 (1.4)	24.6 (1.4)	24.6 (1.4)	24.7 (1.4)
Census region						
Northeast	15.2	16.4	13.9	13.7	16.3	11.1
North Central	28.1	33.1	22.7	25.6	29.3	21.8
South	43.9	30.4	58.8	48.6	32.6	65.0
West	12.8	20.2	4.6	12.1	21.8	2.1
Urban (vs. rural)	77.6	72.6	83.2	76.1	74.5	77.8
Migrated between counties	23.6	29.7	16.8	19.6	24.1	15.0
Children						
None	59.2	68.8	48.5	51.5	60.2	42.5
Non-residential	24.0	12.2	37.1	27.2	17.8	36.9
Residential	16.8	19.0	14.4	21.3	22.0	20.6
Married	14.8	19.0	10.1	17.9	22.4	13.3
Parents' highest education						
HS or less	52.8	46.0	60.2	53.0	46.8	59.6
Some college or associates	22.0	24.6	19.3	21.9	24.1	19.5
Bachelors or higher	16.4	24.1	8.3	16.6	23.9	8.7
No parent information	8.7	5.4	12.2	8.5	5.2	12.1

WORKFORCE DOWNSIZING AND SHAREHOLDER VALUE ORIENTATION AMONG EXECUTIVE MANAGERS AT LARGE U.S. FIRMS

Taekjin Shin

ABSTRACT

In this study, I explore the link between workforce downsizing and the pre-dominance of a corporate governance model that espouses a shareholder value maximization principle. Specifically, I examine how top managers' shareholder value orientation affects the adoption of a downsizing strategy among large, publicly traded corporations in the United States. An analysis of CEOs' letters to shareholders indicates that firms with CEOs who use language that espouses the shareholder value principle tend to have a higher rate of layoffs, after controlling for various indicators of the firm's adherence to the shareholder value principle. The finding suggests that corporate governance models, particularly those advocated by powerful organizational elites, have a significant impact on workers by shaping corporate strategies toward the workforce. The key actors in this process were top managers who embraced the new management ideology and implemented corporate strategy to pursue shareholder value maximization.

Keywords: Downsizing; layoffs; shareholder value; corporate governance; CEOs

Emerging Conceptions of Work, Management and the Labor Market
Research in the Sociology of Work, Volume 30, 185–217
Copyright © 2017 by Emerald Publishing Limited
All rights of reproduction in any form reserved
ISSN: 0277-2833/doi:10.1108/S0277-283320170000030008

Corporate downsizing and mass layoffs in the United States have attracted much attention in the past few decades, particularly in the wake of the recent recession. Public attention to these issues is based largely on widespread concerns about the impact of downsizing on job losses, unemployment, and inequality in the labor market. Downsizing is a corporate strategy that can affect a large number of employees' employment, income, and job security, either directly or indirectly (Osterman, 1999; Uchitelle, 2007). Downsizing has reportedly affected some 43 million people, or nearly one-third of all households in America in the early 1990s (New York Times, 1996). People who lose jobs due to downsizing and layoffs tend to suffer difficulties in finding new jobs and often end up with new jobs that pay less than their former ones (Farber, 2005). Research suggests that downsizing disproportionately targets workers who have weak bargaining power and, therefore, exacerbates inequality in the labor market (Dencker & Fang, 2016; Kalev, 2014). Beyond its impact on job displacement and employment changes, downsizing also affects those who retain jobs, who then face job insecurity and precarious employment (Koeber, 2002; Knudsen, Johnson, Martin, & Roman, 2003).

While downsizing as a strategy is not new in business history, downsizing since the 1990s has been fundamentally different: it has become more severe, pervasive, and enduring than in the past. Instead of being a stigmatizing episode that symbolizes a corporate crisis and impending failure, downsizing has become a standard business practice that corporations routinely adopt in order to boost profits and cut down operating costs even in normal times (Budros, 1999; Lazonick & O'Sullivan, 2000). The rise of this new type of downsizing coincides with a larger trend in the transformation of work and employment relations in the United States: the erosion of labor's bargaining power, the rise of precarious, non-standard employment, and the decline of traditional employment relations that are characterized by internal labor markets, job security, and long-term employment (Hatton, 2011; Kalleberg, 2011; Western & Rosenfeld, 2011). This suggests that there are important connections among these changes. Downsizing and mass layoffs might indicate political dynamics on a larger scale, which is described here as the dominance of corporate power and shareholder value logic over labor (Fligstein & Shin, 2007; Jung, 2015, 2016). The popularity of downsizing and layoffs since the 1980s is a consequence of the rise of a new management orientation and business principle among large corporations. The new management orientation mandates the maximization of shareholder value as the primary goal of publicly traded corporations (Davis & Thompson, 1994; Fligstein & Shin, 2007; Lazonick & O'Sullivan, 2000). One outcome of this new management orientation is a transformation of corporate control, which provides ideological support for shareholder primacy and undermines the power of other stakeholders, including employees.

An important implication of this new principle is that large, diversified conglomerates, which were dominant organizational forms until the 1960s, have become a symbol of inefficiency and management excess in the 1980s and 1990s

(Davis, Diekmann, & Tinsley, 1994). Streamlined companies, with lean operations and focused strategies became popular among investors and stock analysts who increasingly gained power in corporate governance (Zuckerman, 2001). Pressure from shareholders and large institutional investors forced corporations to reduce company size and scope, and to adopt downsizing and mass layoffs (Jung, 2015; Useem, 1996). Another implication of the shareholder value orientation is that corporations started to view employees as a cost to be minimized in order to maximize shareholder value (Appelbaum & Berg, 1996; Lazonick & O'Sullivan, 2000). This view is based on the assumption that shareholders are the ultimate residual claimants of corporate profits (Jensen, 2001; Sundaram & Inkpen, 2004). Accordingly, corporations are no more responsible for the interests of other stakeholders than for the maximization of shareholder wealth, a position that provides the ideological justification for downsizing as a rational business decision.

Recently, sociologists and organizational scholars increasingly have been interested in corporate governance and the shareholder value principle as underlying forces of downsizing. Based on the trend in the transformation of corporate governance (Davis & Thompson, 1994; Fligstein, 2001a), scholars have suggested that the rise of the shareholder value principle as a predominant governance model has prompted firms to focus on maximizing shareholder value and legitimized the use of downsizing as an effective corporate strategy to achieve this goal (Budros, 1999; Lazonick & O'Sullivan, 2000). There is evidence that indicates this link between corporate governance and downsizing. For example, recent research suggests that in addition to economic and institutional determinants of downsizing (Ahmadjian & Robinson, 2001; Baumol, Blinder, & Wolff, 2003; Budros, 1997), corporate governance of a firm, such as the boards of directors and corporate ownership structure, affects the likelihood and magnitude of downsizing (Jung, 2015, 2016; Perry & Shivdasani, 2005; Stavrou, Kassinis, & Filotheou, 2007). Recent studies suggest a link between indirect indicators of shareholder value orientation and corporate downsizing (Fligstein & Shin, 2007; Jung, 2015, 2016), which calls for further investigation of the actual mechanisms involving decision-makers who adopt and implement corporate strategies such as downsizing.

The present study contributes to scholarship on how corporate governance affects downsizing by examining a direct indicator of top managers' shareholder value orientation at the firm level. Specifically, I examine top managers' use of language that expresses the shareholder value principle in public documents and analyze how this indicator is related to workforce downsizing. As publicly visible figures representing the corporation to its environment, top managers such as CEOs routinely use public announcements and corporate communications where they express their views about business and corporate governance (Elsbach, 1994; Pfeffer, 1981). Such expressions of public language provide an important opportunity to investigate the effect of shareholder value discourse on corporate strategy and actions, including downsizing. Even though public language used as a strategic tool may not necessarily reflect the true beliefs of managers, top managers' use of public language plays important roles: it justifies a firm's strategic decisions, sets the overall direction of a firm, and sends useful signals to the environment (Gao, Yu, & Cannella, 2016; Gioia, Thomas, Clark, & Chittipeddi, 1994). Furthermore, research suggests that corporate managers engage in symbolic management tactics to create the appearance of conformity to an institutionally legitimate governance model without necessarily implementing actual strategies that maximize shareholder value (Westphal & Zajac, 1998; Zajac & Westphal, 2004). Therefore, it is important to examine public expressions of the shareholder value principle, controlling for actual strategies of firms. By studying a direct expression of shareholder value orientation, its effect is disentangled from other related indicators deemed to be consistent with shareholder value.

In this study, I argue that top managers strategically adopt the shareholder value orientation to implement downsizing strategy and justify its rationale. The logic of shareholder value maximization legitimizes corporate decisions that prioritize shareholder interests and minimize operational costs, including labor costs. As a consequence, I predict that top managers' public expression of the shareholder value orientation is related to the firm's announcement of downsizing and layoffs. The focus on the announcements, rather than the actual incidents of downsizing, reflects the premise that the shareholder value orientation is fundamentally an institutional logic and a discourse that actors use strategically (Fligstein, 2001b; Thornton, Ocasio, & Lounsbury, 2012). As a discourse, the shareholder value orientation not only reflects a manager's attention and worldview — which in turn shape the actual incidents of downsizing — but also affects the corporation's efforts to manage its environment by announcing important decisions such as downsizing and layoffs. Layoff is defined here as an organization's conscious use of permanent personnel reductions in an attempt to improve its efficiency and/or effectiveness (Budros, 1999; Freeman & Cameron, 1993). Although downsizing is a broader concept than layoff and includes an array of additional options for reducing the workforce (Greenhalgh, Lawrence, & Sutton, 1988), I use layoff and downsizing as interchangeable terms, following the common usage in the literature (Brockner, 1988; Budros, 1997).

The analysis of layoff announcements from the largest U.S. firms supports the hypothesis that a CEO's expression of shareholder value orientation in public documents is significantly associated with the firm's announcements of layoffs. Specifically, the results suggest that firms where the CEO expressed shareholder-value-friendly language in public documents were more likely to announce layoffs than firms where the CEO did not use such language. The findings imply that the predominant governance model affects top managers' expression of business orientation, which in turn determines the overall strategy and policies of workplace organizations (Cobb, 2016; Fligstein, 1990; Shin, 2014). The results suggest that corporate governance models such as the shareholder value principle have a significant impact on workforce downsizing, supporting sociological arguments that highlight a link between corporate governance and workplace outcomes (Fligstein & Shin, 2007; Goldstein, 2012; Jung, 2015).

SHAREHOLDER VALUE ORIENTATION AMONG U.S. CORPORATIONS

Since the 1980s, maximizing shareholder value has been a predominant management principle of large U.S. corporations. In the United States, and increasingly in Europe and Asia, (Ahmadjian & Robbins, 2005; Fiss & Zajac, 2004; Lok, 2010), a widespread and growing belief is that corporations should be run in the interests of shareholders and that this goal be accomplished by maximizing share prices. Although it is not the purpose of the present study to explore the historical evolution of management principles (see Chandler, 1977; Fligstein, 1990), to understand the nature of this new principle, or what Fligstein (1990, 2001a) calls "the conception of control," it is helpful to review the political and economic context from which it emerged.

After the 1960s, macroeconomic and financial conditions spelled decline for American corporations. One cause of major corporations' poor performance was conglomerate mergers among too many unrelated businesses, which became the target of criticism for corporate inefficiency and lack of core competencies. When oil-induced inflation hit the U.S. economy in the 1970s, high interest rates became unattractive to investors, who retreated from the stock market to bond and caused a further fall in share prices. Inflation boosted corporate assets on the books, but depressed the rate of return on assets. Moreover, growing international competition meant American firms began to lose market share in major industries like automobile and consumer electronics. A new business model to revive American economy was needed to address growing competition and declining profitability of U.S. corporations (Fligstein & Shin, 2007; Shin, 2013).

In the 1970s, a group of financial economists proposed a new way to view corporations. Commonly known as agency theory, this approach was radical: corporations were no longer regarded as real organizations with human members, rules, structures, and culture. Instead, agency theory proposed to view corporations merely as a nexus of contracts among atomized constituencies with conflicting interests (Fama & Jensen, 1983; Jensen & Meckling, 1976). Complex organizational issues such as personnel, control, and coordination are reduced to economic problems that can be solved by designing contracts through arm's-length negotiations (see Blair, 1995; Davis, 2005). Thus, owners and shareholders are principals contracting with agents (managers) and delegating the day-to-day operation of the business. In return for this delegation, the owners have claims on the residual value of the profits. Therefore, the task of the managers as agents should be to maximize the owners' wealth. The problem, according to agency theory, is that the agents do not always act in accordance with the interest of the principals; rather, the agents need clear incentives to align their goals to the principals' goals. Because owners tend to lack information on the details of the business, and it is difficult and costly for owners to monitor managers' behavior, agency theorists argue that managers in large corporations are likely to misuse their discretionary power and to pursue activities to enhance their own wealth and status at the cost of the owners' wealth, like conglomerate acquisitions, empire-building efforts, and excessive executive perks. For agency theorists, then, a good corporation is one that minimizes the cost of such abuse, or "agency costs," and maximizes shareholder value. As such, American corporations should reform their governance systems by strengthening the mechanisms to monitor executive behavior and by aligning the interests of managers with those of shareholders.

Agency theory had a profound influence on American business, which was seeking a new model (Jensen & Ruback, 1983; Marris, 1964). First, it provided a theoretical rationale for the 1980s corporate merger movement. Agency theory was deeply rooted in the neoclassical economic belief that the market is always more efficient than human organization, so agency theorists argue that corporate governance reform should be subject to the market mechanism. When a firm is run by inefficient management with high agency costs, a market for corporate control can allow an outsider to acquire the firm and replace its management. Such a market can discipline managers and reduce agency costs.

More importantly, agency theory espouses the primacy of shareholders whose power was weakened during the first three quarters of the twentieth century due to the separation of ownership and control. Because agency theorists view managers as undisciplined and opportunistic agents whose discretionary behavior costs shareholder wealth, they call for more stringent monitoring of managerial behavior through the empowerment of shareholders. During the 1980s and 1990s, large shareholders, particularly institutional investors, gained power (Useem, 1996), and activist investors began to advocate shareholder rights and governance reforms in corporations (Gillan & Starks, 2007; Zorn, Dobbin, Dierkes, & Kwok, 2005).

SHAREHOLDER VALUE AND WORKFORCE DOWNSIZING

The previous section described how the maximization of shareholder value emerged as a new dominant principle in the 1980s with macroeconomic pressure on corporations and academic legitimation by agency theory. In the same timeframe, major U.S. corporations engaged in a restructuring of their organizations and labor forces. Although scholars have noted the changes in business principles and their impact on workforce (Appelbaum & Berg, 1996; Fligstein & Shin, 2007; Goldstein, 2012; Jung, 2015; Lazonick & O'Sullivan, 2000; Useem, 1996), a systematic analysis of the causal link between corporate governance and workforce outcomes is still needed. This study explores such a connection.

Downsizing and layoffs are not new in American business history; companies had always shed workers when business turned bad. What is new about post-1980s downsizing under the shareholder value principle is that firms now downsize even when they are earning profits in order to maximize efficiencies. For example, the American Management Association's (AMA) annual survey of major U.S. companies' layoff practices reports that the number of layoffs was greater in the boom year of 1998 than in any other year in the 1990s (Lazonick & O'Sullivan, 2000). Often the decision to downsize was made to conform to investor preferences and to signal the firm's attempt to cut costs and focus on core competencies (Useem, 1996). When major corporations announced restructuring plans, the stock market often welcomed the news by raising share prices (Worrell, Davidson, & Sharma, 1991). As a result, since the 1980s layoffs have become a standard business practice (Budros, 1997, 2004).

The spread of downsizing as a legitimate business practice defies pure economic logic. Studies show that workforce downsizing often leads to undesirable financial and organizational costs and generally fails to deliver their intended benefits of increased efficiencies and reduced costs (see Datta, Guthrie, Basuil, & Pandey, 2010, for a review). Scholars have documented the negative impacts of downsizing on employee morale and productivity, product innovation and quality, firm performance, and reputation (Brockner, 1988; Cascio, 1993; De Meuse, Vanderheiden, & Bergmann, 1994; Dougherty & Bowman, 1995; Love & Kraatz, 2009; Morris, Cascio, & Young, 1999). The continued popularity of downsizing and layoffs flies in the face of this evidence. McKinley, Sanchez, and Schick (1995) argue that the widespread adoption of downsizing among corporations can be explained by the legitimation of downsizing as an institutionalized norm, consistent with institutional theory's view that organizations adopt institutionalized practices regardless of their effectiveness (Meyer & Rowan, 1977; DiMaggio & Powell, 1983). During the 1980s and 1990s, downsizing gradually acquired the status of a legitimate, taken-for-granted corporate practice. As Budros (1999) argues, early incidences of downsizing were described as "puzzling" and it took "guts" to implement them. As downsizing became more popular and viewed as business-as-usual, the prevalence of downsizing created legitimation pressures that triggered more layoffs (Budros, 1999, p. 78).

Downsizing and layoffs are inherently related to changes in corporate governance and the rise of shareholder value principle (Fligstein & Shin, 2007; Jung, 2015). The shareholder value model espouses corporate strategies that increase shareholder value, and restructuring and downsizing are good news that investors value. In the powerful market for corporate control, corporate raiders bought large corporations and broke them into pieces in so-called "bust-up" takeovers and shed large numbers of employees. Shareholders became increasingly powerful and effective, disciplining executive behavior and altering the strategies of the largest corporations (Jung, 2015; Useem, 1996). Lazonick and O'Sullivan (2000) argue that changes in corporate control in favor of shareholder power led to a marked shift in strategic orientation of top managers away from "retain and reinvest" and toward "downsize and distribute." Before the rise of the shareholder value principle, corporations tended to *retain* both the money they earned and the people they employed, and they *reinvested* in physical and human capital. The shareholder value principle however promotes a new model wherein the job of top managers is to *downsize* the company, boost profits, and *distribute* revenues to shareholders (Lazonick & O'Sullivan, 2000).

The impact of the shareholder value principle on workforce strategies such as downsizing and layoffs can best be understood as part of the tension between a shareholder view of the firm and a stakeholder view of the firm. In answering the question of whose interests public corporations should serve, the shareholder perspective prioritizes a shareholder's right as the residual claimant to the corporate profits. Shareholders receive the residual gain because they financed investment in the productive assets of the enterprise in which they hold shares. Shareholders are also entitled to the premium because they bear risk associated with the corporate enterprise. To shareholder value advocates, maximizing value for shareholders is equivalent to maximizing the social value of corporations, and it follows that it would be socially optimal to ensure that shareholder value is maximized (Shin, 2013; Sundaram & Inkpen, 2004).

The stakeholder perspective rejects the shareholder view in part because shareholders are rarely the only residual claimants (Freeman, 1984). Employees also bear risks associated with certain kinds of investments, particularly investments in human capital: the skills they develop over time at a specific firm are a highly specialized form of investment. As a result, employees have a stake in the company that is at risk. Corporate profits are created by a complex interaction between technological and organizational innovation that includes specialized input by skilled employees, and not just shareholder financial investment (Blair, 1995; O'Sullivan, 2000). Therefore, the objective of a public corporation is to balance the interest of various stakeholders and to maximize the total wealth for stakeholders – employees as well as shareholders (Freeman, 1984).

The contrast between the two perspectives suggests that the firm's dominant business principle, or the conception of control (Fligstein, 1990, 2001a) should have an impact on its strategies toward the employees. Proponents of the shareholder value principle argue that when shareholder value is maximized, the interests of other non-shareholding stakeholders, including employees, are improved as well (Jensen, 2001; Sundaram & Inkpen, 2004). Job loss and displacement are inevitable by-products of efficiency-maximizing tactics such as downsizing and layoffs, which in the long run create shareholder value that out-weighs short-term cost borne by stakeholders (Dial & Murphy, 1995). The shareholder value principle went beyond the arcane world of academic econom-ics and diffused widely to the business community during the 1980s and 1990s. Financial economists who developed agency theory actively promulgated the shareholder value orientation outside academia through publications in the popular media (Jensen, 1987, 1989) and in MBA classrooms (Khurana, 2007). Finance professionals – particularly investment bankers and management consultants – actively espoused the shareholder value model, aggressively pro-moted shareholder-value-maximizing tactics such as downsizing, restructuring, and hostile takeovers, and as a result prospered in the era of financialization (Ho, 2009; Lin, 2015; Lin & Tomaskovic-Devey, 2013). Firms that are managed under the shareholder value principle – either by top executives who espouse such a principle, or by strong pressure from influential outsiders such as large institutional investors – are expected to engage in personnel strategies such as downsizing and layoffs.[1] This should hold even after controlling for the eco-nomic determinants of layoffs, such as lower sales and profitability. In these firms, layoffs are more readily chosen as a legitimate, business-as-usual course of action, compared to other firms in a similar financial situation.

Sociologists have empirically tested this argument by identifying firms or industries that adopt the shareholder value orientation. To do so, these scholars often examine observable indicators that show whether or not the shareholder value orientation is predominant within a given firm or industry. For example, studies examine corporate practices aligned with the shareholder value principle such as mergers and acquisitions (Fligstein & Shin, 2007), existence of pressures from corporate constituencies, such as outside directors and institutional inves-tors that monitor top management (Jung, 2015, 2016), and top managers' func-tional background in finance (Shin, 2014). While these studies consistently show a significant link between the indicators of shareholder value orientation and corporate policies toward the workforce, this approach suffers one impor-tant limitation: these indicators are inherently indirect. Although the indicators are believed to be closely correlated with the actual attribute that the researcher aims to measure, that is, shareholder value orientation of the firm, it is not nec-essarily the case that they exclusively reflect shareholder value orientation of the firm's top decision-makers. Moreover, institutional theory suggests that organizations under institutional pressures tend to decouple formal policies from actual organizational practices (Meyer & Rowan, 1977). Companies often formally adopt shareholder-value-maximizing policies in order to satisfy share-holder demands but fail to implement them (Westphal & Zajac, 1998; Zajac & Westphal, 2004). Examining the firm's formal adoption of shareholder-value strategies would risk confounding the effect of managerial orientation and the symbolic management gestures.

This calls for a more direct way to measure top managers' adherence to shareholder value orientation, while controlling for formal strategies of the firm.

In the present study, I examine the CEO's use of the language that expresses adoption of the shareholder value principle as a direct measure of the manager's shareholder value orientation. Following the perspective that characteristics of top managers reflect the overall values and the orientation that guide the entire organization (Fligstein, 1990; Hambrick & Mason, 1984), studies show that the CEO's cognition or worldview is significantly associated with important outcomes of the firm (Chin, Hambrick, & Trevino, 2013; Finkelstein, Hambrick, & Cannella, 2009; Fligstein, 2001a; Shin, 2014). In the present study, I focus on the CEO's use of the language in public documents. Researchers often rely on public documents, such as corporate annual reports, as an important source of information for managerial characteristics and cognition (Abrahamson & Hambrick, 1997; Cho & Hambrick, 2006; Eggers & Kaplan, 2009; Fanelli, Misangyi, & Tosi, 2009; Salancik & Meindl, 1984; Shin & You, 2017).

The CEOs' letters to shareholders published in corporate annual reports is one outlet for CEOs to express their adherence to the shareholder value principle. CEOs as visible leaders strive to portray a consistent message in their public image (Fiol, 1995; Khurana, 2002). Based on the premise that the language in the letters to shareholders reflects the CEOs' shareholder value orientation, I argue that the CEOs who express their shareholder value orientation are more likely to adopt corporate strategies congruent with the shareholder value principle, including workforce downsizing strategy, compared to the CEOs who do not express shareholder value orientation. As top managers may decouple their language from the actual implementation of a certain strategy (Westphal & Zajac, 1998; Zajac & Westphal, 2004), studying the CEO language provides an opportunity to isolate the effect of language from the effect of decoupling by controlling for implementation of shareholder-value-maximizing strategies of the firm. Therefore, I predict that controlling for other factors that determine the likelihood of workforce downsizing, *firms where the CEOs use the shareholder-value language more frequently are more likely to engage in downsizing than firms where the CEOs do not use the shareholder-value language frequently.*

DATA AND METHODS

The main sample for this study comes from 100 largest (by revenue) U.S. firms from 1998 to 2005. This time period encompasses significant cyclical changes that occurred in the U.S. economy, including the dot-com boom and bust, the 2001 recession, and subsequent boom in the early 2000s. Due to missing values in several variables, the final sample includes 73 unique firms. The dataset has a panel structure with repeated annual observations for each firm. Information for the data came from various sources, including the Compustat, RiskMetrics Directors dataset, Thomson Financial's 13f Institutional Holdings (CDA/Spectrum s34), and Executive Compensation database commonly known as ExecuComp. CEOs' functional backgrounds were collected from various sources including *Who's Who in Finance and Industry, Gale Biography Resource Center*, annual CEO compensation survey on *Forbes* magazines, and corporate annual reports as described in detail below.

The dependent variable in the regression model is a binary variable indicating whether or not a firm announced a layoff in a given year. Similar to other studies in the literature (Baumol et al., 2003; Farbar & Hallock, 2009; Fligstein & Shin, 2007; Jung, 2015), I used articles in the *Wall Street Journal* as the main source of information. Through close examination of the articles, layoffs that involved more than 50 U.S. employees were identified. Two undergraduate coders worked independently and read entire articles which contained any of the following words, word combinations, or any word variations of them: "layoff," "lay off," "laid off," "downsize," "downsizing," "workforce," "work force," "employee," "staff," "job," or "position." Because a single event of layoff could be covered by more than one article and the list could include some highly speculative forecasts based on rumors, the coders carefully examined each article's contents for redundancy and certainty. Layoffs involving more than 50 employees were counted because layoffs at a smaller scale may not always attract the media's attention. In cases where the two coders did not agree, I examined the case in greater depth to determine whether a layoff was actually announced.

The focus on layoff announcements rather than the actual incidents of layoffs is well suited to the purpose of the study, which is to examine how top managers use the shareholder value logic to justify corporate decisions to downsize. A significant part of the motives to downsize is to conform to the institutional pressure and to gain organizational legitimacy by creating an appearance of the shareholder value orientation (Shin & You, 2017). A layoff announcement publicly displays the organization's adoption of the shareholder value logic and its plan to implement a tactic that conforms to this logic. Coverage in business media has an essential role in diffusion of specific management practices throughout the organizational field by demonstrating the firms' conformity to an institutional logic (Bednar, Boivie, & Prince, 2013; Strang & Soule, 1998). Since the sample of this study consists of the largest firms, it is reasonable to assume that any significant personnel decisions are covered in the *Wall Street Journal*. Moreover, as some of the announced layoffs may not actually take place,[2] a conservative approach is to examine the public announcements rather than the actual occurrence of layoffs.

CEOs with shareholder value orientation were identified by examining the language in CEOs' letters to shareholders published in corporate annual reports. In this study, I do not aim to measure true cognition of the managers.

Instead, I treat the language in the CEOs' letters as a visible example of top managers' public communications in which the CEOs as organizational leaders express the official position of the firm regarding important issues about the direction of the company (Salancik & Meindl, 1984; Staw, McKechnie, & Puffer, 1983). Consistent with this approach, there is evidence that the contents of shareholder letters do not deviate significantly from other forms of corporate communication. In a study comparing shareholder letters to internal planning documents, Fiol (1995) found that for non-evaluative components of communications, the two sources of information generally match. Therefore, I believe it is reasonable to assume that the language in the shareholder letters serves as a representative reflection of the CEOs' public communication habit in general. Following this premise, studies have examined the language in shareholder letters and reported meaningful findings (Abrahamson & Hambrick, 1997; Cho & Hambrick, 2006; Eggers & Kaplan, 2009; Fanelli et al., 2009; Salancik & Meindl, 1984; Shin & You, 2017).

I collected CEOs' letters from various sources, including Mergent, OneSource, ProQuest, SEC filings, and company websites. I used dtSearch, a software application that performs text search, to identify all valid references to shareholder value. I used the following keywords: (share*er* or stock*er* or investor*) and (value* or return*). I excluded all references to "total stockholder equity" or any related expressions, because they are simple references to accounting results rather than the shareholder value orientation. The appendix lists common expressions that qualify as references to shareholder value.

My approach incorporates best practices from existing studies that aim to measure the shareholder value-related concepts. Wade, Porac, and Pollock (1997) counted the number of sentences in corporate proxy statements that contained the keywords related to the shareholder concept. These keywords were very similar to mine. Zajac and Westphal (1995) and Westphal and Zajac (1998) manually coded the contents of the proxy statements. They reported little ambiguity in identifying texts that use an agency-theoretic justification of executive compensation.

For each letter, I counted the number of references to shareholder value. Fig. 1 shows the distribution of the number of references to shareholder value. On average, the shareholder-value language appears in each shareholder letter 2.2 times. I then divided the count by the total number of words in the letter and then multiplied it by 1,000 to facilitate the presentation of coefficient estimates in regression models. Therefore, this variable denotes the frequency of references to shareholder value per 1,000 words in each letter.

The models include variables that represent economic and financial determinants of layoffs (Budros, 1997, 1999). *Firm size* is measured by total assets in logarithm. Two measures of firm performance are included: *return on assets (ROA)* and one-year *total shareholder returns*. Using return on equity (ROE) instead of ROA did not change the substantive findings. *Employee productivity* is controlled for by measuring total revenues per employee. Finally, the models

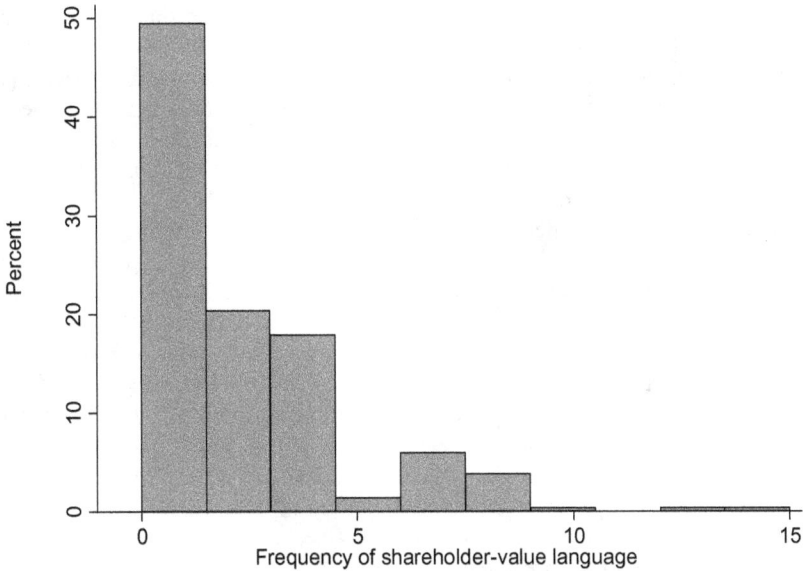

Fig. 1. Frequency Distribution of Shareholder-Value Language in CEOs' Letters to Shareholders.

include a variable that measures the firm's *cumulative number of layoff announcements* since 1998 in order to address unobserved heterogeneity among the firms in terms of underlying tendency to announce layoffs (Allison, 1984).

The models also control for characteristics of the CEO. CEO-chair duality is considered as an indicator of CEO power over the board of directors (van Essen, Otten, & Carberry, 2015). *CEO duality* is a binary variable coded as one if the CEO also held a position of board chair and zero otherwise. CEO tenure at the job represents several important attributes of the CEO including the CEO's experience, skills, and institutionalization of the CEO's leadership (Hambrick & Fukutomi, 1991). *CEO tenure* is a continuous variable that measures the time in years since the CEO was appointed to the job. Layoffs may be more frequent around the time when the CEO succession occurs (Billger & Hallock, 2005). Two binary variables are included to control for differences in layoff rates during the time of CEO succession: *CEO succession in the current year* (year *t*) and *CEO succession in the previous year* (year *t-1*).

Although the focus of the analysis is on the language that expresses the shareholder value orientation, it is important to control for related indicators of the shareholder value orientation. Based on the studies in the literature, five types of shareholder value indicators are controlled for. First, shareholder value proponents argue for the alignment of managerial incentives with the interest of shareholders by providing managers with stock-based compensation packages (Jensen & Murphy, 1990). Jung (2015, 2016) found that stock options granted to CEOs facilitate announcements and implementation of downsizing. In the present study, I use two variables for managerial incentive alignment: (1) the proportion of *incentive-based compensation*, which includes long-term incentive payouts, restricted stock grants, and the Black-Scholes value of stock option grants, to the total compensation awarded to the CEO, and (2) the percentage of *company shares owned by the CEO*.

Second, the CEO's functional background in finance is often regarded as an indicator of the CEO's worldview that is congruent with the shareholder value orientation, as finance and financial economics provide a foundational paradigm of the shareholder value principle (Fligstein, 2001a; Shin, 2013). Based on this reasoning, Budros (1999) predicted that downsizing would be more prevalent in firms managed by CEOs with a finance background rather than other backgrounds. I coded predominant functional background of a CEO's professional education (e.g., advanced degree in law or medicine) and early career (e.g., first job in a marketing department) into five categories: (1) general management including operation and administration, (2) finance, (3) sales and marketing, (4) technical (e.g., engineering, medicine, etc.), and (5) legal. General management is the reference category omitted in the regression models.

Third, I controlled for firms' concrete actions that are congruent with the shareholder value principle. I used two measures: dividends and stock repurchase. Because firms can distribute corporate profits to shareholders in the form of dividends or stock repurchase (Jagannathan, Stephens, & Weisbach, 2000), these measures can be interpreted as two alternative ways in which firms implement shareholder-value strategies. Shareholder value proponents advocate a greater use of dividend payouts and stock repurchase to maximize shareholder value and reduce agency costs (Jensen, 1986; Zajac & Westphal, 2004). Studies have treated these as valid indicators of shareholder-value strategies (Lazonick & O'Sullivan, 2000; Fligstein, 2001a; Sanders & Carpenter, 2003; Zajac & Westphal, 2004). In the present study, *dividend per share* is measured as the total amount of dividends paid during the fiscal year divided by the total number of shares outstanding (Julio & Ikenberry, 2004). *Stock repurchase* is measured in the dollar value (in logarithm) of common stock repurchases as reported in Compustat (Jagannathan et al., 2000).

Fourth, institutional investors constitute a strong force which monitors the companies that they invest in and pressures the firms to pursue shareholder value maximization (Davis & Thompson, 1994; Useem, 1996). Pressure from institutional investors can urge top managers to downsize the workforce in order to maximize profits and share prices (Jung, 2015, 2016; Lazonick & O'Sullivan, 2000). Jung (2015, 2016) found that the presence of large and active institutional investors is related to greater rates of downsizing announcements and implementation. In the present study, institutional ownership is measured by using two variables: (1) the *percentage of shares held by institutional investors* and (2) the *concentration of institutional ownership*. The two variables are not significantly correlated with each other. For the ownership concentration variable, I use a Herfindahl index of concentration.[3] It is computed as the sum of the squared ownership stakes of all institutional investors for each company. Specifically, Herfindahl index H is defined as:

$$H = \sum_{i=1}^{k} \left(\frac{s_i}{N}\right)^2$$

where s_i is the number of shares owned by the ith institutional owner, N is the total number of shares outstanding, and k is the total number of institutional owners. In order to make the index range from 0 to 1 regardless of the number of institutional owners, I use the adjusted Herfindahl index H_{adj} defined as:

$$H_{adj} = \frac{H - \frac{1}{k}}{1 - \frac{1}{k}}.$$

Finally, boards of directors function as an internal monitoring mechanism, whereas institutional investors provide external monitoring (Walsh & Seward, 1990). Shareholder value advocates call for the appointment of independent outside directors and the strengthening of board monitoring beyond rubber-stamping managerial decisions (Fama & Jensen, 1983). Jung (2015, 2016) found that internal monitoring by boards of directors composed of a high proportion of independent outsiders tends to facilitate downsizing announcements and implementation. In the present study, I measure board independence by *the proportion of independent outside directors* on the board. An outside director is defined as a board member who is not a current or former employee of the company, who (or whose employer) does not provide any professional services to the company, and who is not a major customer of the company, a recipient of charitable funds, an interlocking director, or a family member of a director or executive of the company. All dollar values in the variables are adjusted for inflation by using the Consumer Price Index (CPI) for all urban consumers. Tables 1 and 2 present descriptive statistics and correlation coefficients for the variables.

For the analysis, I use discrete-time event history methods (Allison, 1984) and estimate random-effects logit models with robust standard errors. Fixed-effects logit models would delete many cases (29 firms or 76 firm-year observations) from the analysis due to all positive (i.e., a layoff announcement every year) or all negative (i.e., no layoff announcements in all years) values on dependent variable. Using alternative estimation methods such as fixed-effects logit, random-effects complementary log−log (cloglog), and logit with standard errors clustered by the firm resulted in the findings similar to those from random-effects logit models. All independent variables are lagged by one year to facilitate interpretation. All models include dummy variables for fiscal year,

Table 1.   Descriptive Statistics.

	Mean	S.D.	Min.	Max.
Layoff announcement (binary)	.29	.45	.00	1.00
Assets[a]	10.42	1.18	7.97	13.95
ROA	4.27	5.67	−38.61	24.35
Total shareholder return	10.65	38.85	−92.38	265.73
Productivity	.54	.60	.03	5.32
Cumulative layoffs	1.14	1.36	.00	6.00
CEO-chair duality	.85	.36	.00	1.00
CEO tenure	6.19	6.71	.00	38.00
CEO succession (current year)	.13	.34	.00	1.00
CEO succession (previous year)	.14	.34	.00	1.00
CEO incentive pay	.66	.22	.00	1.00
CEO ownership	.90	4.23	.00	32.68
CEO background: general	.33	.47	.00	1.00
CEO background: finance	.27	.45	.00	1.00
CEO background: marketing & sales	.12	.33	.00	1.00
CEO background: technical	.17	.38	.00	1.00
CEO background: legal	.11	.31	.00	1.00
Dividend per share	.83	.70	.00	3.01
Stock repurchase[a]	3.95	3.08	.00	8.72
Percent institutional ownership	64.18	14.28	15.91	100.00
Institutional ownership concentration	.05	.07	.01	1.00
Proportion outside directors	.72	.16	.11	1.00
Shareholder-value language[b]	.11	.13	.00	.80

[a]In logarithm.
[b]Number of references to shareholder value per 1,000 words.

and all models except for fixed-effects models include dummy variables for 2-digit Standard Industrial Classification (SIC) industries.

RESULTS

Table 3 reports the results of regression models predicting the rates of layoff announcements. Coefficients and standard errors for year and industry dummies are not reported. Models 1 and 2 are the results from random-effects logit models. Consistent with Budro's (1999) prediction and Jung's (2015) results, firms with a finance CEO are more likely to announce layoffs, although the

Table 2. Correlation Matrix.

	1.	2.	3.	4.	5.	6.	7.	8.	9.	10.	11.	12.	13.	14.	15.	16.	17.	18.	19.	20.	21.	22.
1. Layoff announcement (binary)																						
2. Assets[a]	.19*																					
3. ROA	-.24*	-.27*																				
4. Total shareholder return	-.17*	-.02	.16*																			
5. Productivity	-.17*	-.04	-.06	.21*																		
6. Cumulative layoffs	.51*	.27*	-.16*	-.03	-.16*																	
7. CEO-chair duality	.05	.06	.13*	-.03	.01	.00																
8. CEO tenure	-.08	.31*	-.05	.01	.09	-.10*	.16*															
9. CEO succession (current year)	.10*	-.08	-.11*	-.15*	-.05	.07	-.12*	-.06														
10. CEO succession (previous year)	.06	-.11*	-.01	.08	-.05	.07	-.18*	-.30*	-.10*													
11. CEO incentive pay	-.03	.03	.07	-.01	.02	-.07	-.07	-.01	.08	-.05												
12. CEO ownership	-.09*	.15*	-.07	.00	.00	-.13*	.03	.54*	-.05	-.07	.04											
13. CEO background: general	.05	-.06	.02	-.03	-.09	.03	.02	-.15*	.07	.02	.06	-.07										
14. CEO background: finance	-.08	.37*	-.09	.01	.23*	-.13*	-.02	.23*	.00	.00	.06	.22*	-.43*									

Table 2. (Continued)

	1.	2.	3.	4.	5.	6.	7.	8.	9.	10.	11.	12.	13.	14.	15.	16.	17.	18.	19.	20.	21.	22.
15. CEO background: marketing & sales	-.09*	-.34*	.14*	-.01	-.13*	.04	-.03	.00	-.02	.02	-.13*	-.06	-.26*	-.23*								
16. CEO background: technical	.08	-.07	.06	.05	-.05	.06	.01	-.02	-.05	-.05	.00	-.07	-.32*	-.28*	-.17*							
17. CEO background: legal	.05	.01	-.13*	-.03	.01	.02	.01	-.07	-.03	.01	-.05	-.06	-.24*	-.21*	-.13*	-.16*						
18. Dividend per share	.06	.14*	.11*	-.05	-.01	.03	.20*	-.01	-.04	-.05	-.06	-.21*	-.02	-.03	-.14*	.07	.13*					
19. Stock repurchase[a]	-.07	-.09	.40*	.08	-.06	-.10*	.16*	-.06	-.07	-.03	.06	-.19*	-.02	-.06	.00	.07	.04	.01				
20. Percent institutional ownership	-.10*	-.31*	-.01	.11*	.00	.07	-.12*	-.05	-.01	.02	.07	-.07	-.09	-.04	.21*	.02	-.07	-.23*	-.11*			
21. Institutional ownership concentration	.02	-.14*	-.01	-.06	.18*	-.04	.00	-.04	.14*	.01	-.03	-.02	.11*	-.09	.04	-.04	-.04	.09	.02	.01		
22. Proportion outside directors	.04	.07	.04	.04	.07	.23*	.08	-.26*	-.05	.00	.03	-.33*	.07	-.06	-.09	.06	.00	.33*	-.02	.08	-.04	
23. Shareholder-value language[b]	.01	.02	-.04	.01	.09	.05	.04	-.06	-.01	-.03	-.01	-.12*	-.06	.06	-.06	.02	.05	.17*	.06	.00	.04	.10*

*p < .05.

[a] In logarithm.

[b] Number of references to shareholder value per 1,000 words.

Table 3. Regression Results Predicting Layoff Announcements.

	Model 1 Random-Effects Logit	Model 2 Random-Effects Logit	Model 3 Fixed-Effects Logit	Model 4 Random-Effects Cloglog	Model 5 Logit	Model 6 Random-Effects Logit	Model 7 Random-effects logit
Assets[a]	-.34	.24	-.38	.30	.24	.24	-.32
	(66)	(.60)	(1.59)	(.34)	(.60)	(.60)	(.51)
ROA	-.05	.08	.06	.04	.08	.08	.02
	(.08)	(.09)	(.10)	(.06)	(.09)	(.09)	(.07)
Total shareholder return	-.01	-.02*	-.02	-.01*	-.02*	-.02*	.00
	(.01)	(.01)	(.01)	(.01)	(.01)	(.01)	(.01)
Productivity	-.88	-1.25	-1.57	-.78	-1.25	-.96	-1.25
	(1.14)	(89)	(1.36)	(.83)	(.89)	(.82)	(1.21)
Cumulative layoffs	2.14**	2.23**	3.98**	1.54**	2.23**	2.28**	2.30**
	(.30)	(.43)	(.84)	(.33)	(.43)	(.42)	(.35)
CEO-chair duality	.26	.13	.23	-.04	.13	.40	.17
	(.96)	(.87)	(1.17)	(.44)	(.87)	(.81)	(.74)
CEO tenure	.05	.00	.18	.01	.00	-.01	.06
	(.04)	(.05)	(.11)	(.03)	(.05)	(.05)	(.04)
CEO succession (current year)	.62	1.24*	1.30	1.05*	1.24*	1.45*	.77
	(.71)	(.62)	(.83)	(.42)	(.62)	(.57)	(.62)
CEO succession (previous year)	.29	.20	.93	.15	.20	.18	.56
	(.62)	(.67)	(1.05)	(.45)	(.67)	(.64)	(.60)
CEO incentive pay	.60	.79	.67	.83	.79	.83	.49
	(.96)	(.77)	(1.26)	(.63)	(.77)	(.75)	(.88)
CEO ownership	-.10	.39	-.65	.28+	.39	.47+	-.16
	(.20)	(.26)	(.52)	(.16)	(.26)	(.27)	(18)

Table 3. (Continued)

	Model 1 Random-Effects Logit	Model 2 Random-Effects Logit	Model 3 Fixed-Effects Logit	Model 4 Random-Effects Cloglog	Model 5 Logit	Model 6 Random-Effects Logit	Model 7 Random-effects logit
CEO background: finance[b]	1.49+	1.59*	.33	1.52*	1.59*	1.45*	1.30+
	(.90)	(.71)	(1.45)	(.68)	(.71)	(.72)	(.72)
CEO background: marketing & sales[b]	-.64	.04	-.01	.57	.04	.02	-.74
	(1.42)	(1.48)	(2.15)	(1.08)	(1.47)	(1.46)	(111)
CEO background: technical[b]	-.07	-.02	1.96	.49	-.02	-.03	-.19
	(.67)	(.71)	(1.81)	(.48)	(.71)	(.67)	(.62)
CEO background: legal[b]	1.11	1.15	2.68	1.28*	1.15	.80	1.57+
	(.85)	(.84)	(2.77)	(.65)	(.84)	(.82)	(.93)
Dividend per share	-.23	-.01	-.25	-.26	-.01	-.16	-.23
	(.41)	(.36)	(1.04)	(.31)	(.36)	(.35)	(.36)
Stock repurchase[a]	-.05	-.18+	-.12	-.12+	-.18+	-.18+	-.15
	(.10)	(.09)	(.16)	(.07)	(.09)	(.10)	(.10)
Percent institutional ownership	-.02	.02	.02	.01	.02	.03	-.01
	(.03)	(.03)	(.06)	(.02)	(.03)	(.03)	(.03)
Institutional ownership concentration	10.51	17.51	.42	19.20*	17.51	15.95	13.86
	(10.34)	(13.73)	(22.54)	(8.20)	(13.73)	(13.39)	(12.86)
Proportion outside directors	.18	-1.50	6.64	.48	-1.50	-2.56	-1.56
	(2.33)	(2.63)	(4.69)	(1.69)	(2.63)	(2.82)	(199)
Shareholder-value language[c]		6.86**	5.94*	4.06*	6.86**		
		(2.58)	(2.82)	(1.69)	(2.58)		

Shareholder-value language (binary)						1.89**	
						(.71)	
Shareholder-value language (within-CEO average)							9.83**
							(2.95)
Constant	−3.37	−13.76+		−12.50*	−13.75+	−13.93+	−1.20
	(7.97)	(8.01)		(5.13)	(8.01)	(7.37)	(7.39)
Year dummies	Included	Included	Included	Included	Included	Included	Included
Industry dummies	Included	Included	Not included	Included	Included	Included	Included
Log likelihood	−90.46	−84.05	−36.72	−85.39	−84.05	−82.74	−99.83
N	271	288	212	288	288	288	306

Note: Robust standard errors are in parentheses.
+$p < 0.10$; *$p < 0.05$; **$p < 0.01$ (two-tailed test).
[a]In logarithm.
[b]Omitted reference category is general management background.
[c]Number of references to shareholder value per 1,000 words.

effect is marginally significant in Model 1. Model 2 includes the variable for the CEO's expression of shareholder-value language found in the letters to share-holders. Consistent with the prediction, the coefficient estimate is positive and statistically significant ($\beta = 6.86$, $p < .01$, two-tailed test). This supports the argument that the shareholder value orientation of the CEO is associated with a higher rate of workforce downsizing.

Models 3–5 present robustness checks using alternative estimation methods. Model 3 is a fixed-effects logit model. Because firms' industry membership does not change over time, the fixed-effects model omits industry dummies. Moreover, the model drops all firms that had a layoff announcement in every year as well as firms that had no layoff announcements during the study period. Model 4 is a random-effects complementary log–log (cloglog) model. Model 5 is a logit regression model with robust errors clustered by the firm. All three models show a similar finding: the CEO's use of language that expresses the shareholder value principle is related to a higher rate of layoff announcements.

As further robustness checks, I tested using alternative measures of the shareholder-value language. In Model 6, I used a dichotomized measure, which is coded one for a presence of any reference to the shareholder value principle (identified in the same way as described in the "Data and Methods" section) and zero otherwise. In the sample, 54.9 percent of the letters contained at least one reference to shareholder value, while 45.1 percent had no references. In Model 7, I averaged the count of shareholder-value language over each CEO's tenure as CEO. In both models, the results are consistent with the prediction that shareholder-value language is associated with a higher rate of layoff announcements.

As top managers often use language and symbolic gestures to justify past actions (Staw et al., 1983; Wade et al., 1997), it may be possible that CEOs use the language to justify past layoff decisions. To investigate this, I ran regression models testing a reverse causal order. The dependent variable was the CEO's use of shareholder-value language per 1,000 words in each letter, and the key independent variable was layoff announcement in the previous year. Table 4 shows the results using various estimation methods: fixed-effects model (Model 1), random-effects model (Model 2), and random-effects model with industry dummies (Model 3). In Model 4, I used a dichotomized version of the share-holder-value language variable as dependent variable and estimated a random-effects logit model. All models include year dummies. In all models, layoff announcement in the previous year was not significantly associated with share-holder-value language. Therefore, I found no evidence of post hoc justification. The use of shareholder-value language as an indicator of the CEO's share-holder value orientation seems to be causally prior to the decision to downsize.

A related concern is a possibility that the shareholder-value language may reflect the firm's performance problems and the CEO's effort to appease share-holders by signaling a message that the company is committed to shareholder value. If this is the case, the shareholder-value language variable might not

Table 4. Regression Results Predicting the Use of Shareholder-Value Language.

	Model 1 Fixed-Effects	Model 2 Random-Effects	Model 3 Random-Effects	Model 4 Random-Effects Logit
Layoff announcement	.00	.00	.00	.24
	(.02)	(.01)	(.02)	(.42)
Assets[a]	.07	.00	.01	.30
	(.05)	(.01)	(.02)	(.28)
ROA	.00	.00	.00	−.01
	(.00)	(.00)	(.00)	(.04)
Total shareholder return	.00	.00	.00	.00
	(.00)	(.00)	(.00)	(.00)
Productivity	.04+	.03+	.01	.86*
	(.02)	(.02)	(.02)	(.43)
CEO-chair duality	−.05+	−.02	−.01	.57
	(.03)	(.03)	(.03)	(.48)
CEO tenure	.01*	.00	.00	−.01
	(.00)	(.00)	(.00)	(.05)
CEO succession (current year)	−.02	−.01	−.01	−.15
	(.03)	(.02)	(.02)	(.49)
CEO succession (previous year)	.00	.00	.00	−.42
	(.03)	(.03)	(.03)	(.46)
CEO incentive pay	.01	.00	.00	−.99
	(.04)	(.04)	(.04)	(84)
CEO ownership	.00	.00	−.01	−.30
	(.01)	(.00)	(.01)	(.51)
CEO background: finance[b]	−.07**	−.04+	−.08**	−.55
	(.03)	(.03)	(.03)	(.45)
CEO background: marketing & sales[b]	.07	.01	.03	.87
	(.05)	(.04)	(.05)	(1.00)
CEO background: technical[b]	−.04	−.01	−.02	−.19
CEO background: legal[b]	(.05)	(.03)	(.04)	(.45)
	.04	−.02	−.01	.57
	(.06)	(.04)	(.05)	(.96)
Dividend per share	.01	.04*	.03	.42
	(.04)	(.02)	(.02)	(.36)
Stock repurchase[a]	.01**	.01**	.01*	.13*
	(.00)	(.00)	(.00)	(.06)
Percent institutional ownership	.00	.00	.00	.01
	(.00)	(.00)	(.00)	(.02)

Table 4.   (*Continued*)

	Model 1 Fixed-Effects	Model 2 Random-Effects	Model 3 Random-Effects	Model 4 Random-Effects Logit
Institutional ownership concentration	−.11	−.57*	−.69	−20.81[+]
	(.64)	(.28)	(.61)	(10.63)
Proportion outside directors	−.08	−.02	−.01	1.31
	(.10)	(.06)	(.09)	(1.80)
Constant	−.55	.06	.04	−5.55[+]
	(.54)	(.17)	(.25)	(3.34)
Year dummies	Included	Included	Included	Included
Industry dummies	Not included	Not included	Included	Included
R^2	.16	.10	.25	
Log likelihood				−160.08
N	302	302	302	285

Note: Robust standard errors are in parentheses.
[+]$p < 0.10$; *$p < 0.05$; **$p < 0.01$ (two-tailed test).
[a]In logarithm.
[b]Omitted reference category is general management background.

measure the shareholder value orientation of the firm. The statistical association between shareholder-value language and downsizing might actually be explained by firm performance: poor performance might determine both shareholder-value language and downsizing. To address this concern, I tested whether poor performance of the firm in the previous year predicts the use of shareholder-value language. There is no evidence in support of this possibility. Models in Table 4 include firm performance measures: ROA and total shareholder returns. Neither of them is significantly associated with the use of shareholder-value language. Using ROE instead of ROA does not change the finding. The results suggest that top managers use shareholder-value language both in good times and bad times. This implies that shareholder-value language is a reasonable measure of the underlying orientation of the firm, rather than simply an expedient tool adopted during a time of crisis.

Another issue is whether the CEO's use of language is symbolic in nature so that it is decoupled from actual implementation of shareholder value strategy. In the context of corporate governance, empirical studies have found that CEOs tend to endorse a prevailing model of governance in order to gain legitimacy in the institutional environment while failing to implement concrete practices of the governance model that they have endorsed (Westphal & Zajac, 1998; Zajac & Westphal, 2004). Language in public domain plays an important role in this decoupling process (Fiss & Zajac, 2004; Zajac & Westphal, 1995).

In my data, the shareholder-value language variable is uncorrelated with most indicators of the shareholder value principle: CEO incentive compensation, CEO background, stock repurchase, and institutional ownership (see Table 2). Shareholder-value language is positively correlated with dividend payouts and board independence, whereas it is negatively correlated with CEO ownership. In a multivariate analysis shown in Table 4, most of the shareholder-value indicators as independent variables were not significantly associated with shareholder-value language as dependent variable. Only stock repurchase variable was significantly associated with shareholder-value language in all four models. It appears that the CEOs' use of shareholder-value language is often decoupled from various indicators of the shareholder value principle.

To address the issue further, I ran random-effects logit models predicting layoff announcements with an interaction term between shareholder-value language and each of the indicators of shareholder value principle. None of the interaction effects was significant (results available upon request). This suggests that the decoupling of language and other indicators does not significantly affect layoff announcements. Regardless of whether the language is decoupled from concrete practices of the firm or it is tightly coupled with them, the shareholder value orientation of the CEO as measured by the language seem to predict a significant part of the firm's decision to downsize.

DISCUSSIONS AND CONCLUSION

Although corporate downsizing has been widely studied and debated, few attempts have been made to link downsizing to the issues of corporate governance. This study explored such a link. I developed a hypothesis that a governance model that espouses shareholder value orientation affects corporations' announcements of downsizing. The results from a sample of large U.S. firms supported the prediction that the CEO's use of language congruent with the shareholder value principle would be significantly associated with higher rates of layoff announcements, after controlling for indirect indicators of the shareholder value principle.

The present study contributes to the literature on corporate downsizing, corporate governance, and shareholder value. First, the findings of this study deepen our understanding of downsizing by emphasizing a fundamental cause of the decision to downsize, namely the top managers' cognition. Although environmental pressure on the organizations is an important force prompting firms to adopt new practices like downsizing, the top managers as leaders of the organizations are the ones who recognize the value of such practices and call for their implementation. For such an action to occur, the new practices must be accompanied by a compelling rationale that demands top managers' attention and justifies the use of organizational resources necessary for adopting the practices. I argue that CEOs use the prevailing norm of maximizing shareholder value as the rationale for adopting shareholder-value-maximizing practices including workforce downsizing. Although the literature suggests that several indicators of the shareholder value orientation – for example, stock-based compensation for executive managers and more stringent monitoring mechanisms – are associated with downsizing (Budros, 1997; Fligstein & Shin, 2007; Jung, 2015, 2016), such indicators seem to be consequences of top managers' shareholder value orientation rather than a fundamental cause of downsizing. The CEOs who embraced the shareholder value principle were open to the set of governance mechanisms that shareholder value proponents recommended. By examining a more proximate measure of top managers' cognition, the CEO's use of language, the present study highlights the role of managerial cognition as an underlying force that drives organizational action.

Second, this study holds a broad implication for the link between corporate governance and workforce outcomes. As sociologically oriented scholars of corporate governance argue (Aguilera & Jackson, 2003; Fligstein & Shin, 2007; Jung, 2016; Shin, 2013), the existing literature on corporate governance focuses extensively on the relationships among corporate elites such as executive managers, boards of directors, and large investors, while ignoring the role of labor. This is an important limitation for two reasons: first, labor constitutes important participants that shape corporate governance processes (Aguilera & Jackson, 2003; Gourevitch & Shinn, 2005), and second, corporate governance has a significant impact on employees as stakeholders (Goldstein, 2012; Jung, 2015, 2016; Shin, 2014). This study's findings are consistent with recent studies that show the impact of corporate governance dynamics on workforce downsizing (Jung, 2015, 2016). Moreover, the present study suggests that the normative side of the governance model drives corporate policies affecting the employees rather than the objective side of corporate governance such as monitoring mechanisms and managerial compensation schemes.

Finally, the present study highlights an important implication for the institutionalization of the shareholder value principle within the United States. Whereas scholars describe political and economic environments that gave rise to the shareholder value principle as a predominant governance model in the United States (Davis & Thompson, 1994; Fligstein & Shin, 2007; Lazonick & O'Sullivan, 2000; Shin, 2013), the actual process of how individual actors espouse the shareholder value principle is not well understood. The findings of the present study shed light on this issue when considered together with evidence in other studies. Brookman, Chang, and Rennie (2007) showed that CEO compensation significantly increases after announcing layoffs. Henderson, Masli, Richardson, and Sanchez (2010) found that the relationship between layoffs and CEO compensation depends on the CEO's power over the board of directors: as the layoffs intensify, more powerful CEOs experience smaller reductions in their bonuses and a greater increase in stock-based compensation compared to less powerful CEOs. In addition, there is evidence that CEOs who use shareholder-value language in public documents tend to receive greater compensation (Shin & You, 2017). Putting these together with the present study's findings, I argue that CEOs – particularly those with greater power over the boards – have financial incentives to publicly espouse the shareholder value principle and to announce layoffs. Such actions of the CEOs are highly visible and bring tangible benefits to the executives in the form of lucrative compensation. If this process continues over time, I suggest that the financial incentive could have facilitated the institutionalization of the shareholder value principle across the firms. This was possible through the actions of the top managers who actively participated in the diffusion of the new governance model by embracing it publicly.

Some limitations of this study should be noted. First, the sample was limited to the largest firms in the United States. Future studies need to expand the scope of the research in order to test generalizability of the findings in a broader setting, for example among smaller firms or non-U.S. firms. Second, although my measure of the shareholder value orientation is considered as a more direct indicator of what top managers think and say than other available measures, it is still a proxy of the managers' actual beliefs. Future studies would benefit from even more proximate indicators of dominant business principles and ideologies held by top managers. As presented in this study, textual data offers ample opportunities for analysis of rich and subtle information (Fanelli et al., 2009; Tuggle, Sirmon, Reutzel, & Bierman, 2010). Finally, workforce downsizing, albeit important and timely, is one of many dimensions of outcomes that impact workers. Other important outcomes including wages, benefits, and opportunities for upward mobility (Cobb, 2015; Lin, 2015) should also be studied in relation to the shareholder value principle in particular and corporate governance in general.

This study suggests that corporate downsizing needs to be understood within a larger context of the transformation of corporate governance. These findings imply that beyond the immediate impact on the laid off workers, a corporate downsizing strategy represents the rise of shareholder primacy and the deterioration of labor power. The key actors in this process are top managers who publicly embrace the shareholder value principle in response to external pressure from the investors and conform to the new management ideology. As Gordon (1996) observed two decades ago, managers were far from the victims of aggressive efforts to downsize. The pursuit of shareholder value strategies paradoxically increased supervisory requirements over labor and intensified demand for managerial talent, resulting in firms that became fatter at the top (Goldstein, 2012). This implies that one of the conspicuous consequences of this mechanism is the rising inequality between average workers who have suffered job loss and insecure employment relations and the corporate executives who accumulated wealth by aligning with shareholders.

NOTES

1. Budros (1999) proposes a related hypothesis that downsizing will be less popular among employee-centered firms than among those that are less-employee-centered, without explicitly linking this to the shareholder/stakeholder views. Budros (1997) tested this hypothesis by comparing downsizing rates across different industries, based on the assumption that industries have different cultures. He found that downsizing rates were higher in banking, finance, and utility industries, which he considers to have a service-oriented culture, than in manufacturing and retail industries, which he assumes to have a competition-oriented culture.

2. For example, AT&T eliminated 7,700 jobs in 1996, and hired about the same number of employees in the company's fast growing wireless, Internet, and other operations. At the end of 1996, the total number of employees stayed about the same as in the beginning of the year (Keller, 1996).

3. Alternatively, I also used the percentage of institutional ownership held by top-five investors as a measure of ownership concentration among institutional investors. This did not change substantive findings.

REFERENCES

Abrahamson, E., & Hambrick, D. C. (1997). Attentional homogeneity in industries: The effect of discretion. *Journal of Organizational Behavior, 18*(Special Issue), 513–532.

Aguilera, R. V., & Jackson, G. (2003). The cross-national diversity of corporate governance: Dimensions and determinants. *Academy of Management Review, 28*(3), 447–465.

Ahmadjian, C. L., & Robbins, G. E. (2005). A clash of capitalisms: Foreign shareholders and corporate restructuring in 1990s Japan. *American Sociological Review, 70*, 451–471.

Ahmadjian, C. L., & Robinson, P. (2001). Safety in numbers: Downsizing and the deinstitutionalization of permanent employment in Japan. *Administrative Science Quarterly, 46*, 622–654.

Allison, P. D. (1984). *Event history analysis: Regression for longitudinal data.* Newbury Park, CA: Sage.

Appelbaum, E., & Berg, P. (1996). Financial market constraints and business strategy in the USA. In J. Michie & J. G. Smith (Eds.), *Creating industrial capacity: Towards full employment.* New York, NY: Oxford University Press.

Baumol, W. J., Blinder, A. S., & Wolff, E. N. (2003). *Downsizing in America: Reality, causes, and consequences.* New York, NY: Russell Sage Foundation.

Bednar, M. K., Boivie, S., & Prince, N. R. (2013). Burr under the saddle: How media coverage influences strategic change. *Organization Science, 24*(3), 910–925.

Billger, S. M., & Hallock, K. F. (2005). Mass layoffs and CEO turnover. *Industrial Relations: A Journal of Economy and Society, 44*(3), 463–489.

Blair, M. (1995). *Ownership and control: Re-thinking corporate governance for the twenty-first century.* Washington, DC: Brookings Institution.

Brockner, J. (1988). The effects of work layoffs on survivors: Research, theory and practice. *Research in Organizational Behavior, 10*, 213–255.

Brookman, J. T., Chang, S., & Rennie, C. G. (2007). CEO cash and stock-based compensation changes, layoff decisions, and shareholder value. *Financial Review, 42*(1), 99–119.

Budros, A. (1997). The new capitalism and organizational rationality: The adoption of downsizing programs, 1979-1994. *Social Forces, 76*(1), 229–250.

Budros, A. (1999). A conceptual framework for analyzing why organizations downsize. *Organization Science, 10*(1), 69–82.

Budros, A. (2004). Causes of early and later organizational adoption: The case of corporate downsizing. *Sociological Inquiry, 74*(3), 355–380.

Cascio, W. F. (1993). Downsizing: What do we know? What have we learned? *Academy of Management Executive, 7*, 95–104.

Chandler, A. D. (1977). *The visible hand: The managerial revolution in American business.* Cambridge, MA: Harvard University Press.

Chin, M. K., Hambrick, D. C., & Treviño, L. K. (2013). Political ideologies of CEOs the influence of executives' values on corporate social responsibility. *Administrative Science Quarterly, 58*(2), 197–232.

Cho, T. S., & Hambrick, D. C. (2006). Attention as the mediator between top management team characteristics and strategic change: The case of airline deregulation. *Organization Science, 17*(4), 453–469.

Cobb, J. A. (2015). Risky business: The decline of defined benefit pensions and firms' shifting of risk. *Organization Science, 26*(5), 1332–1350.

Cobb, J. A. (2016). How firms shape income inequality: Stakeholder power, executive decision making, and the structuring of employment relationships. *Academy of Management Review, 41*(2), 324–348.

Datta, D. K., Guthrie, J. P., Basuil, D., & Pandey, A. (2010). Causes and effects of employee downsizing: A review and synthesis. *Journal of Management, 36*(1), 281–348.

Davis, G. F. (2005). New directions in corporate governance. *Annual Review of Sociology, 31*, 143–162.

Davis, G. F., Diekmann, K., & Tinsley, C. (1994). The decline and fall of the conglomerate firm in the 1980s: The deinstitutionalization of an institutional form. *American Sociological Review, 59*, 547–570.

Davis, G. F., & Thompson, T. (1994). A social movement perspective on corporate control. *Administrative Science Quarterly, 39*, 141–173.

De Meuse, K., Vanderheiden, P., & Bergmann, T. (1994). Announced layoffs: Their effect on corporate financial performance. *Human Resource Management, 33*, 509–530.

Dencker, J. C., & Fang, C. (2016). Rent seeking and the transformation of employment relationships: The effect of corporate restructuring on wage patterns, determinants, and inequality. *American Sociological Review, 81*(3), 467–487.

Dial, J., & Murphy, K. J. (1995). Incentives, downsizing, and value creating at general dynamics. *Journal of Financial Economics, 37*, 261–314.

DiMaggio, P. J., & Powell, W. W. (1983). The iron cage revisited: Institutional isomorphism and collective rationality in organizational fields. *American Sociological Review, 48*, 147–160.

Dougherty, D., & Bowman, E. (1995). The effects of organizational downsizing on product innovation. *California Management Review, 37*, 28–44.

Eggers, J. P., & Kaplan, S. (2009). Cognition and renewal: Comparing CEO and organizational effects on incumbent adaptation to technical change. *Organization Science, 20*(2), 461–477.

Elsbach, K. D. (1994). Managing organizational legitimacy in the California cattle industry: The construction and effectiveness of verbal accounts. *Administrative Science Quarterly, 39*, 57–88.

Fama, E. F., & Jensen, M. C. (1983). Separation of ownership and control. *Journal of Law and Economics, 26*(2), 301–325.

Fanelli, A., Misangyi, V. F., & Tosi, H. L. (2009). In charisma we trust: The effects of CEO charismatic visions on securities analysts. *Organization Science, 20*(6), 1011–1033.

Farbar, H. S., & Hallock, K. F. (2009). The changing relationship between job loss announcements and stock prices: 1970–1999. *Labour Economics, 16*, 1–11.

Farber, H. S. (2005). What do we know about Job Loss in the United States? Evidence from the Displaced Workers Survey, 1981–2004. *Economic Perspectives*, Federal Reserve Bank of Chicago, (Second Quarter), *29*(2), 13–28.

Finkelstein, S., Hambrick, D. C., & Cannella, A. A. (2009). *Strategic leadership: Theory and research on executives, top management teams, and boards.* New York, NY: Oxford University Press.

Fiol, C. M. (1995). Corporate communications: Comparing executives' private and public statements. *Academy of Management Journal, 38*(2), 522–536.

Fiss, P. C., & Zajac, E. J. (2004). The diffusion of ideas over contested terrain: The (non)adoption of a shareholder value orientation among German firms. *Administrative Science Quarterly, 49*, 501−534.

Fligstein, N. (1990). *The transformation of corporate control*. Cambridge, MA: Harvard University Press.

Fligstein, N. (2001a). *The architecture of markets: An economic sociology of twenty-first-century capitalist societies*. Princeton, NJ: Princeton University Press.

Fligstein, N. (2001b). Social skill and the theory of fields. *Sociological Theory, 40*, 397−405.

Fligstein, N., & Shin, T. (2007). Shareholder value and the transformation of the U.S. economy, 1984−2000. *Sociological Forum, 22*(4), 399−424.

Freeman, R. E. (1984). *Strategic management: A stakeholder approach*. New York, NY: Cambridge University Press.

Freeman, S., & Cameron, K. (1993). Organizational downsizing: A convergence and reorientation framework. *Organization Science, 4*, 10−29.

Gao, H., Yu, T., & Cannella, A. A. (2016). The use of public language in strategy: A multidisciplinary review and research agenda. *Journal of Management, 42*(1), 21−54.

Gillan, S. L., & Starks, L. T. (2007). The evolution of shareholder activism in the United States. *Journal of Applied Corporate Finance, 19*(1), 55−73.

Gioia, D. A., Thomas, J. B., Clark, S. M., & Chittipeddi, K. (1994). Symbolism and strategic change in academia: The dynamics of sensemaking and influence. *Organization Science, 5*(3), 363−383.

Goldstein, A. (2012). Revenge of the managers: Labor cost-cutting and the paradoxical resurgence of managerialism in the shareholder value era, 1984 to 2001. *American Sociological Review, 77*(2), 268−294.

Gordon, D. (1996). *Fat and mean: The corporate squeeze of working Americans and the myth of managerial downsizing*. New York, NY: Free Press.

Gourevitch, P. A., & Shinn, J. (2005). *Political power and corporate control: The new global politics of corporate governance*. Princeton, NJ: Princeton University Press.

Greenhalgh, L., Lawrence, A. T., & Sutton, R. I. (1988). Determinants of work force reduction strategies in declining organizations. *Academy of Management Review, 13*(2), 241−254.

Hambrick, D. C., & Fukutomi, G. D. (1991). The seasons of a CEO's tenure. *Academy of Management Review, 16*(4), 719−742.

Hambrick, D. C., & Mason, P. A. (1984). Upper echelons: The organization as a reflection of its top managers. *Academy of Management Review, 9*(2), 193−206.

Hatton, E. (2011). *The temp economy: From Kelly girls to permatemps in postwar America*. Philadelphia, PA: Temple University Press.

Henderson, B. C., Masli, A., Richardson, V. J., & Sanchez, J. M. (2010). Layoffs and chief executive officer (CEO) compensation: Does CEO power influence the relationship? *Journal of Accounting, Auditing and Finance, 25*(4), 709−748.

Ho, K. (2009). *Liquidated: An ethnography of wall street*. Durham, NC: Duke University Press.

Jagannathan, M., Stephens, C. P., & Weisbach, M. S. (2000). Financial flexibility and the choice between dividends and stock repurchases. *Journal of Financial Economics, 57*(3), 355−384.

Jensen, M. C. (1986). Agency costs of free cash flow, corporate finance, and takeovers. *American Economic Review, 76*(2), 323−329.

Jensen, M. C. (1987). A helping hand for entrenched managers. Wall Street Journal, November 4.

Jensen, M. C. (1989). Is leverage an invitation to bankruptcy? Wall Street Journal, February 1.

Jensen, M. C. (2001). Value maximization, stakeholder theory, and the corporate objective function. *Journal of Applied Corporate Finance, 14*(3), 8−21.

Jensen, M. C., & Meckling, W. H. (1976). Theory of the firm: Managerial behavior, agency costs and ownership structure. *Journal of Financial Economics, 3*, 305−360.

Jensen, M. C., & Murphy, K. J. (1990). CEO incentives: It's not how much you pay, but how. *Harvard Business Review, 68*(3), 138−153.

Jensen, M. C., & Ruback, R. S. (1983). The market for corporate control. *Journal of Financial Economics, 11*, 5–50.

Julio, B., & Ikenberry, D. L. (2004). Reappearing dividends. *Journal of Applied Corporate Finance, 16*(4), 89–100.

Jung, J. (2015). Shareholder value and workforce downsizing, 1981–2006. *Social Forces, 93*(4), 1335–1368.

Jung, J. (2016). Through the contested terrain: Implementation of downsizing announcements by large U.S. firms, 1984 to 2005. *American Sociological Review, 81*(2), 347–373.

Kalev, A. (2014). How you downsize is who you downsize: Biased formalization, accountability, and managerial diversity. *American Sociological Review, 79*(1), 109–135.

Kalleberg, A. (2011). *Good jobs, bad jobs: The rise of polarized and precarious employment systems in the United States, 1970s–2000s.* New York, NY: Russell Sage Foundation.

Keller, J. J. (1996). AT&T to end year with same size work force. Wall Street Journal, December 30.

Khurana, R. (2002). *Searching for a corporate savior: The irrational quest for charismatic CEOs.* Princeton, NJ: Princeton University Press.

Khurana, R. (2007). *From higher aims to hired hands: The social transformation of American business schools and the unfulfilled promise of management as a profession.* Princeton, NJ: Princeton University Press.

Knudsen, H. K., Johnson, J. A., Martin, J. K., & Roman, P. M. (2003). Downsizing survival: The experience of work and organizational commitment. *Sociological Inquiry, 73*(2), 265–283.

Koeber, C. (2002). Corporate restructuring, downsizing, and the middle class: The process and meaning of worker displacement in the "new" economy. *Qualitative Sociology, 25*(2), 217–246.

Lazonick, W., & O'Sullivan, M. (2000). Maximizing shareholder value: A new ideology for corporate governance. *Economy and Society, 29*(1), 13–35.

Lin, K. H. (2015). The financial premium in the U.S. labor market: A distributional analysis. *Social Forces, 94*(1), 1–30.

Lin, K. H., & Tomaskovic-Devey, D. (2013). Financialization and US income inequality, 1970–2008. *American Journal of Sociology, 118*(5), 1284–1329.

Lok, J. (2010). Institutional logics as identity projects. *Academy of Management Journal, 53*(6), 1305–1335.

Love, E. G., & Kraatz, M. (2009). Character, conformity, or the bottom line? How and why downsizing affected corporate reputation. *Academy of Management Journal, 52*(2), 314–335.

Marris, R. L. (1964). *The economic theory of managerial capitalism.* London: Macmillan.

McKinley, W., Sanchez, C. M., & Schick, A. G. (1995). Organizational downsizing: Constraining, cloning, learning. *Academy of Management Executive, 9*(3), 32–44.

Meyer, J. W., & Rowan, B. (1977). Institutionalized organizations: Formal structure as myth and ceremony. *American Journal of Sociology, 83*(2), 340–363.

Morris, J. R., Cascio, W. F., & Young, C. E. (1999). Downsizing after all these years: Questions and answers about who did it, how many did it, and who benefited from it. *Organizational Dynamics, 27*(3), 78–87.

New York Times. (1996). *The downsizing of America.* New York, NY: Random House.

O'Sullivan, M. (2000). *Contests for corporate control: Corporate governance and economic performance in the United States and Germany.* New York, NY: Oxford University Press.

Osterman, P. (1999). *Securing prosperity: The American labor market: How it has changed and what to do about it.* Princeton, NJ: Princeton University Press.

Perry, T., & Shivdasani, A. (2005). Do boards affect performance? Evidence from corporate restructuring. *The Journal of Business, 78*(4), 1403–1432.

Pfeffer, J. (1981). Management as symbolic action: The creation and maintenance of organizational paradigms. In B. M. Staw & L. L. Cummings (Eds.), *Research in organizational behavior* (Vol. 3, pp. 1–52). Greenwich, CT: JAI Press.

Salancik, G. R., & Meindl, J. R. (1984). Corporate attributions as strategic illusions of management control. *Administrative Science Quarterly, 29*(2), 238–254.

Sanders, W. G., & Carpenter, M. A. (2003). Strategic satisficing? A behavioral-agency theory perspective on stock repurchase program announcements. *Academy of Management Journal*,
46(2), 160−178.

Shin, T. (2013). The shareholder value principle: The governance and control of corporations in the
United States. *Sociology Compass*, *7*(10), 829−840.

Shin, T. (2014). Explaining pay disparities between top executives and nonexecutive employees: A
relative bargaining power approach. *Social Forces*, *92*(4), 1339−1372.

Shin, T., & You, J. (2017). Pay for talk: How the use of shareholder-value language affects CEO
compensation. *Journal of Management Studies*, *54*(1), 88−117.

Stavrou, E., Kassinis, G., & Filotheou, A. (2007). Downsizing and stakeholder orientation among
the Fortune 500: Does family ownership matter? *Journal of Business Ethics*, *72*, 149−162.

Staw, B. M., McKechnie, P. I., & Puffer, S. M. (1983). The justification of organizational performance. *Administrative Science Quarterly*, *28*(4), 582−600.

Strang, D., & Soule, S. A. (1998). Diffusion in organizations and social movements: From hybrid
corn to poison pills. *Annual Review of Sociology*, *24*, 265−290.

Sundaram, A. K., & Inkpen, A. C. (2004). The corporate objective revisited. *Organization Science*,
15, 350−363.

Thornton, P., Ocasio, W., & Lounsbury, M. (2012). *The institutional logics perspective: A new
approach to the culture, structure, and process*. New York, NY: Oxford University Press.

Tuggle, C. S., Sirmon, D. G., Reutzel, C. R., & Bierman, L. (2010). Commanding board of director
attention: Investigating how organizational performance and CEO duality affect board
members' attention to monitoring. *Strategic Management Journal*, *31*(9), 946−968.

Uchitelle, L. (2007). *The disposable American: Layoffs and their consequences*. New York, NY:
Alfred A. Knopf.

Useem, M. (1996). *Investor capitalism: How money managers are changing the face of corporate
America*. New York, NY: Basic Books.

van Essen, M., Otten, J., & Carberry, E. J. (2015). Assessing managerial power theory: A meta-ana-
lytic approach to understanding the determinants of CEO compensation. *Journal of
Management*, *41*(1), 164−202.

Wade, J. B., Porac, J. F., & Pollock, T. G. (1997). Worth, words, and the justification of executive
pay. *Journal of Organizational Behavior*, *18*, 641−664.

Walsh, J. P., & Seward, J. K. (1990). On the efficiency of internal and external corporate control
mechanisms. *Academy of Management Review*, *15*(3), 421−458.

Western, B., & Rosenfeld, J. (2011). Unions, norms, and the rise in U.S. wage inequality. *American
Sociological Review*, *76*(4), 513−537.

Westphal, J. D., & Zajac, E. J. (1998). The symbolic management of stockholders: Corporate governance reforms and shareholder reactions. *Administrative Science Quarterly*, *43*(1), 127−153.

Worrell, D. L., Davidson, W. N., & Sharma, V. M. (1991). Layoff announcements and stockholder
wealth. *Academy of Management Journal*, *34*(3), 662−678.

Zajac, E. J., & Westphal, J. D. (1995). Accounting for the explanations of CEO compensation:
Substance and symbolism. *Administrative Science Quarterly*, *40*(2), 283−308.

Zajac, E. J., & Westphal, J. D. (2004). The social construction of market value: Institutionalization
and learning perspectives on stock market reactions. *American Sociological Review*, *69*(3),
433−457.

Zorn, D., Dobbin, F., Dierkes, J., & Kwok, M.-S. (2005). Managing investors: How financial markets reshaped the American firm. In K. K. Cetina & A. Preda (Eds.), *The sociology of financial markets*. New York, NY: Oxford University Press.

Zuckerman, E. W. (2001). Focusing the corporate product: Securities analysts and de-diversification.
Administrative Science Quarterly, *45*, 591−619.

APPENDIX EXAMPLES OF REFERENCES TO SHAREHOLDER VALUE

The following list shows common expressions in shareholder letters that qualify as references to shareholder value. The search terms are italicized. The company names and the fiscal years are in the parentheses.

During the year, we continued to sharpen our strategic focus and review our operating platforms, shaping MetLife for heightened market leadership in the years ahead and increased *shareholder value* (Metlife, 2001).

We look to the future with great confidence as we pursue business strategies to further distinguish ourselves within the defense sector and, in doing so, enhance *shareholder value* (Northrop Grumman, 1999).

We must deliver *shareholder value* (Electronic Data Systems, 1998).

Our goal is to use our growing financial capacity to maximize *value* for *shareholders* (Time Warner, 2003).

In fact, I am more convinced than ever that 3M is indeed an excellent company, but more importantly, a very strong company with the potential to become truly great in all aspects, and especially in delivering sustainable and superior *returns* to our *shareholders* (3M, 2005).

Throughout 2003, our operating companies implemented long-standing strategies to grow their brands and, as an enterprise, we remain steadfast in pursuing our overriding objective to deliver superior *returns* to *shareholders* over the long term (Altria Group [formerly Philip Morris], 2003).

I firmly believe that if Office Depot surpasses the expectations of our employees and customers, and we do so better than any of our competitors, our growth will be consistent, our earnings will be predictable and our return to investors will be exceptional (Office Depot, 2000).

ABOUT THE EDITOR

Steven Vallas is Professor of Sociology at Northeastern University, USA, where he teaches contemporary social theory and the sociology of work. He is the author of numerous books and articles on a wide array of topics, including the shifting nature of authority relations at work, racial, and ethnic boundaries among employees, the commercialization of the life sciences, and the disruptions that new technologies provoke within the firm. Most recently, he is the author of *Work: A Critique* (Polity, 2012) and co-editor of *The SAGE Handbook of Resistance* (2016), with David Courpasson.

INDEX

Affordable Care Act (ACA), 120, 129, 134

Agency, 38, 61, 63, 77, 79, 81–82
theory, 189–190

Agency for Health Care Research And Quality, 121

American Hospital Association, 121

American Management Association (AMA), 191

AT&T, 212*n*2

Audience segregation, 4, 17, 18, 24, 27

The Birth of Biopolitics (Foucault), 5

Boundaryless careers, 37–38, 45, 47, 49, 52

Budros, A., 212*n*1

Callback, 143, 149–151, 154–155, 157–159, 160, 167–169

Call-centres, 60, 61, 63, 64, 66, 73, 75, 81–83

CEOs, 194, 195–198, 206, 208–211

Clinton, H., 22

"Company of one", 36, 44, 52

Context collapse, 18, 29*n*7

Continuous improvement, 88, 99, 101

Corporate governance, 187–191, 208–211

Crew Resource Management, 128

Crossing the Quality Chasm (Institute of Medicine), 119

Decoupling, 89, 90, 102, 106, 110–112

Digital inequality, 4

Digital technologies, 2–4, 19

Disciplinary power, 5

Dividend per share, 198

Downsizing, dealing with, 34–35
boundaryless careers and, 37–38, 45, 47, 49, 52
co-management of career paths and, 47–48
data and methods, 39–43
discussion, 51–53
financial service careers and, 39
large financial firms becoming precarious and, 43–44
new organizational careers and, 38–39
in financial services, 44–46
variation in, 48–51
precarious work and insecurity and, 35–37

Facebook, 8–9, 11, 17, 22

Flexible working, 118, 119, 133

Foucault, M., 5, 20, 26–28, 28*n*1, 29*n*9

Gawande, A., 118

Goffman, 16–18, 28*n*1

Great Recession, 143, 145–146, 148, 150, 151, 153, 170

Health care industry, 118, 119, 122, 123, 129, 134
See also Lean production in healthcare, deployment of

Herfindahl index, 199

Hiring, 142–144, 146–149, 151, 152, 154, 159, 167, 170–172, 173*n*5

Homosocial reproduction, 144
Human resources, 2, 101
HyperRESEARCH, 125

Insecurity, 34−35, 38−39, 43−44,
        52−54
    precarious work and, 35−37
Institute for Healthcare
        Improvement, 121
Institute of Medicine, 119, 121
Institutional entrepreneurs, 91−92
Institutional investors, 198
Institutional Review Board (IRB),
        124
Institutional theory, 193
Institutional translation, 88, 91
Intensive care, 118−120
    discussion, 133−136
    hospital restructuring and, 129
        ICU expansion, 133
        rationalizing labor, 131−132
        service lines, 130
    medical authority and rise of
        teamwork and, 120−121
    methods and settings, 123−124
        analytic process, 125
        interviews, 124−125
        observations, 124
    and teamwork
        as culture, 127−129
        in ICU, 125−127
        meaning, 121−123
Internet, 2, 4, 22, 23, 27, 29n8

Job search and digital intermediaries,
        3−6
Joint Commission, 121

Labor queues, 143, 144, 146−148,
        167, 169−171
Labour process theory (LPT), 60
Lakeview Associates, 89−90, 93,
        102−103

frame alignment, 104
implementation, 104−111
Lean's deployment organizing,
        103−104
Lane, C. M., 35
Layoff, 186, 188, 191−193, 195−197,
        199, 200, 203, 206,
        209−211
Lean production in healthcare,
        deployment of, 87−90
    cases and methods, 92−94
    Lakeview Associates and, 102−103
        frame alignment, 104
        implementation, 104−111
        lean's deployment organizing,
                103−104
    lean medicine and, 90
    management models and divergent
        change, 91−92
    Riverside Hospital and, 94−95
        frame alignment, 96−100
        implementation, 100−102
        Lean's deployment organizing,
                95−96
LinkedIn, 8−11, 14, 15, 17−18, 29n4
    membership rise of, 9

Managing for Excellence (ME), 105,
        109−110
Mass-customized services, 60, 61, 63,
        66, 82, 83
Mass-services, 60, 63, 82
Microsoft OneNote, 125
Model attenuation, 89, 111
Model entrepreneurs, 89−90, 94, 96,
        97, 101, 102, 104, 107, 108,
        111, 112
Model translations, 89, 92
Monster.com, 2

National Longitudinal Survey of
        Youth 1997 (NLSY97),
        143, 153

survey results
between-group differences,
165–166
main effects and difference-in
difference, 159–165
variables and statistical analyses,
153–154
Neo-normative control and value
discretion, in interactive
service work, 60–62, 68,
72–73
case study and methods, 66–67
control and discretion at work,
62–66
discussion, 80–83
management approach, 70–72
recruitment and selection and,
68–70
task discretion and, 77–78
range and degree of
performance offered and,
79–80
range and degree of service
offered and, 78–79
value discretion and, 73–77,
80–83
New organizational careers, 38–39,
48, 52
in financial services, 44
internal movement as evidence,
44–45
loyalty as evidence, 45–46
variation in, 48–49
serial monogamy model, 49–50
spiral staircase model, 50–51

One-profile dilemma, 16–21
One Stop center, 7–8, 29n3
One-way honor system, 36, 52
Outside director, 199

Patient Safety Curriculum Guide,
121

Practice managers, 102–104,
106–111
Precarity, 27–28
Professionalism, 120
Pugh, A. J., 36

Race, recession, and social closure, in
low-wage labor market,
142–143
discussion, 169–172
field experiment results
between-group differences,
157–159
main effects and difference-in-
difference, 154–157
limitations and strengths, 166–169
methods
field experiment, 150
sampling and experimental
procedures, 150–151
survey data, 153–154
variables, 151–152
NLSY97 survey results
between-group differences,
165–166
main effects and difference-in
difference, 159–165
theoretical background, 143
great recession effect on
individuals, 145–146
inequality durability, 148–150
labor queues and social closure,
146–148
racial discrimination and
employment disadvantage
sources, 143–144
Racial inequality. *See* Race,
recession, and social
closure, in low-wage labor
market
Recession. *See* Race, recession, and
social closure, in low-wage
labor market

Reciprocity, virtue of, 70, 72
Responsible autonomy, 62, 71, 82
Return on assets (ROA), 196, 208
Return on equity (ROE), 196, 208
Reverse networking, 9, 24
Riverside Hospital, 89, 92−95
　frame alignment, 96−100
　implementation, 100−102
　Lean's deployment organizing,
　　95−96
Robert Wood Johnson Foundation,
　121

Search engine optimization (SEO), 14
Serial monogamy career, 48, 53
　of new organizational careers,
　　49−50
Shareholder value and workforce
　downsizing, 190−194
　orientation among U.S.
　　corporations and, 189−190
Social closure, 142, 143, 146−149,
　167, 169−171
Social networking sites and labor
　　market, 2−3
　data and methodology, 6−7
　double-edged exposure of, 10−11
　exposure and one-profile dilemma
　　and, 16−21
　exposure of one's image and,
　　11−16
　implications, 24−28
　job search and digital
　　intermediaries and, 3−6
　lure and benefits of, 7−10
　social-political self exposure and,
　　21−24
Society for Human Resource
　　Management (SHRM), 2,
　　25
Spiral staircase model, 50−51,
　53
Stakeholder perspective, 192

Stock repurchase, 198
Street level bureaucrats, 65

Task discretion, 77−78
　range and degree of performance
　　offered and, 79−80
　range and degree of service offered
　　and, 78−79
Taylor, F. W., 62
TeamSTEPPS, 121
Team work. See Intensive care
To Err is Human (Institute of
　　Medicine), 119
Trust and care, as virtue, 62, 65,
　70−72, 74, 78, 80
Twitter, 21

U.S. Bureau of Labor Statistics, 153,
　174n10
U.S. Census Region, 153
U.S. Department of Labor, 153
U.S. National Bureau of Economic
　　Research (NBER), 151

Valorization process, 81
Value discretion, 65−66, 73−77,
　80−83

Wall Street Journal, 195
Weberian closure theory, 142
Workforce downsizing, 186−189
　data and methods, 194−200
　discussion, 209−211
　results, 200−209
　shareholder value and, 190−194
　orientation among U.S.
　　corporations and,
　　189−190
"Workforce 2015: Strategy Trumps
　　Shortage" (American
　　Hospital Association), 121

YouTube, 14, 21

www.ingramcontent.com/pod-product-compliance
Lightning Source LLC
Chambersburg PA
CBHW052001270326
41929CB00015B/2743